MASTERCLASS
in Japanese
Cooking

MASTERCLASS
in Japanese
Cooking

EMI KAZUKO

PAVILION

Dedication

To my late parents who provided me with a good foundation in life and food, and to my darling Toby whose canine existence has enriched my life enormously.

First published in Great Britain in 2002 by
PAVILION BOOKS
(an imprint of Chrysalis Books)
64 Brewery Road
London N7 9NT

A member of **Chrysalis** Books plc

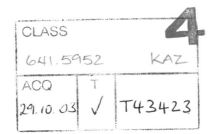
Designed by Nigel Soper
Publishing Director: Vivien James
Senior Editor: Zoe Antoniou

Colour reproduction at Colourpath in London
Printed and bound at Imago, Singapore

2 4 6 8 10 9 7 5 3 1

This book can be ordered direct from the publisher. Please contact the Marketing Department. But try your bookshop first.

All recipes suitable for vegetarians are marked with a [v]

Japanese knives courtesy of Nippon Kitchen. www.nipponkitchen.com

Picture Library Credits
Japanese Cultural Centre, pp8, 9 and 14; The Anthony Blake Photo Library, pp17 and 20; Corbis, pp10, 11, 12, 13, 15, 16, 19, 21 and 22; Jean Cazals, pp35, 51, 65, 85, 103, 168 and 181.

Picture on page 2 shows the vegetable Myoga, by Gus Filgate

Acknowledgements
My thanks to the late Kenneth Lo, who first introduced me to the joy of writing cookery books in English, my mentor Dehta Hsiung for his friendship and support, and my life-long friend Katsuko Hirose for her unceasing willingness to assist in research from Japan. I would also like to thank all my food writer friends, especially Marlena Spieler, for their professional interest in Japanese food and cooking. Most of all, my heartfelt thanks go to my editor Zoe Antoniou, without whose undeserving belief in me, encouragement and patience, this book would never have happened.

contents

Introduction

I have watched with much interest the rapid rise of the popularity of Japanese cuisine in the past decade. It has gathered pace with the sushi phenomenon that swept the world towards the end of the nineties. To add to my delight, sushi has brought Japanese food to the attention of a much wider public than ever before, and helped to create a new wave of Japanese cooking along the way. It is an exciting development and one that I feel privileged to witness and to contribute to helping provide a wider understanding of what was once the most mysterious cuisine of the world.

It was mysterious in the eyes of Westerners, most probably because we ate raw fish. Now that this alien act has been transformed into fashion in the name of sushi, it is mysterious no more. However, the concept of Japanese cooking remains quite different from that of any Western countries. Traditional Japanese cooking is uncomplicated, while Western cooking is more complex. It is a natural way of cooking: if you can eat anything straight from the ground or out of the water, it's the best – if not the only – way to experience the natural taste of food. This is the core of the Japanese philosophy of eating, and most of our cooking is kept very simple. Fundamentally, Japanese cooking is based on cooking with water, unlike nearly all other countries which cook with oil. If we use oil at all it is only sparingly and the oiliness is often reduced in a light sauce before eating. Tempura, for instance, is lightly fried with a very thin batter, and eaten dipped in a dashi (fish stock or broth) sauce, which washes off the excess oil as well as adding flavour.

In the past, European chefs have also tried to create new-wave cooking – eclectic, Pacific Rim or fusion – making use of the increasingly available exotic ingredients. What's really exciting is that Japanese chefs, with their natural feel for and knowledge of their unique cuisine, detailed techniques, subtle flavouring and meticulous presentation, are creating something very new. In Tokyo I have tasted lightly grilled foie gras presented on top of long-simmered daikon in a dashi sauce, and even a Gorgonzola miso soup, and in London a classic *katsuo no tataki* (bonito or skipjack tuna seared sashimi) is being made into a salad dressed with mustard shoyu (Japanese soy sauce). Meanwhile, in New York and London, the simple, miso-marinated and grilled fish is transformed into a grand banquet dish using not widely available – thus expensive – black cod. What they are doing is presenting Japanese cuisine in a Westernized fashion. The result is very interesting in that it remains within the Japanese traditions yet has universal appeal.

Twenty very stimulating chefs, cooks, teachers, writers and broadcasters from around the world feature in this book, telling us all about Japanese cuisine today. They have been chosen because they are all expert in Japanese cooking, from very traditional *kaiseki* (multi-course meal) to the modern, new-wave cooking. All are highly respected professionals in their own field and their recipes reflect their specialities. A masterclass dish from the contributors is highlighted in each chapter, with detailed step-by-step instructions giving valuable expert's tips on how to handle individual ingredients and to make a complete dish.

Twelve contributors from Japan cover the wider spectrum of the cuisine, ranging from the authentic *ryotei* (old-style entertainment house) in Kyoto to modern restaurants in Tokyo. Many of the chefs are well known at home for their appearances on television and in magazines, but are little known outside Japan. Most of the established *ryotei* in Kyoto are still run by a descendant of the founder, and it is a privilege to have three such distinguished chef/patrons included in this book.

Eiichi Takahashi was born to the legendary Hyotei, established in 1837, and is a leading figure in the culinary world of Japan. Masahiro Kurusu, of the famous Tankuma, also teaches at a number of well-known cookery schools, while Yoshihiro Murata of Kikunoi is a celebrity chef and presented a *kaiseki* banquet in association with Dom Pérignon in France in 1999. Akihiro Kurita is the young chef/owner of one of the Kyoto speciality counter *kappo* (cooking) restaurants, where he cooks in front of the diners.

A number of television celebrity chefs, famous teachers and new-wave chefs from Tokyo have also been persuaded to reveal the authentic techniques in their handling of ingredients and compiling recipes. Kazunari Yanagihara, descendant of a long line of the *cha-kaiseki* (tea ceremony meal) sect Kinsa-ryu, runs his own prestigious cookery school and has presented a number of Japanese cookery series on television. Kentaro Kobayashi is a television personality chef, specializing in simple home cooking. Takayuki Hishinuma and Minoru Odajima, chef/patrons of Hishinuma and Odajima respectively, belong to a breed of brilliant chefs creating new-wave cooking. From speciality restaurants there is Tetsuya Saotome, tempura chef and owner of the celebrated Mikawa, and Takeshi Yasuge, *fugu* (puffer fish) chef and owner of the wild *fugu* restaurant Asakusa Fukuji. Yuichi Oyama is a sushi chef of the legendary sushi restaurant Yoshino in Osaka, and is the proud guardian of Osaka-style sushi dishes. Nobuo Iwaseya is the chief chef for all overseas Suntory restaurants, and was awarded a Michelin star for the London branch in 1987.

From the United Kingdom I have selected two outstanding restaurants in London. Hisashi Taoka, owner of Kiku, is a fish trader, while Susumu Hatakeyama is the head chef of the well-established Ikeda. From Germany, Hideaki Morita, chef/patron of Matsumi in Hamburg, has contributed recipes that warm your heart as well as the stomach.

Three distinguished chefs from the United States have also given their special recipes. Linda Rodriguez, the only woman and non-Japanese contributor, is the executive chef at New York's celebrated Bond Street restaurant. She was born in Manila but brought up in the United States and Japan, and has worked with the world-famous Nobu Matsuhisa at his New York and London restaurants. Toshi Sugiura, chef/patron of the sushi restaurant Hama in Los Angeles, travelled the world before settling down and becoming the best sushi chef in LA. Ken Tominaga is the young chef/patron of the popular Hana restaurant in the Bay Area, north San Francisco.

From Australia I have chosen Hiroshi Miura, the head chef of an All Nippon Airways restaurant Unkai, in Sydney. He is trained in the tea ceremony as well as in classical cooking. Naoyuki Sato started his career at Nadaman, one of the oldest and most successful *kaiseki* restaurants in Kyoto, and has climbed the ladder to head the army of chefs at the renowned Hong Kong restaurant.

I have complemented the chefs' contributions with a similar number of my own, filling in any gaps there might be in ingredients or techniques. Many of my recipes come from the traditional home cooking I learned from my mother or from the cookery courses I attended in my youth as part of my bridal training, which includes the tea ceremony and *cha-kaiseki* (tea ceremony meal).

It is not difficult to cook Japanese: just take note of what nature is offering, as we say in Japan. I hope this combination of chefs' recipes and mine will help home cooks everywhere to have a deeper understanding of the healthiest, most flavoursome and one of the greatest, cuisines of the world.

EMI KAZUKO

Japanese food and the tea ceremony

In the world of great cuisine, Japanese food, like its culture, stands out as something very different from that of any other country. Its range is enormous, but its individual foods and dishes are relatively simple – even minimalist if you like. This derives from various factors, cultural, religious and social, arising during the centuries-old history of Japan. At the root there is rice, the country's staple food since ancient times, and the invention of vital flavourings such as shoyu (Japanese soy sauce) and miso. The introduction of Buddhism had an enormous impact on the food and cooking of Japan. It also led to the development of the tea ceremony and the food served with it, which formed the basis of the unique style of the cooking and serving of Japanese cuisine.

For the Japanese, rice is so important that the word for cooked rice, *gohan* or *meshi*, also means 'meal', and all other dishes are called *okazu,* mere 'accompaniments'. Rice was probably introduced to Japan from South-East Asia around the second century BC. It was firmly established as the staple food between the eighth and twelfth centuries when aristocratic culture blossomed, and eating and drinking became part of the important social life. The fact that rice yields more per unit of land than any other crop and also stores well has made it possible for the Japanese to rely heavily on it as a staple food ever since. All other food and dishes were created around it or to go with it, and since rice has a clear, mouth-cleansing taste and soft texture, any flavoured food will accompany it well. In addition, many other Japanese foods such as sake, mirin, vinegar and miso were developed from this gem of grains.

Sake was already brewed from rice by the eighth century. It was – and still is – regarded as a sacred liquid, cleansing evil spirits, and is deeply associated with Shinto, the indigenous religion, and its ceremonies and rituals. The first brew of sake from each region is still dedicated to the Shinto shrines every year.

The most prominent development in Japanese culinary history, along with rice and sake, was *hishio*,

the origin of present-day shoyu and miso. This was a mixture of salt with animal or plant fibres and proteins, which resulted in a nutritious, fermented food as well as a seasoning. There were various types of *hishio*, and the grain variety – salt-fermented rice, barley or beans – was gradually developed between the eleventh and sixteenth centuries into the two most important Japanese flavourings, shoyu and miso.

Another type of *hishio,* using fish, was in fact the origin of the now world-famous sushi. Initially, freshwater fish was fermented in salt and cooked rice for almost a year in order to preserve it. Only the fish was eaten and the rice was discarded. This long-pressed sushi is called *nare-zushi*, and the oldest surviving sushi is still made each year in Shiga, near Kyoto, and dedicated to an eighth-century shrine. To hasten the process and prevent the fish from rotting, vinegar was added to the rice, and the preservation period was greatly shortened to about ten days, and the rice was also eaten. It was in nineteenth-century Tokyo that the process was speeded up even more, and the present-day *nigiri-zushi* (finger sushi with a slice of raw fish on top) was developed.

The introduction of Buddhism from the sixth century onwards also played a big part in Japanese cooking. The slaughter and eating of animals was seen as sinful, which eventually led the nation to ban meat eating. Japan's centuries-old vegetarian tendency was thus established. It wasn't until the end of the nineteenth century, when the country was forced to open up to foreigners after 260 years of closure, that meat eating started again, although vegetable- and seafood-oriented cooking persists strongly to this day.

Although Buddhism came through China, and it shares a lot of common ingredients with Chinese cuisine, Japanese cooking is very different. Meat eating continued in China, as well as the use of animal oil for cooking. Chinese cooking is mainly based on quick frying in hot oil so as to retain ingredients' freshness and to save fuel consumption at the same time, while

The Great Buddha at Kamakura has an awesome presence. It is an eternal reminder of the impact of Buddhism on Japanese culture and food.

Japanese cooking on the other hand did not use oil, and resolved the problem of lack of fuel by grilling directly over a fire or simmering in a minimum amount of water for the minimum length of time. Chinese cooking uses many different ingredients and flavours whereas Japanese cooking is almost a single-ingredient cuisine and a sauce is normally served separately.

In the twelfth century the rather more severe Zen Buddhism was introduced, and contributed to the development of the tea ceremony and vegetarian cooking. Tea was first introduced from China in the eighth century, but it was the Zen monks who spread the habit of tea drinking among the aristocratic and samurai classes. Mere tea drinking gradually evolved into an appreciation of tea in tranquillity, away from wars, during the turbulent period of the fifteenth and sixteenth centuries, and with more emphasis on the Zen philosophy of serenity and simplicity, the tea ceremony was born. The tea ceremony (a generally agreed translation of *chadō* or *sadō*, literally meaning 'way of tea') is not just a ritual afternoon tea, but also, philosophy apart, the very backbone of Japanese culture itself, which embraces all forms of visual art such as painting, pottery, flower arrangement, architecture, and food and its presentation. The tea ceremony and vegetarian cooking came together to form the *cha-kaiseki* (tea ceremony meal), and *chaji*.

The meal, *cha-kaiseki*, served at the *chaji*, formal, full tea ceremony, originally consisted of only bowls of rice and soup and two or three dishes. It is served before the tea ceremony so as to appreciate the tea itself. The word *kaiseki*, 'embraced stone', comes from a warmed stone monks carry close to their bosom to help them endure hunger as well as the cold. Present-day *cha-kaiseki* is normally made up of rice, soup, hors d'oeuvres, a simmered dish, a grilled dish, clear soup, a main dish, salted vegetables and hot water. Sake is also served. The ingredients and presentation should all reflect the season in which the *chaji* is held.

Visiting a traditional *kaiseki* restaurant in Japan is an intriguing experience even for the Japanese. It is not really a restaurant, but an old-style house, which you enter through a gate by stepping on freshly watered stones in a bamboo-lined passage. In a screened entrance hall you step onto the raised floor, leaving your shoes behind, before being led through a long wooden corridor to an individual *tatami* (thick straw mat) room, overlooking a beautifully tended, serene garden. Inside, one of the walls has a decorative alcove where a seasonal scroll and flowers are displayed.

After a ritual greeting by the lady of the house, food chosen by the chef will be brought, dish by dish, by a kimono-clad woman, bowing before and after serving. Overwhelmed by the whole atmosphere, you will soon realize that the food is only one part of a more total experience combining place, garden, atmosphere and etiquette with food. Not only the decorative objects in the room, but also the dishes and even the chopstick rests change according to the season. On the hors d'oeuvre plate you will see foods of the season from mountain, sea and land. The *kaiseki* is the ultimate eating experience and an ideal way to appreciate nature's gifts of food to us.

While the tea ceremony is no longer a part of Japanese everyday life and has become a mere hobby of well-to-do men and women, these *kaiseki* restaurants are firmly established. Though this traditional cooking is still at its backbone, the Japanese culinary scene is now quite a mixture. Foreign-influenced dishes such as *tonkatsu* (pork cutlet) and ramen have developed and are among the popular dishes on menus in many restaurants. Another unique feature of Japanese restaurant culture is that there are many that specialize in only one dish or ingredient, such as a sushi or tempura. In Japan, people normally decide what they want to eat before going to a restaurant, and choose a restaurant that specializes in this particular type of food. The time has now come for the world to discover Japanese cuisine.

The tea ceremony is an ancient art, bringing together food, drink and culture. It is still practised today, although there are now less intricate forms of the ceremony that can be experienced.

The regions and their food and drink

Japan's geographical position makes it one of the world's most perfect countries to live in: the climate is fairly mild, and there are four seasons, each lasting almost equal length. Agricultural produce differs markedly from season to season, and this is clearly reflected in Japanese cuisine's emphasis on seasonal food. Also, Japan is a long, narrow country (roughly the size of California), stretching across 20 degrees of latitude – a distance equal to that between the north of Scotland and the north of Africa. So it is blessed with produce ranging from rice to sugar cane, apples, mango and papaya. Although it is also a mountainous country with huge mountain ranges covering up to 80 per cent of the land, it is still an arable country. In addition, the clash of warm and cold currents around the coastal plains makes Japan one of the world's richest fisheries.

Japan was largely an agricultural country before World War II, but owing to rapid industrialization the country now relies heavily on food imports, chiefly from other South-east Asian countries. However, in this world of increasing globalization and mass production, it is a minor miracle that in Japan numerous small family businesses still thrive, whether it is *konbu* (kelp) picking and drying operations in Hokkaido or vegetable pickling farms all over Japan. These local specialities are now available anywhere in Japan through mail order and flourishing online sales. However, seasonal specialities are still important and are sampled at local restaurants, at home or through the special *bento* (lunch box) found in local shops and at platform kiosks in the mainline railway stations.

The country has 47 *ken* or prefectures, of which Tokyo counts as one, which derived from the *han* (domains) the old warlords used to govern during the Shogunate era of the sixteenth to nineteenth centuries. While the *han* (now *ken*) features and characteristics of the people still persist today, the country can be divided geographically into the following seven regions. Rice is produced almost all over Japan, but the

A local man shops for octopus at Tsukiji fish market, Tokyo.

rich rice regions are in the north, as is the production of sake. The southern regions are more tropical, and so produce tropical fruits and vegetables.

Hokkaido (*the northern island*)

The climate and the landscape of Hokkaido are very similar to parts of Europe, particularly Scotland, and its population is sparse. This is the least developed island, and it was only around the early twentieth century that the government encouraged people to move here to develop the land. Apart from the indigenous people, the Ainu, the inhabitants are from all over Japan, so it is a culturally mixed, fairly liberal region.

Like Scotland, it is famous for its abundance of seafood, most notably salmon. Any salmon that is not used for fresh consumption is mostly salted immediately. Its eggs, *ikura,* are also salted and used for sushi and hors d'oeuvres. Another Hokkaido speciality is crab. There are three types: *taraba-gani* (king crab), *kegani* (horsehair crab) and *hanasaki-gani* (hanasaki crab). Herring roe, *kazunoko,* immediately salted and dried, is one of the special items for the New Year's Day feast. It is used for sushi as well. Other seafood includes clams such as *hokki-gai* (surf clam), squid, scallops, several varieties of prawn (shrimp) and saury.

Despite the cold climate and craggy mountain ranges in the centre of the island, vegetables such as

Brightly coloured cans of crab are stocked in a shop in Tokyo.

A fish stall in a local market lays out its fresh dried fish for customers. Fish is by far the most common protein to be used in Japanese cooking.

Tohoku (*the northern part of the main island, Honshu*)

The huge mountain ranges that run down the centre of Japan start at the northern tip of the main island. The Siberian wind clashes with the central mountain range, bringing heavy snowfall to the Sea of Japan side, covering the region with snow for half of each year.

Fish such as salmon, squid, cod and scallop are caught in the surrounding Sea of Japan, Pacific Ocean and Tsuruga Straits, which separate Hokkaido from Honshu. The Pacific coastline of this region has the unique feature of many craggy estuaries, which are used to farm oysters, *wakame* (young seaweed) and scallops. Sharks are also caught off the coast here. Freshwater fish such as *ayu* (sweetfish), *iwana* (char), *dojo* (weatherfish), trout and carp are also available.

However, this is Japan's prime rice region, and the richest rice belt runs from here along the Sea of Japan coast to the next region, producing many top-quality brand names including one of Japan's best, if not the best, Sasanishiki. Despite the cold winter this region produces some vegetables and fruits too, but it is most famous for its apples such as Fuji. The mountains provide numerous varieties of *sansai* (wild mountain vegetables) and mushrooms. These are mostly made into various types of pickles. Utilizing the inactive time during the severe winters, high technology has been used to preserve all sorts of food. The legendary Japanese beef, *Shonai-gyu*, is reared in Yamagata-ken, facing the Pacific, along with *Shonai*, the pedigree black pig.

This region has many speciality dishes using or accompanying rice. One such, *kiritanpo*, is a stick with rice pasted around it, grilled over a charcoal fire, then cooked in soup. A hotpot dish called *shottsuru*, which uses local fish *hata hata* (sailfin sandfish) is a winter speciality. *Hata hata* is also salted to make sushi. Sendai, a large city facing the Pacific, produces Sendai miso and fish products such as *sasa kamaboko* (ground fish cake wrapped in bamboo leaves).

The snow-melted water from the high mountains, together with the region's prized rice, helps it to produce some of the finest sake. There are about 300 breweries in this region, and four out of six are among the top ten sake-producing prefectures of Japan.

potatoes, sweetcorn, onions, kabocha squash and asparagus, and even melons are produced in the remaining very limited lowland area. The island's prized potato, *danshaku* (baron), is named after its developer Baron Kawada. Hokkaido is the only place in Japan where sheep are reared.

Ishikari-nabe (fresh salmon and vegetables cooked in miso soup) is a typical Hokkaido speciality. Pregnant *shishamo* (a type of smelt), lightly grilled whole, is a national favourite for sake drinkers. Crab flakes on top of rice is a typical *ekiben* (station *bento*) in this region, and there are a lot of street stalls selling boiled crabs during the summer tourist season. *Ghenghis Khan-nabe* (lamb barbecue) can also be eaten here. Ramen (Chinese-style noodles), in particular *miso-ramen*, was first developed in Sapporo, the capital of Hokkaido, and has since led to the ramen craze that has now spread not only all over Japan but also abroad. There is even a ramen village in Hokkaido.

Hokkaido is one of the largest rice-producing regions, but their rice is mainly used for making sake. The water from the melting snow of the high mountains is very suitable for sake brewing. Due to the long, cold winter, the brewing tends to be slow, producing a slightly dry and light sake. Some of the finest wines are produced on the Tokachi plains.

Kanto (*Tokyo and its environs*)

This region, centred around the capital, is the political, economical and cultural centre of Japan. The Kanto plains, the largest lowland area, are shielded from the Siberian wind by the mountains to the north, and face the warm current of the Pacific Ocean in the east and south. The northern and the western areas towards the adjacent regions are covered by mountains, making this region strikingly varied in its population distribution as well as its landscape. The Pacific coastline from here to Osaka, the second largest city, has the most balanced warm climate, and is therefore Japan's most populated area with some 80 per cent of the country's 125 million inhabitants. People come from all over Japan and indeed the world to live and work in Tokyo, so its cuisine is very varied. You can get any food or drink in any season, and all regional cuisine and dishes from any part of the world are available here. At Tokyo's Tsukiji fish market, some 3,000 types of fish are traded every day.

The east of the region facing the Pacific has access to rich fisheries and here they catch more *katsuo* (bonito or skipjack tuna) than in any other prefecture. Sardines and shellfish such as abalone, *sazae* (spiny top shell or turban shell), *asari* (Manila clam) and *hamaguri* (hard clam) are also caught. The Pacific coastline's nori, the indispensable ingredient for rolled sushi, is one of the highest in quality. Clearwater fish are made into ready-to-eat foods such as *kabayaki* (steamed and grilled with *taré* sauce) using eel, and *tsukudani* (simmered for a long time in rich shoyu sauce) using all sorts of fish and shellfish.

Chiba-ken, west of Tokyo, is Japan's foremost vegetable-producing prefecture for daily items such as daikon, mangetout, *sato-imo* (taro), *gobo* (burdock) and *nashi* pear. Their speciality fruit, *Boshu biwa* (the loquat or Japanese medlar, an apricot-like fruit) is reputed to be the king of fruits. The northern and western mountainous areas produce some vegetables and very Japanese ingredients such as *konnyaku* (yam-like potato cake) and *kanpyo* (dried gourd ribbon). Mito, north-east of Tokyo, is famous for its *natto* (fermented soya bean (soybean product) production, where soya beans (soybeans) are still fermented, and sold in straw in the traditional manner. This is also the

main shoyu- producing region. The city of Noda in Chiba-ken has 270 years of successful shoyu-making history. It also produces miso.

Apart from sushi, there is no major regional dish here – the cuisine is both national and international. Sushi is now an international dish, but the best-known *nigiri-zushi* (finger sushi with a slice of raw fish on top) was first developed in nineteenth-century Tokyo. The *nigiri-zushi* is also known as *Edo-maé* (Tokyo style), Edo being the old name for Tokyo. Some other popular dishes such as *oden* (fish cakes hotpot), also known as *Kanto-daki* (Kanto cooking), were developed in Tokyo, but many are now considered national dishes.

Sake is also produced throughout this region; even in Tokyo there are fourteen breweries, although they are relatively small-scale operations. Interestingly, the north-east of the Kanto plain has an almost 100-year history of wine making.

Chubu (*the central region*)

With the northern part facing the cold Sea of Japan, the south the warm Pacific Ocean, and the middle amid the highest mountains of Japan, this region varies greatly in landscape, climate and produce. Whereas the north and the central mountain area are snow-covered for several months of the year, the warm current of the ocean brings the Pacific coastline a pleasantly mild climate all year round.

Tsukiji fish market displays its fresh catches of the day for customers to admire. Fresh tuna are in the foreground.

With good fishing along the coast of the Sea of Japan, this region has a variety of unique fish such as *hotaru-ika* (firefly squid) and winter *buri* (Japanese amberjack). The notorious, toxic *fugu* (puffer fish) is caught off the Sea of Japan. Shellfish such as *zuwai-gani* (red snow crab) and *bai-gai* (ivory shell) are also this region's speciality. Fisheries along the Pacific also thrive with sea bream, snapper, crab, *katsuo* (bonito or skipjack tuna), abalone, *sazae* (spiny top shell or turban shell), eel, trout and lobster.

The northern area is the continuation of Japan's richest rice belt, and the northernmost Niigata-ken is a synonym for rice, being blessed with Koshihikari, along with Sasanishiki, one of the country's two most cherished brands. Despite the long and severe winter, a variety of vegetables such as *sato-imo* (taro), and kabocha squash are also produced. The central mountain area produces Japan's best soba noodles, called *Shinshu soba*.

The southern area, on the other hand, is reputed for its thriving strawberry and tea production. Although facing the Pacific, it is fairly mountainous with Japan's symbolic Mount Fuji right in the centre, and its hills and plateaus are used for tea cultivation. This region produces three of the top Japanese beef cattle, namely *Matsuzaka-gyu* in the southern lowland, *Hida-gyu* in the central mountain area, and *Wakasa-gyu* in the north-west lowland. Nagoya, Japan's third city after Tokyo and Osaka, situated in the south of this region, produces

dark red miso, *haccho*, which is used in place of shoyu (Japanese soy sauce) for flavouring in the Nagoya area.

Nagoya has many speciality dishes. Among the most famous are *kishimen* (flat ribbon udon noodles) and *hitsumabushi* (*kabayaki* eel dish). Because of its good rice, the northern region has numerous rice speciality dishes such as *ika-meshi* (squid rice) and *masu-zushi* (trout sushi).

Rice and sake go hand in hand, and Niigata is one of the top sake producers. Due to the soft water and severe cold climate enabling brewing to be kept at a low temperature for a long time, Niigata's sake tends to be light and dry. In the Kofu basin in the south-east of the mountain area good wine is produced. This region also produces *shochu* (distilled rice spirit) and beer.

Kinki (*Osaka and its environs*)

Unlike all the other regions, this is fairly flat, except in the centre of the Kii peninsula, stretching out to the Pacific Ocean. The two big cities, Osaka and Kyoto, dominate this region's central plain. The climate is mild on the whole and the area from Osaka along to the peninsula is particularly warm.

The Pacific coastline along the Kii peninsula has access to fish such as mackerel, horse mackerel, *tachiuo* (Atlantic cutlass fish) and lobster. To the north of Kyoto lies the Wakasa Bay, which is regarded as one of the best fishing areas in Japan, providing *buri* (Japanese amberjack), *katsuo* (bonito or skipjack tuna) and also squid.

Although Kyoto, the old capital, is considered the birthplace of Japanese haute cuisine, Osaka is now the culinary heart of Japan. There are many small-scale, family-business food manufacturers in both cities, notably of hand-made *yuba* (tofu skin) and various pickles in Kyoto, and of *konbu* (kelp) in Osaka. The Tanba hills, north-west of Kyoto, are well known for their speciality vegetables such as *kabura* (a giant turnip) and *matsutake* mushrooms, which are sought after by the top *kaiseki* restaurants in Kyoto. The region produces two of the best varieties of Japanese beef cattle, *Kobe-gyu* and *Ohmi-gyu*, which were first introduced to this region as early as 1844. Good rice is grown in the Ohmi plains, east of Kyoto. Due to its mild climate, the Kii peninsula provides *mikan* (satsuma),

An attractive collection of exotic vegetable pickles are displayed for sale.

plum, *kaki* persimmon and *nashi* pear. The peninsula has wild boar, which in winter is eaten in a hotpot. The ancient capital of Nara also produces some vegetables and fruits, and is especially famous for its pickles, *Nara-zuke* (marrow pickled in mirin). The somen (fine noodles) produced in Miwa city are among the best.

Ohtsu City by the Biwa Lake in Shiga, the largest lake in Japan, is regarded as the birthplace of sushi. Sushi was originally the method of preserving fish in rice and salt, which were then discarded. The lake's freshwater fish such as *funa* (a type of carp), *dojo* (loach) or *namazu* (catfish) were pressed and fermented in salt and rice for a year. The original *funa-zushi* has continued to be made at a shrine in Ohtsu since the eighth century. Although Kyoto produces many specialities such as vegetable pickles and a cinnamon biscuit called *yatsuhashi* for the tourist market, its culinary contribution centres on the cooking and serving style of *kaiseki* rather than speciality dishes. Osaka has produced many interesting dishes such as *kushi-yaki* (fried skewered food) and *udon-suki* (udon hotpot), but these have now become national dishes.

The most prominent feature of this region is the sake breweries, and Hyogo and Kyoto are Japan's top two sake-producing prefectures. Since Nada in Hyogo and Fushimi in Kyoto are the places where most sake breweries are based, the region's sake brands are called Nada and Fushimi respectively. Nada is blessed with locally produced Yamada Nishiki, widely recognized as the king of sake rice, coupled with a good local source of spring water. Nada's sake is said to be 'masculine' due to its hard water, making it dry and strong, in contrast to the soft Fushimi's 'feminine' character.

Chugoku (*the western region*) and Shikoku

This western end region of Honshu has two sides, one on the Sea of Japan and the other on the inland Seto Sea, with a mountain range in the middle, and its climate varies accordingly. The island of Shikoku, situated south of Chugoku region, is the smallest of the four main islands, again with a mountain range running through the centre. With the northern region facing the calm inland sea of Seto and the southern the warm Pacific Ocean, the island has a very mild climate.

The northern, Sea of Japan, side has some fish and seaweed such as *ago* (flying fish), squid, sea urchin, nori and *wakame* (young seaweed), whereas the Seto side is well known for its oyster farming and black sea bream. The furthest western city, Shimonoseki, is famous for its infamous *fugu* (puffer fish), the poisonous fish. It has toxic substances, particularly in its liver and ovaries, and is so deadly poisonous that you need a licence to handle it in Japan. Shimonoseki's wild *fugu* is regarded as the best and there are many restaurants that specialize in serving this fish. On the southern coast of Shikoku fresh seafood is abundant all the year round as the warm current of the Pacific flows close to this region. Seafood processing such as drying prawn (shrimp), *jako* (small fish), plaice and seaweed (to make nori, *wakame* and *hijiki*), or long-simmering shellfish are all carried out locally. *Anago* (sea eel) *kabayaki* (steamed and grilled or broiled) as well as fish products such as *kamaboko* and *chikuwa* are also prevalent. Wild eel, now rare, is caught in the south.

The Chugoku region is among the top three for producing the king of Japanese mushrooms, *matsutake*, along with shiitake, and the relatively warm climate on the Seto side brings this region a lot of vegetables and fruits. This region also rears a variety of Japanese beef cattle. Tosa is the old name for Kochiken, south of Shikoku, and is still used fondly to name local products: *Tosa Jiro* is the region's *jidori*, a special local chicken, and *Tosa-no tataki* is the area's famous seared *katsuo* (bonito or skipjack tuna) sashimi. Local speciality dishes here are dominated by *katsuo*.

A busy shopping street in Tokyo attracts visitors with its bright and busy array of banners and stalls overflowing onto the pavement.

Sanuki, the old name for Kagawa-ken, north-east of Shikoku, is famous for its udon and somen (types of noodles). Olives and olive oil are not used greatly in Japan, but due to the popularity of Italian food, Kagawa is now one of the few places to produce olive oil. Various citrus fruits are also produced such as *mikan* (satsuma), *yuzu* and *sudachi* to name but a few.

Despite the fact that this region is fairly mild all year round, sake is also produced all over the region.

Kyushu (*the southern island*) and Okinawa

Kyushu contains the large industrial cities in the north, with a strip of lowland along the coast, and huge volcanic mountains in the centre. The climate is very mild and the southern islands are sub-tropical. The southern islands are scattered between Kyushu and Taiwan, and halfway to the Philippines, and Okinawa, the largest island, lies midway. It lies at about the same latitude as North Africa, so it has a more Mediterranean-like climate.

The north of Kyushu, facing the Sea of Japan, has great access to *fugu* (puffer fish), mackerel and squid. The surrounding sea from the south of Kyushu to Okinawa is too warm for the good oil-rich fish found in all the other regions of Japan.

The sub-tropical climate also accounts for Kyushu's huge variety of citrus fruits, strawberry, mango and

grape. The region also produces rice, and vegetables such as lotus root, onions, and shiitake. Dried shiitake from Ohita-ken, in the north-west of Kyushu, are regarded as the best quality in Japan. *Hogo-gyu* is the local Japanese beef and there is also a *jidori* (local pedigree chicken). In Okinawa wild boar and black pig are also reared from which are produced sausage, bacon and ham. The tropical climate results in Okinawa's tropical fruits such as pineapple, papaya, mango and passionfruit as well as numerous citrus fruits.

Satsuma, the old name for Kagoshima, the southern-most prefecture in Kyushu, has left notable marks in Japanese culinary history. It has a lot of foreign influence in its food and cooking. *Satsuma-imo* (sweet potato) came from southern Asia; *Satsuma-age* is a fried fish paste, a very common food in all countries of South-East Asia, and *Satsuma-jiru* is a type of miso soup containing pork, chicken and vegetables. Satsuma is also the first place from which *mikan* was exported to the West, hence the Western name 'satsuma' for this sweet citrus fruit. The word 'soy' in soy sauce and soya bean (soybean) is Satsuma dialect for shoyu, since it was from there that shoyu (Japanese soy sauce) was first brought to the West by Dutch traders in the sixteenth century.

Local specialities include *mentaiko* (salted cod's roe) and ramen from Hakata, the largest city in the north of Kyushu. The ramen in rich pork soup is so popular that you will find Hakata ramen restaurants all over Japan. Nagasaki, the western prefecture, is really the birthplace of ramen, with its invention of Nagasaki *chanpon* (ramen with a mixture of vegetables and meat). In Kumamoto, the central-west prefecture at the foot of the volcanic mountain Aso, horsemeat is eaten raw as sashimi! Okinawan food and cooking has been influenced by the Chinese and its specialities include *champuroo* (stir-fried tofu with vegetables), *irichee* (simmered pork with various ingredients) and *unbushee* (various ingredients cooked in miso sauce).

Surprisingly, despite the warm climate here, sake brewing is also very widespread. Okinawa's drink is a *shochu* (distilled rough sake, made from not only rice but also many other grains and even potato) called Awamori, which is made from Thai rice with black *kohji*. Throughout the southern islands black sugar *shochu* is made from sugar cane.

A food counter within a department store food hall offers a variety of cooked dishes for weary shoppers searching for tonight's dinner.

The Japanese store cupboard

Japanese ingredients are increasingly making their way into Western supermarkets, and it is now quite possible to enjoy Japanese cooking without having to visit Japanese supermarkets. This selection includes some of the essential items, while the recipes show how to handle each ingredient.

Beans

Azuki (azuki bean). This small red bean – *azuki* actually means 'small bean' – is mainly used to make a sweet paste called *an* for cakes and desserts.

Daizu (soya bean or soybean). This is the basis of tofu and the most important Japanese sauces such as miso and shoyu. It is so nutritious that it is called 'beef of the field' and is actually used to make meat substitutes as well.

Edamamé (fresh green soya (soy) bean in pod). This is a fresh young green *daizu* (see above) still in the pod, which is simply boiled, and eaten from the pod with a little salt sprinkled on. Freshly boiled *edamamé* is an indispensable accompaniment to aperitifs at home as well as in restaurants, and is also popular abroad. It is often sold on the stalk.

Natto (fermented soya (soy) beans). *Natto* is a regular item on the Japanese breakfast table. It is used for *norimaki* (nori-rolled sushi) or mixed with grated daikon, spring onions (scallions), shoyu (Japanese soy sauce) and mustard.

Flavourings

Miso and shoyu are the two most important, indeed indispensable Japanese flavouring sauces. They are more often used as condiments for dipping or as flavouring for cooking.

Mirin. Mirin is a sweet cooking sake made from *shochu* (distilled rice spirit) mixed with steamed glutinous rice and *koji* (a yeast-like culture made from rice). It is brewed and compressed to absorb the liquid, and then filtered. Mirin adds to food not only a mild sweetness but also a shiny glaze and slightly alcoholic flavour. It is used mostly for simmering dishes and in glazing sauces such as *teriyaki* sauce.

Miso. Miso is made from boiled soya beans (soybeans), crushed, then mixed with a culture called *koji*, which is made from wheat and rice, barley or beans. The fermented mixture is allowed to mature for up to three years. There are three basic grades of strength of flavour and colour to match: *shiro-miso*, white and light; ordinary miso, khaki and medium; and *aka-miso*, red and strong. There is also a speciality miso called *kuro-miso*, which is dark and strong. Miso is a versatile ingredient and is simply diluted into dashi (fish stock or broth) to make soups, used as part of the seasoning for simmered dishes or dipping sauces, and also as a marinade for meat and fish.

Shoyu (Japanese soy sauce). Shoyu is made from soya beans (soybeans), wheat and salt. First the mixture of soya beans (soybeans) and wheat is made into a culture called *koji*, helped by active mould, which is then mixed with salt and water. This mash is left to ferment and brew for one year. It is then compressed

Trays of beans and other dried pulses are displayed on a stall.

to exude liquid, which is then refined. (Mass-produced shoyu does not necessarily follow this authentic process but uses chemicals instead to hasten it.) All manufactured shoyu is pasteurized and has preservatives added. Shoyu is used as a dip on its own for sushi, sashimi, pickles and many other dishes. For a dip, use it very carefully and sparingly, by pouring only one or two tablespoons into your sauce plate at a time and do not fill the dish.

Yonezu (rice vinegar). Yonezu is used for Japanese cooking but unless it is labelled 'pure rice vinegar' it normally contains some other grains as well. The acidity of Japanese rice vinegar is 4 to 4.5 per cent, a lot milder than most Western vinegars. Therefore, if you use white wine vinegar as a substitute, use slightly less than suggested in the recipe, or dilute it with a little water.

A bunch of daikon is displayed in a market stall.

Fruits

Japan produces numerous citrus fruits for flavouring as well as eating. The two favourite fruits used in sauces and dressings are *daidai* and *yuzu*.

Daidai is a citrus fruit, too sour to eat as a fruit, which is often mixed with shoyu for dipping sauces to eat mainly with *nabé* (pot) dishes.

Yuzu is among the many varieties of citrus fruits used in Japanese cooking but is the most popular and is used almost entirely for its exquisitely aromatic rind. Tiny pieces and slivers of the bright yellow skin are scraped and used to garnish soups, salads, simmered dishes, pickles, relishes and sweets. The fruit is too sharp to eat, though its juice is used in dressings and sauces. There is also a citrus flavouring called *ponzu*, and it is made commercially in jars to resemble *yuzu*.

Umeboshi (salted and dried Japanese apricots) is a unique Japanese pickle, usually eaten with rice for breakfast. It is regarded as having a tonic quality, aiding digestion and keeping the intestinal tract clear. It is often pickled with red *shiso* leaves for flavour as well as for colour, and used for nori-rolled sushi.

Herbs and spices

In Japanese cooking herbs and spices are used in a very subtle way. Garlic is not normally used, and for flavouring root ginger is almost always grated and only the juice is used.

Goma (sesame seeds). In Japanese cooking black and white seeds are used. They are roasted, called *iri-goma* or *atari-goma*, and are available in packets from oriental supermarkets. It's best to lightly roast them again before use to bring out the aroma.

Sansho. Although *sansho* means 'mountain pepper', it is not actually a pepper plant but a prickly ash tree. Its refreshingly piercing fragrance is used to mask the smell and balance the taste of fatty foods. The delicate young sprouts, *kinome*, the tiny greenish-yellow flowers, *hana-zansho*, and the bitterly pungent berries, *mi-* or *tsubu-zansho* are all used in daily cooking in Japan. The ripened seed pods are dried, and the green pods are powdered to make *kona-zansho* (powdered *sansho*), which is used as a condiment most famously for *kabayaki* eel and other grilled dishes such as *yakitori*.

Shiso. Shiso is a herb from the mint family, unique to Japan (known by the Americans bizarrely as beefsteak plant). There are two types, green and red, and the whole *shiso* plant, from berries to flowers, is used as a herb or garnish for Japanese dishes. The green variety is used for its exquisite flavour and the red for colouring as well as its aroma. Normally only green *shiso* is used as a herb and garnish for dishes such as sashimi, tempura and vinegared salads, and red *shiso* for making *umeboshi* (salted and dried Japanese apricots) and other pickles. Its berries, stems and flowers are used to garnish sashimi, soup and sauces.

Shoga (root ginger). To use as a spice, ginger is normally grated, and the juice is then squeezed. Vinegared fresh root ginger is the most popular accompaniment to sushi, and is eaten to cleanse the palate after each course.

Taka-no-tsumé (dried red chilli). *Taka-no-tsumé*, meaning 'hawk's claw', usually dried, is extremely hot, probably three times hotter than fresh chilli, so use sparingly. It is used for making *momiji-oroshi*, a dipping sauce with grated daikon for hotpot dishes. It is also used in piquant marinades and pickling mixtures for vegetables.

Shichimi-togarashi (seven-spice chilli powder). This is made of powdered dried chilli mixed with other seeds including sesame, poppy, rape, hemp, *shiso* and *sansho*, as well as nori, and is used as a condiment for sprinkling over soups and grilled (broiled) meat and fish.

Wasabi. Wasabi is a mountain hollyhock and although it is sometimes introduced as the Japanese equivalent to Western horseradish, the two are not related. The grated fresh root of wasabi has a milder fragrance and less sharp pungency than horseradish. However, freshly grated wasabi is a rarity even in Japan and is more commonly used in its powdered and paste forms, which will normally contain horseradish for extra pungency. Wasabi paste is always used for sashimi and sushi. It is also used for pickling vegetables and in salad dressings.

Mushrooms

Enoki-daké (enoki mushroom). This bundle of tiny berry cap mushrooms is one of the regular ingredients for hotpot dishes such as *shabu shabu*, and is also used for seasoned salads and in soups.

Matsutake (pine mushroom). *Matsutake* is the king of Japanese mushrooms. This relatively large, dark brown fungus with a thick, meaty stem grows only in the wild in undisturbed stands of red pine trees in Japan. It is often compared with European cep or porcini, but it's more delicate and rarer, thus much more expensive. Unfortunately, *matsutake* is never dried, so it's very difficult to obtain outside Japan. It's eaten lightly grilled, or in clear soup, *dobinmushi* (teapot steam) and cooked with rice.

Nameko (nameko mushroom). *Nameko*, meaning 'slippery mushroom', is available only in jars or tins, since the fresh *nameko* has a very short life. The most popular use of *nameko* is in miso soup. It is also used for hors d'oeuvres.

Shiitake. These are the most popular and well known among numerous Japanese mushrooms. Also known, incorrectly, as Chinese mushroom, the shiitake actually originated in Japan. There are various types, but the one called *donko*, winter mushroom, which has a small, thick and dense, dark cap, is the best. Dried shiitake have a richer aroma and flavour, and the water they are soaked in can be used in place of dashi (fish stock or broth) for vegetarian cooking.

Shimeji. This is a popular Japanese mushroom making its way into the Western culinary scene. Its fresh but not strong character suits most delicate Japanese cooking, in clear soup, or for grilled (broiled) and fried dishes. It is a common ingredient for hotpots.

Somen noodles are some of the most popular noodles, along with ramen. This somen is tied specially for use in the somen with sea bream recipe.

Noodles

The Japanese love noodles, and have developed numerous types of noodle dishes. Ramen in particular has now been accepted as a popular part of the Western diet.

Ramen, literally meaning 'stretched noodles', originated in China but the Japanese have developed it to a finer, more sophisticated form. It is made into a dough with *kansui*, alkali water, the chemical reaction of which makes the wheat dough smooth and able to be stretched into very fine noodles. Its crunchiness and the style of serving rich soup with a lot of toppings have caught the attention of young people the world over. It is available fresh, dried or frozen from supermarkets and oriental shops. So-called instant ramen, a block of dried ramen with sachets of soup and spices in packets, is regarded as one of Japan's most successful inventions, and billions of packets are now consumed the world over each year.

Soba (buckwheat noodle). As noodles made from just buckwheat flour lack elasticity and stickiness, wheat flour is usually added as a smoothing, binding agent. According to how finely the buckwheat seeds were ground, the colour of the noodles varies from dark brownish-grey to light beige. There is also a green-coloured soba called *chasoba*, to which powdered tea has been added. Soba is eaten dipped in a dashi (fish stock/broth)-based sauce or cooked in soup.

Udon (wheat noodle). Udon is available in dried or cooked form in packets. Dried udon usually takes just over ten minutes to cook in boiling water. *Hiyamugi,* thin white noodles, are made in the same way but cut very thinly. Somen, very fine noodles, are also made from wheat, but the dough is stretched with the help of vegetable oil to very thin strips and air-dried. Very fine somen cooks in 1–2 minutes.

Rice

Rice is the staple food of Japan, and other grains such as glutinous rice and barley are also used in Japanese cooking.

Japanese rice is the short grain variety, as opposed to the long grain rice of neighbouring South-east Asian countries. There are over 300 different types of short grain rice grown throughout Japan, and brand names such as Koshihikari and Sasanishiki are among the most popular. They are grown in water-filled paddy fields. However, most of the Japanese rice sold in the West is in fact produced in California on dry land, while some comes from Spain. There are slight variations in hardness, but Kahomai (the hardest), Nishiki, Maruyu, Kokuho (all Californian) and Minori (Spanish, the softest) are some of the popular brand names available. There are other varieties such as *genmai* (unpolished brown rice) and *mochigome* (glutinous rice), mainly used for making *mochi* (rice cakes).

Seafood and seafood products

Japanese cooking means mainly vegetable and seafood cooking, and numerous fish, shellfish and seaweeds are eaten every day in Japan. Some fish are unique to the seas around Japan, but an increasing number of fish are appearing on the Western market.

Dashi. Dashi is a fish stock (broth), which is an important feature of many dishes, particularly soups. It is best made fresh, as shown on page 56 – Clear Soup with Egg and Prawns (Shrimp). However, if you want to prepare just a single and quick dish, use dashi granules, which is available in Japanese supermarkets or specialist shops.

Hijiki (hijiki seaweed). This is small, twiggy, black, marine algae, normally sold dried in packets. It is often stir-fried and then simmered in a shoyu-based sauce with other vegetables. It is also used to garnish rice dishes, its black, twig-like shape contrasting well with the white rice.

Ikura (salmon caviar). In Russia all fish eggs are called *ikura* but it is used only for salmon eggs in Japan. This is a great delicacy and mainly used for sushi and for making hors d'oeuvres. It is salted and widely available in jars from supermarkets.

Kabayaki (grilled or broiled eel). Kabayaki is either filleted *unagi* (eel) or *anago* (sea eel), steamed and then grilled (broiled) with a thick, sweet shoyu sauce. It is usually eaten with hot boiled rice with the accompanying sauce sprinkled with *shichimi* (seven-spice chilli powder) or *sansho* (Japanese green pepper). It is also used for sushi, and is available ready-to-eat in packets, frozen or vacuum packed.

Each region has a variety of speciality pickled vegetables, and they are freshly made and sold at a market.

Kanten (agar-agar). Taken from *tengusa* seaweed, *kanten* is a freeze-dried, pure substance that works like a gelatine, and is mainly used for making desserts and cakes. It makes a slightly opaque jelly, and begins to set at higher than room temperature.

Katsuo (bonito or skipjack tuna). *Katsuo* is one of the most important and versatile fish in Japanese cooking. It is commonly translated as 'bonito' (skipjack tuna), but they are in fact slightly different fish. The red meat of *katsuo* is firmer and crunchier than tuna. The most cherished *katsuo* dish is *tataki* (seared, then sliced), eaten with ginger, garlic and spring onion (scallion) mixed in shoyu (soy sauce).

Kazunoko (herring roe). As it comes salted and dried (the whole ovary with roe inside), *kazunoko* needs to be soaked in water overnight to soften and desalt it before use. It is usually eaten with a little shoyu and dried fish flakes as an hors d'oeuvre. It is one of the special items for the New Year's Day celebration brunch and is also used as a sushi topping.

Kezuribushi or hanagatsuo (dried fish flakes). *Katsuo* (bonito or skipjack tuna), is cooked and sun-dried to a hard block (*katsuobushi*) and then shaven for use. This is the source of dashi (fish stock or broth) and is also used for sprinkling on vegetables or fish as an additional flavouring. Mixed with a little shoyu (Japanese soy sauce) it makes a good accompaniment to hot boiled rice or stuffing for rice balls.

Konbu (kelp). The most important role this large dark seaweed plays in Japanese cooking is in the making of dashi, along with *kezuribushi* (dried bonito or skipjack tuna flakes). It is also used for extra flavour in the boiling of rice for sushi, for simmering with vegetables, fish and meat or in hotpots.

Maguro (tuna). Blue-fin tuna with its deep red meat is supposed to be the best among several kinds of tuna, and is used for sashimi (prepared fish) and sushi. There are two kinds of tuna meat, *akami* (red meat) or *toro* (oily meat), and *toro* is classified by the degree of its oiliness into *chu-toro* (middle *toro*) and *o-toro* (big *toro*). It is generally thought that *toro* is superior, thus more expensive.

Tarako (cod's ovary with roe). *Mentaiko* is a salted version and *karashi mentaiko* a pungent chilli version. They are normally coloured slightly red with

vegetable colouring to look more attractive. It is lightly grilled (broiled) and eaten with hot boiled rice or used for making nori-rolled sushi.

Uni (sea urchin ovary). Fresh *uni*, eaten raw, is one of the regular items for sushi toppings. It also provides a golden coating for other seafood.

Wakame (young seaweed). Wakame, meaning young leaf, is brownish orange algae, available mostly in dried or salted form. It is one of the most popular soup ingredients and is also good as a salad with a vinegary dressing. Cut *wakame* in packets, which softens almost instantly, is widely available from oriental supermarkets.

Tofu and tofu products

Tofu came to Japan from China in the eighth century and has been one of the most important foods in Japanese cooking ever since. There are numerous products developed from tofu, some of which are listed below.

Abura-agé (thin deep-fried tofu). *Abura-agé* is often used as a substitute for meat for vegetarians. It can be slit open like pitta bread and stuffed with vegetables or sushi rice. It is also used in soup and hotpot dishes.

Koya-dofu (freeze-dried tofu). Also known as *kogori-dofu* (frozen tofu), it is believed to have been invented by Buddhist monks on the *Koya* mountain

Various fish and tofu products are available for home cooking.

many centuries ago, hence its name. It has a spongy texture and rich taste even after it has been soaked in water, and is used for simmering with vegetables in a rich soup. It is also used for *shojin-ryori*, Buddhist monks' vegetarian cooking.

Tofu (soya bean or soybean curd). Tofu is made from soya beans (soybeans), and is regarded as extremely healthy food. There are two types: firm and soft. There is also lightly seared tofu called *yaki-dofu*, which is available from Japanese shops and mainly used in hotpot dishes. The pulp after exuding the soya milk for making tofu is not wasted; it is called *okara* and is used in the cooking of vegetables. It is occasionally available in Japanese supermarkets.

Yuba (tofu skin). This is the filament of soya milk carefully removed from the surface of heated soya bean (soybean) milk and left to dry. It is one of the specialities of Kyoto and is often used in clear soup, for *shojin-ryori* (vegetarian cooking) and in Kyoto-style *kaiseki* (multi-course meal). In Kyoto, fresh *yuba* is available. It comes in various sheet forms in packets such as flat, rolled and cut or thick strips.

Vegetables

In Japanese cooking, the cutting of ingredients is so important that different cuts and shapes have their own names such as *sengiri* (shreds), *wagiri* (rounds), *hangetsu* (half-moons), *tanzaku* (poem card – thin rectangles), *hyoshigi* (clapper board – thick rectangles), *sainome* (cubes), *arare* (dice), *sasagaki* (shavings) and *hanagiri* (flowers). The following typical Japanese vegetables are available from Western or oriental supermarkets.

Daikon (white long radish). Daikon, also known by its Indian name mooli, is a member of the radish family. It is a versatile vegetable, cooked in soup, chopped for salad, shredded for a sashimi garnish or most notably grated as a condiment. It is also pickled to make *takuan*, the bright yellow pickle often used for nori-rolled sushi.

Ginnan (gingko nut). The Japanese maple tree bears this exquisite nut, which is available from Japanese supermarkets either fresh in its shell, shelled in packets, or shelled and cooked in tins or jars. Simply fried gingko nuts sprinkled with salt are often served as hors d'oeuvres: a Japanese delicacy and a good accompaniment to sake. They are also used for simmered and fried dishes, and in soups.

Gobo (burdock root). Its grey flesh is quite stringy but *gobo* adds a unique texture and flavour. It is used for making *kinpira*, stir-fried shredded carrot and *gobo* with chilli and shoyu (Japanese soy sauce). Fresh *gobo* is sometimes available from Japanese supermarkets, where tinned, cooked *gobo* is also sold.

Hakusai (Chinese cabbage or leaf). Hakusai, meaning white vegetable, is one of the most popular vegetables in Japanese cooking. It is salted to accompany freshly cooked hot rice, and is also used in simmered dishes, hotpots and steamed dishes.

Kabocha (kabocha squash). Simply steamed or boiled, kabocha squash makes a very delicious and nutritious snack. It is also used for frying in tempura as well as for simmering with other vegetables and chicken meat. It is increasingly available from many general supermarkets.

Kanpyo (dried gourd ribbon). Kanpyo is made from the flesh of the calabash gourd, a member of the marrow family. Cut into strips and dried, it plays an unusual role in Japanese cooking for tying foods together or for making a decorative bow on food, as well as for simmering with vegetables and meat. Cooked in sweet shoyu, it is used for sushi dishes.

Renkon (lotus root). This adds a unique feature to a dish as it contains several holes that run the full length of the root. Its crunchiness as well as unique pattern is most appreciated. It is used for simmering dishes and for salad with vinegar dressing. It is also popular for tempura and mixed sushi. Fresh lotus root is available in abundance in winter from most oriental supermarkets, while the cooked and tinned or frozen ones are found all year round.

Sato-imo (taro). A kind of potato, *sato-imo* has dense grey-white flesh and a gorgeous nutty flavour. Underneath its hairy, striped dark skin there is a unique slipperiness, which makes peeling very easy. Plain boiled or steamed and dipped in shoyu (Japanese soy sauce), it is a popular snack, a much healthier alternative to crisps. It is also excellent for simmered dishes and soups.

Satsuma-imo (sweet potato). This used to be the number one snack before the days of fancy cakes and sweets. It is used for simmered, fried and steamed dishes and is also good for barbecues. It is also an ingredient in cakes and desserts, and plain boiled or steamed *satsuma-imo* still makes a enjoyable snack.

Shungiku. These are the leaves of the chrysanthemum family, and with their slight bitter taste, they are used in soups, hotpots and simmered dishes.

Takenoko (bamboo shoots). Takenoko are a very seasonal delicacy, available from late spring to early summer in Japan. Simply cooked, fresh bamboo shoots in dashi (fish stock or broth) sauce is one of the most popular dishes. The young, tender shoots are also cooked with rice, while the older shoots are used for either slow cooking with other vegetables and chicken, or stir-frying.

Takuan (pickled daikon). This is pickled in *nuka*, dry rice bran and salt, and the end result is a soft but crunchy, delicious yellow daikon. This pickle is said to have been invented by the seventeenth-century Buddhist monk, Takuan, hence the name. It is salty with a hint of sweetness and is a good accompaniment to hot boiled rice. It is also a regular ingredient for nori-rolled sushi and other rice dishes.

Other products

Fu (dried gluten cakes). Fu was originally developed as a substitute for meat in Zen Buddhist cooking, but is now used mainly as a decorative garnish. It is a

dried starch cake extracted from wheat flour. It comes in many colours, sizes and shapes and is used to garnish soups and also hotpots.

Harusame ('spring rain' noodles). This is a fine translucent filament made from various starchy roots such as potato and sweet potato, or sometimes green beans. It is used in cooked salad, soup, hotpot or as a coating for frying fish and vegetables.

Konnyaku (yam cake). Also known as devil's tongue, *konnyaku* is an unusual, dense, gelatinous cake made from the rugged root of the *konnyaku* plant, a kind of yam potato. Fresh *konnyaku* is eaten raw, like sashimi, or is used for cooking with other vegetables and meat or for soups and hotpots. The slippery texture may not appeal to non-Japanese people, but it is regarded as a slimming food as it is very filling although it has no nutrients and is supposed to cleanse the stomach. It is eaten only for its texture.

Shirataki (konnyaku noodle). Meaning 'white waterfall', it is a noodle but is used as a vegetable in *nabé* (pot) and cooked salad dishes. It is made in the same way as *konnyaku* but, as the name implies, only as a thin white filament form. Parboil and roughly cut (since it is a long noodle) before use.

Various types of miso are ready for weighing in a shop near Ikebukuro, Tokyo.

Alcoholic drinks

Sake (rice wine). Sake is the prime alcoholic drink of Japan, and is also used for cooking. It is made from refined and then steamed rice, *koji* (a yeast-like culture made from rice) and water, and it's a simple but very labour-intensive process. Unlike wine, it keeps well, but once a bottle is opened, it should be drunk as soon as possible. Store in a cool, dark place away from the sunlight.

Shochu (distilled rice spirit). Literally translated as 'fiery spirits', it is a distilled spirit made from rice and other various grains or even sweet potatoes. The alcohol content is quite high at 20–25 per cent – some are as high as 45 per cent – so it's normally drunk diluted with water, hot or cold depending on the season. It is also used for making *umeshu*, plum (Japanese apricot) liqueur.

Umeshu (Japanese apricot liqueur). *Umeshu* is sold as plum liqueur, but it is made of white spirit, Japanese apricots and sugar. In Japan it is also made at home. It's a sweet liqueur, which is drunk on the rocks or diluted with ice-cold water.

A note on kitchen utensils

If your kitchen is equipped with a good selection of knives, chopping-boards and other usual cooking utensils, it is not necessary to buy any Japanese utensils. However, the following items will be particularly useful and will make your Japanese cooking easier and more enjoyable.

Daikon oroshi or oroshi-gane (daikon grater). This is the most useful tool for Japanese cooking, which uses a lot of grated daikon and fresh root ginger. This grates not only very finely but also captures the juices from the ingredients in the curved compartment at the bottom. If you want to add just one Japanese tool to your kitchen, this is the one.

Handai or hangiri (wooden rice tub). This tub is used to mix cooked rice with the vinegar mixture for sushi making. The wood is gentle to the rice and absorbs extra moisture so as not to make the rice soggy.

Hashi (Japanese chopsticks). *Hashi*, or more politely *ohashi*, are not meant to for chopping, as in Japanese cooking food is normally served in properly cut sizes, so chopsticks is the wrong word for this, the most elegant cutlery in the world. There are also wooden as well as metal *hashi* for cooking. They come in different sizes from a little longer than eating *hashi* to about 40cm/16in. The longer ones are good for handling deep-frying so that your hands remain reasonably distant from the hot oil. There are also serving *hashi*, which are more decorative than cooking *hashi*.

Hocho (cooking knives). Cutting is so important in Japanese cooking that a set of personal knives is the Japanese chef's heart and soul. You do not need to have a set of Japanese knives, but it is essential to have a good carving knife and a vegetable knife.

Makisu (sushi rolling bamboo mat). This is a piece of bamboo mat, the size of a tablemat, which is used as an aid to roll sushi or egg omelette, or squeeze excess water out of tofu and cooked vegetables. This is an essential tool for sushi lovers, and as it can be folded into the size of a pencil-case it doesn't take up much space in your kitchen.

Otoshi-buta (drop lid). The light pressure of this wooden lid, placed directly on the food in the pan, keeps delicate ingredients, such as vegetables and tofu, securely on the base of the pan.

Suribachi and surikogi (Japanese mortar and pestle). The *suribachi* is a large mixing bowl made of clay, with numerous sharp ridges on the inside surface so that ingredients as diverse as sesame seeds and minced meat can be ground into a paste with the *surikogi*, a pestle made of hardwood. The *suribachi* can then be used as a mixing bowl.

Také-gushi (bamboo skewers). Bamboo skewers are very useful tools to have in the kitchen. They make grilling (broiling) on direct heat easier, particularly for small pieces of food, and are also useful for checking how food is cooking without breaking it or making obvious holes in it.

Zaru (strainer). The Japanese mesh strainer is made of bamboo or stainless steel, and is extremely effective as it can be used to strain even tiny grains of rice and very fine noodles. It comes in various sizes and shapes for different usage.

1

Appetizers

Daikon and salmon kinuta roll

Daikon kinuta-maki

AKIHIRO KURITA has cooking in his genes: his father runs a restaurant in Kyoto, where he trained for 12 years, and many of his relatives either own or work at a restaurant. A young chef/patron himself of a small Kyoto-cuisine restaurant, Kurita, situated in the town centre, his cooking is based on old *kaiseki* (formal banquet meal), but is more approachable and affordable. The main part of the restaurant is the counter, which seats about a dozen people and is where he cooks in front of the diners. He has therefore developed many small dishes he can prepare beforehand and assemble in a small space and in a short time. This pretty and delicious dish is one of them.

MAKES 8 ROLLS

300g/10oz salmon fillet
1 large daikon, peeled
salt

FOR THE SWEET VINEGAR MARINADE:

8 tablespoons *yonezu* (Japanese rice vinegar)
4 tablespoons granulated sugar
½ teaspoon salt
1 red chilli, de-seeded and finely chopped

In Kyoto, a kabura *(giant turnip) is used for this dish for its soft and smooth texture, but it is not easily obtainable elsewhere, even in Tokyo, so I suggest here that daikon is used instead. If you do not wish to use chilli,* yuzu *or lemon rind will add an extra aroma. This is a useful starter for dinner parties as it can be made two or three days beforehand. AK*

1 Salt the salmon generously and leave in the refrigerator overnight. Using a damp cloth or kitchen paper (paper towel) wipe off the salt from the salmon and cut into 1cm/½in square, 7–8cm/3–3½in long cylinders. You'll need 8 pieces.

2 For the sweet vinegar marinade mix the vinegar, sugar and salt in a saucepan, and place on a low heat, stirring until the sugar and salt have dissolved. Remove from the heat, then add the chopped chilli and set aside.

3 Cut the daikon crossways into 7–8cm/3–3½in pieces (you may need 2–3 pieces). Using a sharp knife shave off 3–4 thin sheets (*katsura-muki*, see page 42), about 3mm/⅛in thick and 20cm/8in long, from each daikon inserting the blade lengthways like peeling off the skin. You will need 8 daikon sheets of 7–8cm/3–3½in wide and 20cm/8in long. Alternatively, (this is a lot easier to do) cut a 20cm/8in

piece crossways from the thick end of the daikon, and halve lengthways. Carefully slice a 3mm/⅛in thick sheet from the cut end of each daikon piece. Repeat this until you have 8 daikon sheets of 7–8cm/3–3½in wide and 20cm/8in long.

4 Mix 1 litre/1¾pints/4½ cups water and 2 tablespoons of salt in a large mixing bowl. Soak the daikon sheets in the bowl and leave to wilt for 5–10 minutes. Drain and wipe the water with kitchen paper (paper towels).

5 Place a daikon sheet on a chopping-board and tightly roll in a salmon piece. Repeat this until you have 8 rolls, and put all in a mixing bowl. Pour over the sweet vinegar marinade, then place a small plate upside down to cover the daikon rolls inside the bowl and put a weight (a stone or unopened can of food) on top. Leave to marinate in the refrigerator. After about 3 days, it is ready to eat. Serve 2 rolls each on individual plates.

Salad with sashimi

Sashimi dé salada

KENTARO is a celebrity cookery personality on television, Japan's answer to England's 'Naked Chef', Jamie Oliver. In fact the two met in Japan and became firm friends since they share a lot of common interests and tastes, cooking and non-cooking alike. Like Jamie's, Kentaro's cooking style is carefree and easy-going, and appeals particularly to the busy, younger generation. His philosophy of Japanese cooking is to make it as simple as possible, yet not to economize on time and ingredients when necessary. He thinks there are too many ambiguous words and must-dos in 'ye olde' Japanese haute cuisine, which deter younger people from cooking. Here is one of his simplest dishes using ready-made ingredients.

SERVES 4

4 portions any sashimi pack from
    Japanese shops or 4–6 fillets (depending
    on size) very fresh salmon, tuna, marlin
    or sole
1 salad lettuce
10cm/4in piece of daikon, peeled
4 spring onions (scallions)
1–2 teaspoons each black and white sesame
    seeds, lightly roasted

FOR THE DRESSING:

½ Spanish onion, grated
1–2 cloves garlic, grated
2 tablespoons shoyu (Japanese soy sauce)
2 tablespoons sesame oil

They say you must at least be able to fillet fish before tackling Japanese cooking. I'd say that's nonsense. If you cook a very good fish dish with ready-made fillet, but then want to make it even better next time using freshly filleted fish, you may then make an effort to learn how to fillet fish yourself. Even if you don't, it doesn't make much difference to your whole life! It's much more fun for you to do cooking that is quick and enjoyable rather than long and tiresome, however authentic the result. Let's do it the way you feel like doing it is my idea of cooking. For this salad you can use any ready-prepared sashimi bought from a Japanese supermarket, or prepare slices of your own fillet of a very fresh fish such as salmon, tuna, marlin, turbot or sole. You can also use squid or scallops. KK

1 If the fillets come with the skin, skin them first: place a fillet skin-side down on a chopping-board, then insert the blade in between the flesh and skin at the tail-end. Holding down the tail-end with the fingers of one hand, run the blade along the skin towards the head. Place the skinned fillet on a chopping-board skin-side down, and cut diagonally into thin (about 0.5–1cm/¼–½in) slices to make sashimi. Repeat this sashimi process with the rest of the fillets.

2 Tear the salad lettuce by hand roughly into bite-sized pieces. Cut the daikon in half to make 2 5cm/2in cylinders, slice each lengthways into 5mm/¼in thick squares and then each square, lengthways, into thin shreds. Cut the spring onions (scallions) into 3cm/1¼in long pieces.
3 Mix all the dressing ingredients in a small mixing bowl.
4 Mix all the sashimi and vegetables in a large mixing bowl and arrange on 4 individual plates, or in one salad bowl. Sprinkle with the sesame seeds and pour the dressing over the salad before serving.

Foie gras with simmered daikon

Foie gras daikon-ni

MINORU ODAJIMA used to be a keen mountaineer, and went to work in Paris in the late sixties so that he could climb the Alps. He learned about wine and cooking meat there, and when he got back to Japan in the seventies and started his own restaurant, he adapted the not-so-popular meat dishes to Japanese cooking, matching wines to the dishes. This foie gras dish is one of his long-running dishes at his restaurant, Odajima in Sangen-jaya, a suburb of Tokyo.

SERVES 4

12cm/5in piece of daikon (from the thick end)
4 asparagus stalks
1 tablespoon vegetable oil
4 pieces (approximately 30g/1oz each) of
   foie gras
salt

FOR THE SAUCE:
225ml/8fl oz/1 cup dashi (see page 56)
2 tablespoons shoyu (Japanese soy sauce)
1 tablespoon granulated sugar

My motto in cooking is 'simple is the best', and all my recipes are made as simple as possible. Simple cooking is not always the easiest because you need the freshest of fresh ingredients prepared with meticulous precision and cooked to just the right softness. The crucial point in this dish lies in the cooking of the daikon. Daikon is one of the most versatile and popular vegetables for Japanese cooking, but can easily be ruined if not cooked correctly. MO

1 Peel the hard skin off the daikon, and cut into 4 rings, about 3cm/1in long. Using a sharp knife, carefully cut off from each piece about 2mm/⅛in diagonally round the sharp edges – this prevents vegetables from becoming misshapen while cooking. Put the daikon pieces in plenty of water in a saucepan, bring to the boil, then lower the heat and cook on a moderate heat until soft. It takes 40–50 minutes depending on the quality of the daikon. Remove from the heat, drain and place under running water to wash off its bitterness.

2 Put all the sauce ingredients in a saucepan and bring to the boil, stirring until the sugar dissolves. Add the daikon and simmer over a low heat for 15 minutes until the daikon absorbs the flavour.
3 Meanwhile, boil the asparagus in lightly salted water for 2–3 minutes until soft but still crunchy, and drain. Cut into about 3cm/1in long pieces.
4 Heat a frying-pan, add the vegetable oil, and fry the foie gras over a high heat for 1–2 minutes on both sides until it is golden brown. Remove from the heat and then sprinkle with a pinch of salt.
5 Place a flavoured daikon ring on each of 4 individual, deepish dishes and a foie gras on top of each. Pour over a little sauce, garnish with asparagus and serve hot.

Prawn (shrimp) 'chrysanthemum' and smoked salmon 'persimmon' sushi

Kiku mitaté ebi-zushi to kaki mitaté salmon-sushi

MASAHIRO KURUSU, the current chef/patron of Tankuma, introduces one of his breathtakingly beautiful sushi dishes, which can be eaten as a starter or main course. Most of the established *kaiseki* restaurants in Kyoto are still run by the descendant of a long line of *kaiseki* chefs, and Tankuma, established in 1928, is one of them. It can be found in Kyoto, Osaka, Tokyo, Hakata and Kyushu.

MAKES 4 OF EACH SUSHI

FOR THE *TOSA-ZU*:
110ml/4fl oz/½ cup water
3 tablespoons *yonezu* (Japanese rice vinegar)
1½ tablespoons light shoyu (Japanese soy sauce)
1 teaspoon granulated sugar
2–3cm/about 1in dried *konbu* (kelp)
1–2 tablespoons *kezuribushi* (dried fish flakes)

FOR THE CHRYSANTHEMUM SUSHI:
4 giant prawns (shrimp) with shells
1 hard-boiled (hard-cooked) egg (only yolk is needed)
pinch of salt
150g/5oz/1 cup *sumeshi* (cooked vinegared rice)
shungiku (chrysanthemum leaves), to garnish (optional)

FOR THE PERSIMMON SUSHI:
4 slices (approximately 5cm/2in square) smoked salmon
8cm/3½in dried *konbu* (kelp)
150g/5oz/1 cup *sumeshi* (cooked vinegared rice)

The word mitaté, *meaning 'imaging', is more often used in* kaiseki *cooking than anything else since it is traditional for* kaiseki *to express the season by visualizing nature in the cooking. This often results in the representation of flowers and birds through the food on the plate. This dish, expressing the images of chrysanthemum and persimmon, is an autumn starter, and fun to make.* Tosa-zu *is used here to flavour the fish and consists of rice vinegar with* kezuribushi *(dried bonito or skipjack tuna flakes). Tosa is an area in Shikoku island with a good katsuo (bonito or skipjack tuna) fishery, hence the name. MK*

1 Mix all the ingredients of the *Tosa-zu*, except the *kezuribushi*, in a small saucepan, and bring to the boil on a moderate heat. Add the *kezuribushi* and remove from the heat as soon as it comes back to the boil. Allow the *kezuribushi* to settle to the bottom of the pan, then strain through a fine cloth or fine mesh laid with kitchen paper (paper towels). Allow to cool.

2 Make the chrysanthemum sushi: take the head off each prawn (shrimp), and de-vein, retaining the shell. Tightly curl each into a round shape and fix it with a cocktail stick (toothpick). Cook the curled prawns (shrimp) in lightly salted boiling water for 2 minutes until bright red, and drain. Remove the cocktail sticks (tooth-picks), then peel and slice each prawn (shrimp) horizontally into two rings.

3 Press the hard-boiled (hard-cooked) egg yolk through a fine mesh into a small saucepan, add a pinch of salt, and then toss over a low heat, stirring vigorously for 1–2 minutes to make into fine egg crumbs. Remove from the heat and set aside to cool down.

4 Plunge a piece of prawn (shrimp) in the *Tosa-zu*, and place it, shell-side down, on a sheet of cling film (plastic wrap), about

20 x 20cm/8 x 8in. Spoon a heaped tablespoonful of rice on top, and wrap the cling film (plastic wrap) around the rice to make a slightly flat ball. Remove from the cling film (plastic wrap). Repeat with the remaining halves and rice.

5 Place a small amount of egg yolk crumbs on the centre of each chrysanthemum sushi. To make it look more like a chrysanthemum arrange chrysanthemum leaves around the sushi.

6 Make the persimmon sushi: soak the smoked salmon slices in the *Tosa-zu* for 3 minutes, and drain. Wipe the *konbu* with vinegar-soaked kitchen paper (paper towels), and cut it into the shape of a persimmon calyx (see picture).

7 Place a salmon slice on a piece of cling film (plastic wrap), about 20 x 20cm/ 8 x 8in, and put 1 heaped tablespoonful of rice on top. Aided by the cling film (plastic wrap), wrap the smoked salmon round the rice to make a ball, and then shape it like a persimmon. Place a *konbu* calyx on it. Make a hole with a cocktail stick (toothpick) from the top in the centre, and insert a piece of *konbu*, to look like a stem of the persimmon. Repeat to make another 3 with the remaining ingredients.

Salted hakusai roll with spinach

Horenso no hakusai-maki [v]

There are numerous methods of pickling vegetables in Japanese cooking from simple salting to pickling in rice bran. Hakusai, known as Chinese leaves in the West, is best salted; the transformation from the somewhat bland and crispy leaf into a richly flavoured, soft vegetable is quite remarkable. Chop the vegetable into bite-sized pieces, then put into a large freezer bag in layers with some salt, and leave to wilt in the refrigerator for 3–4 days, mixing from time to time. Drain and squeeze out the excess water with your hands before eating on its own or dipped in a little shoyu, or mixed in salad. This recipe is a version of salted hakusai, but instead of cutting, it takes advantage of the large, flexible sheet of shiny white leaf to roll the deep green spinach.

SERVES 4

4 large hakusai leaves
150–200g/5–7oz spinach
1 tablespoon shoyu (Japanese soy sauce)
1 tablespoon sake
1 tablespoon shiitake soaking water or
    vegetable stock (broth), or water
½ teaspoon mustard or wasabi
    paste (optional)
1 tablespoon white sesame seeds
salt

1 Sprinkle salt on both sides of the hakusai leaves and leave to wilt for 10–15 minutes. Squeeze out excess water with your hands and pat dry with kitchen paper (paper towels).
2 Boil the spinach in lightly salted boiling water for 30–60 seconds, drain and squeeze out the excess water with your hands. Spread the spinach on a large plate and sprinkle with the mixture of the shoyu, sake, shiitake soaking water or vegetable stock or water (broth) and the mustard or wasabi, if using. Leave to marinate for 5 minutes. Drain and lightly squeeze out the excess sauce.

3 Place a wilted hakusai leaf on a chopping-board, the inside (the right side) up. Place a quarter of the spinach across the thick end of the hakusai, and roll up toward the top end. Repeat this process with the remaining hakusai and spinach to make another 3 hakusai rolls.
4 Cut each hakusai roll crossways into 4 cylinders and arrange on 4 individual plates. Heat a small dry saucepan and put in the sesame seeds. Roast, constantly shaking the pan, until the seeds start popping up, and remove from the heat. Lightly pound in a mortar with a pestle, and sprinkle over the hakusai rolls. Serve as an appetizer or a pickle with rice.

Swordfish tataki with citrus daikon sauce

Kajiki no tataki oroshi-jyoyu aé

Tataki, literally meaning banging, is a raw fish 'banged' by the blade into tiny pieces then mixed with herbs and spices, as opposed to sashimi, which is simply sliced raw fish eaten with shoyu and wasabi. However, seared or parboiled raw fish slices, not 'banged', are also called tataki, *and the most popular* tataki *in this form is* katsuo *(bonito or skipjack tuna) as shown on page 42 (katsuo no tataki salad).*

SERVES 4

450g/1lb swordfish steak, skinned

salt

cress, to garnish

FOR THE *OROSHI-JYOYU* (CITRUS DAIKON SAUCE):

4 tablespoons finely grated daikon and juice

1 tablespoon light shoyu (Japanese soy sauce)

1 tablespoon sake

1 teaspoon granulated sugar

1 tablespoon lime juice

½ tablespoon root ginger juice

¼ teaspoon finely grated garlic

1 Plunge the swordfish steak into a saucepan of lightly salted boiling water over a high heat, and boil for 30 seconds until the surface turns white but the inside is still uncooked. Drain and immediately put into ice-cold water. Drain and pat dry with kitchen paper (paper towels). Cut the fish into slices 5mm/¼ in thick and 5 x 2.5cm/2 x 1in.

2 Mix all the ingredients for the *oroshi-jyoyu*, and thinly spread a quarter of the sauce on each of 4 individual plates. Arrange decoratively a quarter of the fish slices on the bed of the *oroshi-jyoyu*, sprinkle with cress on top and serve.

Boiled green soya beans (soybeans) in pods

Edamamé [v]

From early spring to late summer edamamé *(green soya beans (soybeans) in pods) come to the market in abundance in Japan. It's often sold still on the stalks. This simple dish is becoming very popular outside Japan, too, and is often found on menus at Western restaurants. At the moment it is only available cooked and frozen in packets from Japanese supermarkets, but it is expected that vegetable growers will soon grow it locally making fresh* edamamé *available. This is a very good accompaniment to chilled beer in summer.*

SERVES 4–8

900g/2lb *edamamé*

salt

1 If the *edamamé* pods are still on the stalks, separate them, and discard the stalks. Sprinkle the pods generously with salt and rub into the bean pods with your hands, then leave for 10–15 minutes. Cook in plenty of boiling water on a high heat for 6–7 minutes until cooked but the beans inside the pods are still crunchy.

2 Drain, and refresh briefly under running water (this stops further cooking and brightens the green colour). Arrange heaped in a basket or on a large serving plate. Sprinkle with a little sea salt all over, and serve warm or cold. Diners pick up a pod with their hand, and squeeze the soya beans (soybeans) into their mouths.

Squid and nori roll grilled (broiled) with sesame seeds

Ika to nori no goma-maki

Squid may be a little chewy for some tastes, but it makes a pretty dish. If it is cut crossways into fine shreds, a raw squid becomes ika somen *(squid noodle), and it is eaten raw with a little shoyu and wasabi. As it has a natural tendency to shrink on the skin-side and curl when heated, if you want to use it as a flat sheet as in this recipe, make criss-cross cuts on the skin-side before heating. You need a* makisu *(sushi rolling bamboo mat) for making this dish successfully.*

SERVES 4

1 medium squid, cleaned and skinned
sesame oil, for brushing
2 tablespoons white sesame seeds
1 sheet nori seaweed
vegetable oil, for oiling the skewers
sea salt

1 Cut the squid's body part lengthways in the centre to make 2 flat pieces. Place a piece on a chopping-board skin-side up and make fine diagonal criss-cross cuts on the skin-side. Repeat this process with the other piece of squid.

2 Place a sheet of cling film (plastic wrap) slightly larger than the size of a squid piece on a chopping-board and brush with sesame oil. Sprinkle 1 tablespoon of white sesame seeds and a pinch of salt evenly over the oiled cling film (plastic wrap). Place a piece of squid skin-side down on it and half a nori sheet on the squid. Tightly roll from the head towards the bottom of the squid piece and secure the roll with an oiled metal skewer. Repeat this process with the other squid.

3 Remove the squid rolls from the cling film (plastic wrap) and grill (broil) the skewered, rolled squid pieces under a moderate heat for about 2–3 minutes on both sides or until the squid is lightly cooked and the sesame seeds become an even golden brown. Remove from the heat and when cool remove the skewers.

4 Cut each squid and nori roll crossways into 4–6 rings and arrange 2–3 squid rings on individual plates as part of an assorted hors d'oeuvre.

Amberjack carpaccio with kanzuri and yuzu vinaigrette

Kanpachi carpaccio, kanzuri to yuzu no vinegrette

KEN TOMINAGA, chef/patron of Hana restaurant in the Bay Area, north of San Francisco, first came to California as a boy with his family, although he also trained as a chef in Tokyo. His cooking is therefore instinctive and very innovative, yet based on the traditional techniques and culinary senses that have earned his restaurant a reputation as one of the best 50 in the Bay Area. This is a simple sashimi salad, with an interesting dressing.

SERVES 4

300g/10oz amberjack or any sashimi fish, thinly sliced

1 Italian tomato, diced

5cm/2in piece of cucumber, diced

4–6 *shiso* leaves (pictured), shredded

1½ tablespoons *tonburi* or fish caviar (optional)

salt and pepper

FOR THE HANA SPECIAL DRESSING:

3 tablespoons white wine vinegar

1 tablespoon extra-virgin olive oil

2 tablespoons shoyu (Japanese soy sauce)

½ white onion, finely grated

½ clove garlic, finely grated

1 tablespoon lemon juice

salt and pepper

FOR THE *KANZURI* AND *YUZU* DRESSING:

1 tablespoon *yuzu* or lime juice

1 tablespoon shoyu (Japanese soy sauce)

3 tablespoons extra-virgin olive oil

1 tablespoon white wine vinegar

1 teaspoon *kanzuri* or chilli oil

1 teaspoon ginger juice

salt and pepper

Amberjack is a red meat fish, similar to skipjack tuna, regarded as one of the most delicious sashimi fish. Alternatively, you can use any sashimi fish, even white fish such as Dover sole, turbot or halibut. At my restaurant we use kanzuri, *a very unique, fermented chilli essence, in the dressing for this dish, but at home you can just use a drop of chilli oil. The garnish,* tonburi, *is the berry of a kind of cypress, and is regarded as 'field caviar'. It is a speciality of Akita, in the north-east of Japan, and a very rare ingredient. You can omit it totally or use any fish caviar instead if you like. KT*

1 Sprinkle salt and pepper over the sliced fish, and divide into 4 individual plates.

2 Mix all the ingredients for the Hana special dressing, pour over the mixture of the diced tomato and cucumber and then lightly toss. Put a quarter on the fish slices in each plate, and garnish with *shiso* shreds and *tonburi* or caviar.

3 Mix together all the ingredients for the *kanzuri* and *yuzu* dressing, and sprinkle over the tomato and cucumber. Serve immediately.

Monkfish liver steamed in salt and sake

Ankimo no sake shio mushi

HISASHI TAOKA is a fish trader and co-owner with his wife Mariko of Kiku restaurant, Mayfair, London. During the tuna season he visits the Mediterranean in search of good tuna, while Mariko holds the fort single-handedly. Though he used to be a wholesaler at Billingsgate market, he now goes there as a customer very early in the morning every day when he's in London. In this recipe, he introduces one of Japan's winter delicacies.

SERVES 4

300g/10oz monkfish liver, soaked in water
for 1 hour to drain off the blood
½ teaspoon salt
3 tablespoons sake
1–2 spring onions (scallions) or chives, finely
chopped, to garnish
5 tablespoons *momiji-oroshi* (see page 124),
to garnish

FOR THE *PONZU* (CITRUS SHOYU) SAUCE:
3 tablespoons lemon juice
2 tablespoons shoyu (Japanese soy sauce)
3 tablespoons dashi (see page 56)

Monkfish liver is so delicious that it is regarded as foie gras from the sea. In my opinion it's much better than foie gras, and it's certainly healthier and a lot cheaper. It is not readily available, but a good fishmonger will be able to get it for you. Try this, and you will be amazed to find how good it is. HT

1 Drain the monkfish liver; it should already have been drained of blood in water. Wash off the thin skin and any dirt, and pat dry with kitchen paper (paper towels). Sprinkle with the salt and leave in the refrigerator for about 1 hour to get rid of excess water.

2 Put the liver in a shallow dish, sprinkle with the sake, and then steam in a boiling steamer over a high heat for 20 minutes. Remove from the heat and leave to cool.

3 Cut the liver into 1cm/½ inch square pieces, and put a quarter into each of 4 small individual bowls. Mix all the ingredients for the *ponzu* sauce in a small measuring cup, and pour some over the liver. Serve, garnished with chopped spring onions (scallions) and *momiji-oroshi*.

Autumn hors d'oeuvres (three kinds)

Aki no hors d'oeuvre san-ten mori [v]

The hors d'oeuvre plate is a good vehicle for reflecting the season, and a kaiseki *course will often start with a plate of three different kinds of food from the mountains, field and sea. In spring you may find on the plate the theme of cherry blossom together with* fuki *(a long stemmed vegetable unique to Japan), young bamboo shoots and perhaps some clams. In summer the host or the chef will endeavour to make the diners feel cool and refreshed by serving sashimi and assorted seaweeds on crushed ice, fern and melon. Autumn brings chefs a huge choice as the mountains are full of nuts and wild mushrooms, fruits grow in abundance and the* katsuo, *salmon and many other fish return from the north. Here is a sample autumn hors d'oeuvre plate so that you create your own using local produce.*

SERVES 4

¼ cucumber (approximately 100g/3½oz)
½ teaspoon salt
2–3g/⅛oz dried, cut *wakame* (young
   seaweed), soaked in water for 10 minutes
8–12 chestnuts, ready-cooked in syrup
4–8 fresh shiitake
shoyu (Japanese soy sauce) and mirin,
   for brushing
4 small, ripe persimmons or sharon fruits
pinch of salt or granulated sugar (optional)
1–2cm/½– ¾in piece of root ginger, peeled
   and finely shredded
1–2 teaspoons mustard

FOR THE *KAKI SANBAIZU*:

1 tablespoon sieved persimmon or sharon
   fruit flesh (see text)
1 tablespoon *yonezu* (Japanese rice vinegar)
½ tablespoon shoyu (Japanese soy sauce)
½ tablespoon mirin
1 teaspoon sesame oil

1 Cut the cucumber in half lengthways, and cut into very thin, almost transparent, half-moons. Put in a mixing bowl, sprinkle with the salt and then mix with your hands, rubbing salt into each piece. Leave salted to wilt for 15 minutes. Drain and squeeze out excess water.

2 Drain the softened and expanded *wakame*, and squeeze out excess water in the same way as for the cucumber. Chop any large piece into a similar size to the cucumber half-moons.

3 Thread 2–3 chestnuts on to a metal skewer and grill (broil) over a high heat, placing the chestnuts about 10cm/4in away from the heat, until a light golden brown. Repeat this until all the chestnuts are grilled (broiled).

4 Lightly grill (broil) the shiitake caps in the same way as the chestnuts. Brush a mixture of equal amounts of shoyu and mirin on the caps and set aside.

5 Cut a third horizontally from the stem of each persimmon or sharon fruit, and scrape the flesh from the body parts to make 4 persimmon cups. The top piece acts as a lid.

6 Pass the scraped persimmon or sharon fruits flesh through a fine sieve, and mix 1 tablespoonful with the rest of the *sanbaizu* ingredients to make the *kaki sanbaizu*.

7 Mix the cucumber and the *wakame* in a mixing bowl, and toss with the *kaki sanbaizu*. Add a pinch of salt, or sugar, if necessary. Arrange a quarter of the salad in each of 4 persimmon cups and garnish with finely shredded ginger on top.

8 Arrange 2–3 chestnuts, 1–2 shiitake with a little mustard on the side, and a persimmon cup on each of 4 individual baskets or plates, and serve with warm sake if desired.

Grilled tuna in avocado with wasabi shoyu

Yaki-toro to avocado no wasabi-joyu aé

TOSHI SUGIURA, chef/patron of the sushi restaurant, Hama, in Los Angeles, is regarded as one of the best sushi chefs in the city. He didn't spend his youth in the confines of a sushi restaurant, but rather travelled the world before reaching Los Angeles in the late seventies. Starting at an upmarket fish restaurant, he soon learned the art of sushi shaping, and graduated to sushi chef of Hama under the previous owner. This is one of his favourite appetizers, using two very popular ingredients in California, tuna and avocado.

SERVES 4

450g/1lb tuna or 4 tuna steaks
   (approximately 120g/4oz each)
vegetable oil, for searing
2 avocados, cut in half and stoned
2 teaspoons wasabi paste
3 tablespoons shoyu (Japanese soy sauce)
1 tablespoon sake
1 tablespoon mayonnaise
salt and pepper
chives, finely chopped, to garnish
4 medium tomatoes, sliced into thin wedges,
   to garnish

As you know, seasons don't exist in California, so the idea of seasonal foods, which is very strong in Japanese cuisine, can't really be applied here. On the other hand, we can use fresh local produce all year round, and avocado is one of them. Tuna, the most popular Japanese ingredient, and avocado go very well together, and this dish is one of our established appetizers. Searing the tuna together with ample wasabi makes this dish appealing even to those who are not keen on raw fish. The tomato garnish also makes a good colour contrast with the green avocado. TS

1 Cut the tuna into 2–3cm/about 1in square cubes and sprinkle with salt and pepper. Heat a frying-pan (skillet) with a little vegetable oil over a high heat, and very lightly sear only the surface of the tuna, keeping the inside rare.

2 Make a few slits inside the avocado halves to make it easier to scoop out the flesh. Put a quarter of the tuna (4–5 pieces) into each of the avocado halves, and pour over a mixture of the wasabi, shoyu, sake and mayonnaise. Sprinkle with finely chopped chives, and serve garnished with tomato wedges around the avocado.

Jellied fish

Nikogori

TAKESHI YASUGE is a *fugu* (puffer fish) chef and owner of the *fugu* restaurant Asakusa Fukuji, in Ginza, Tokyo. *Fugu*, unique to Japan, has an extremely dangerous poison in its ovary and often also its liver so that *fugu* chefs are required to have a special licence. Yet it is one of the most prized fish in Japan, so popular that, according to Mr Yasuge, there are over 1000 *fugu* restaurants in Tokyo, and probably ten times as many in Osaka. Unfortunately, or fortunately for some, *fugu* is not available outside Japan. Here one of Mr Yasuge's most popular hors d'oeuvre dishes is reproduced using skate or monkfish instead.

SERVES 4

60–90g/2–3oz skate or monkfish skins
1–2 skate or monkfish main bones with
 a little meat
1 tablespoon shoyu (Japanese soy sauce)
1 lime, cut into wedges, to garnish

There is no argument that fugu *is the most delicious – thus most expensive – fish in the world. There are numerous types and sizes, but the best one is* tora-fugu, *the biggest, which grows to about 70cm/28in. The fish is so precious that no part is wasted, except the ovaries and liver, which are discarded as soon as the fish is killed. At my restaurant we serve this* nikogori, *made from the skin and bones, as an hors d'oeuvre. Any fish skin and bones can be made into* nikogori, *but you cannot expect it to be as good as the* fugu's. TY

1 Boil plenty of water in a saucepan, add the fish skins and bring back to the boil. Remove from the heat, and immediately put in cold water with ice cubes to chill quickly. Leave in the refrigerator for 30 minutes – this makes cutting otherwise slippery skins easier – before cutting into bite-sized pieces.
2 Put the skin pieces and the bones together with 1½ litres/2½ pints/7 cups cold water in a saucepan, bring to the boil and then simmer on a moderate heat for 30–45 minutes or until the liquid reduces to a third. Keeping on the lowest setting of the heat, take out the bones, pull off bits of fish meat, and put the meat back into the saucepan. Discard the bones. Season the liquid with the shoyu, and add more if necessary. Leave to cool to room temperature.
3 Pour the mixture into a wet mould, about 15 x 13 x 4cm/6 x 5 x 1½in, or a similar sized plastic container, spreading the skin pieces and the bits of fish meat evenly, and put in the refrigerator, preferably overnight, to set.
4 Turn over the mould or plastic container onto a chopping-board, and cut the jellied fish into 8. Arrange 2 pieces on each of 4 individual dishes, and serve garnished with lime wedges.

Skipjack tuna tataki salad

Katsuo no tataki salada shitate

TAKAYUKI HISHINUMA is the young chef/patron of the celebrated Hishinuma, in Tokyo. He was a forerunner of the new-wave Japanese cooking that is now everywhere in Japan, and opened his restaurant when he was only 30 years old. His handling of ingredients is traditional while he shows his modern artistic skills in assembling them.

SERVES 4

½ long fillet of *katsuo* (bonito or skipjack tuna), skin on, about 30cm/12in long and 7–8cm/3–3½in wide, or 225g/8oz tuna or swordfish in a thick oblong shape
3 tablespoons shoyu (Japanese soy sauce)
2–3cm/about 1in piece of root ginger, peeled and finely grated
5cm/2in piece of carrot, peeled
½ cucumber
5cm/2in piece of daikon, peeled
4–5 *myoga* (Japanese bulb vegetable) (optional)
handful of *kaiware daikon* (young daikon leaves) or cress
2–3 spring onions (scallions)
salt
white sesame seeds, lightly roasted, to garnish

FOR THE MUSTARD SAUCE:

1 egg yolk
1 teaspoon powdered mustard
½ teaspoon salt
½ teaspoon granulated sugar
1 tablespoon black pepper, freshly milled
200ml/7fl oz/⅞ cup extra-virgin olive oil
4 tablespoons lemon juice
pinch of salt

The 'first katsuo' *(bonito or skipjack tuna) are so-called as they swim near Japanese shores in spring on their way north. The* katsuo *returning south in late summer have a richer flavour. Use either, or tuna or swordfish here. Tataki is a form of sashimi (prepared raw fish), seared on the outside but raw inside. TH*

1 If you start with a whole *katsuo*, carefully scale, then fillet, and halve each fillet lengthways. Trim off the blood-coloured flesh, in the centre of the fillets. You will have four half-size fillets. For this dish you need only one half fillet for four people as a starter (or two as a main course). Freeze the rest for later use.
2 Place a half fillet, skin-side down, or if using tuna, the whole lot, on a chopping-board, and pierce with 4 metal skewers crossways, close to the skin, in the shape of a fan so that you can hold the skewers together in one hand. Sprinkle salt over it.
3 Fill a deep roasting tin (pan) with water and ice and leave by the stove. Grill (broil) the fish over a high heat, skin-side first, for 30 seconds until the skin is marked with light burns. Turn the fish over and quickly repeat on the flesh-side for no more than 10 seconds until the flesh just browns. Remove from the heat and immediately plunge into the water to stop it cooking.
4 Remove from the water, pat dry with kitchen paper (paper towels), and place the fillet on a chopping-board, flesh-side down. Using a very sharp knife, slice it crossways into pieces about 1cm/½in thick.
5 Mix the shoyu and grated ginger in a flat dish. Plunge the fish into the mixture to give it a basic flavour.
6 Prepare the vegetables: thinly shave pieces of carrot lengthways (*katsura-muki*, see the picture, left), and finely shred. Shred the cucumber and daikon into similar-sized pieces. Trim off the core from the *myoga*, if using, and thinly slice. Cut the *kaiware daikon* or cress into about 3cm/1¼in long pieces. Finely chop the white part of the spring onions (scallions), and cut the rest into 3cm/1¼in shreds. Put all the shreds in a bowl with water and ice to refresh. Drain and dry with kitchen paper (paper towels).
7 Mix together all the mustard sauce ingredients. Place a quarter of the fish on each plate, pour the mustard sauce over, and put some shredded vegetables on top. Sprinkle with the chopped spring onion (scallion) and sesame seeds and serve.

2

Stocks
and Soups

Thick egg soup

Chawan-mushi

NOBUO IWASEYA is the chief chef for all ten Suntory restaurants abroad. Suntory, a leading drinks company, specializing in whisky, liqueur and beer, started in the restaurant business in the seventies, opening its first restaurant in Mexico City in 1970. Since then the company has rapidly expanded to Acapulco, São Paulo, Honolulu, London, Madrid, Taipei, Kuala Lumpur, Shanghai and Singapore, and even opened a second restaurant in Mexico City. The restaurants are renowned for their traditional and authentic dishes of a very high standard throughout the world. Here Mr Iwaseya introduces one of the well-established, traditional recipes, with a twist.

SERVES 4

4 prawns (shrimp), shelled and de-veined
2 tablespoons sake
1 bunch *shimeji* mushrooms, trimmed
4 okra, trimmed and de-seeded
salt
yuzu or lime rind, to garnish

FOR THE EGG SOUP:
3 large eggs, beaten
560ml/1 pint/2½ cups dashi (see page 56)
⅔ tablespoon sake
½ teaspoon salt
⅔ tablespoon shoyu (Japanese soy sauce)

FOR THE *KUZU* SOUP:
225ml/8fl oz/1 cup dashi (see page 56)
¼ teaspoon salt
¼ tablespoon shoyu (Japanese soy sauce)
1 tablespoon *kuzu* (thickening agent) or
    arrowroot, diluted with 1 tablespoon water

Usually, chawan-mushi, *meaning 'steamed rice bowl', is a dish of thick egg soup steamed with other ingredients in the soup, but here ingredients are cooked separately and placed on top with a sauce poured over them. If you prefer the former, you can steam the ingredients together with the seasoned egg soup. Either way, sieve the egg mixture before steaming so that it won't easily make the surface of the soup rough with bubbles. Other stocks (broths) such as chicken, dried scallop or dried shiitake can be used instead of dashi (fish stock). Traditional ingredients include prawns (shrimp), chicken, duck, gingko nuts, shiitake mushrooms, grilled* anago *(sea eel), green vegetables, lily bulb and young bamboo shoots. NI*

1 Finely chop the prawns (shrimp), and put in a small saucepan together with the sake and a pinch of salt. Place the saucepan on a high heat and cook the chopped prawns (shrimp) vigorously, stirring with a fork until cooked and the skin turns bright red. Remove from the heat and set aside.
2 Boil the *shimeji* mushrooms in lightly salted boiling water on a high heat for 2–3 minutes until just cooked, drain and set aside. Chop the okra into about 1cm/½in thick rings, and cook in lightly salted boiling water on a high heat for 1–2 minutes until just cooked but still crunchy. Drain and set aside.
3 Mix all the egg soup ingredients, and stir gently until the salt dissolves. Do not bubble. Sieve the egg mixture through a fine cotton cloth or double-folded gauze. Divide the mixture into 4 individual soup cups, and steam, each cup covered either with a lid or a sheet of aluminium (aluminum) foil, in a boiling steamer on a moderate heat for 15 minutes, or until the egg soup has just hardened. Remove from the heat, and keep warm in the steamer.
4 Heat the dashi for the *kuzu* soup, and season with salt and shoyu. Add the diluted *kuzu* or arrowroot into the soup, stirring continuously until the soup thickens. Remove from the heat.
5 Arrange a quarter of the prawn (shrimp), *shimeji* and okra on top of each of the 4 egg soups, and pour over the *kuzu* soup just to cover all the ingredients. Garnish with a tiny pice of *yuzu* or lime rind and serve hot.

Senba mackerel soup

Senba-jiru

YUICHI OYAMA, executive chef and general manager of the 160-year-old Osaka sushi restaurant Yoshino Sushi, shows how to make the modern and richer version of *Senba-jiru*. Red fish in soup may seem a rather unusual mixture, but its origin is very humble: daikon cooked in soup made from salted mackerel heads. In the nineteenth century it was a common dish fed to apprentice boys and servants employed by wealthy merchants in the Senba area of Osaka, hence the name, *Senba-jiru* (Senba soup).

SERVES 4

1 mackerel fillet, heavily salted for 15 minutes
10cm/4in piece of daikon
675ml/24fl oz/3 cups dashi (see page 56)
1 teaspoon sea salt
1 tablespoon light shoyu (Japanese
   soy sauce)
yuzu or lime rind, to garnish

Yoshino Sushi was established in 1841, and is still run by the same family. It was the third generation who created the legendary hako-zushi *(boxed sushi, a speciality from Osaka, see page 154), and* Senba-jiru *was recreated by the fifth generation. I am very proud to head the operation here and be one of the guardians of the old traditional specialities of Osaka. The* Senba-jiru *we serve is, of course, a restaurant version, and I remember a few years ago an old customer murmured that the one he used to be fed didn't taste so sophisticated. He may have passed away now, but the tradition goes on and on... YO*

1 Wash off the salt from the mackerel fillet, and cut into bite-sized (approximately 2.5cm/1in square) pieces. Parboil in boiling water on a high heat for 30 seconds, then immediately plunge into cold water for 5 minutes to reduce the fishy smell. Drain and set aside.
2 Cut the daikon into about 3mm/⅛in thick rectangular pieces, approximately 1.5 x 4cm/½ x 1½in, and cook in the dashi over a moderate heat for 5–10 minutes until well cooked and almost transparent. Season the soup with salt and shoyu, adding more if necessary.
3 Put a quarter (2–3 pieces) of the mackerel into each of 4 individual soup bowls, add 4–5 pieces of daikon on top and pour over the soup. Garnish with a tiny piece of *yuzu* or lime rind, and serve hot.

Chilled asparagus and ginger soup

Shoga-fumi asuparagasu supu [v]

LINDA RODRIGUEZ has been the executive chef of the celebrated Bond Street restaurant, New York, since it opened in 1998. She was born in Manila, Philippines and raised in the United States. When she was a small child her family was stationed in Yokota Air Force Base in Japan, and that was when her first taste of Japanese cuisine really evolved. This beautiful green soup has a little twist, adding not only ginger but also *yamaimo* (yam) and roasted garlic.

SERVES 4

3 bunches asparagus
350g/12oz spinach
4 shallots, chopped
2 cloves garlic, chopped
vegetable oil, for frying
110ml/4fl oz/½ cup white wine
450ml/16fl oz/2 cups vegetable stock (broth)
225ml/8fl oz/1 cup water
225ml/8fl oz/1 cup plain yoghurt
7 tablespoons root ginger juice
salt and pepper
yamaimo (yam) (optional), to garnish
garlic, chopped and roasted, to garnish

This dish is vegetarian. A summer dish, it's very fresh, very clean and healthy. Before cooking starts, make sure you have a medium bain-marie *or stainless steel container to hold the soup and put in the refrigerator. LR*

1 Blanch the asparagus and spinach separately in lightly salted boiling water until just soft, and drain. Immediately put into cold water with ice to chill quickly, and drain. Squeeze the excess water out of the spinach, and keep both vegetables in the refrigerator.

2 Lightly pan-fry the shallots and garlic in a hot frying-pan (skillet) with a little vegetable oil. Add the white wine, vegetable stock (broth) and water, and then bring to the boil. Lower the heat and simmer for 15 minutes. Remove from the heat and, when it has cooled, chill in the refrigerator.

3 When both the vegetables and soup are chilled, reserve 4 asparagus tips for the garnish, and then combine the vegetables and soup in a large blender. Purée for 3–5 minutes, and strain the soup through a fine sieve.

4 Add the yoghurt and fresh ginger juice to the soup and mix well. Season with salt and pepper to taste.

5 Serve very cold, garnished with the asparagus tips, thin slices of raw *yamaimo*, if using, and roasted garlic.

Steamed teapot soup

Dobin-mushi

The idea of cooking in a teapot is not just for its pretty looks. Cooking soup in a small, closed pot (hence the minimal amount of liquid) gives the ingredients a gently steamed rather than rough boiled effect, hence the name, mushi, *'steaming'. The soup will be drunk like tea.*

SERVES 4

250g/9oz chicken fillet
2 medium *matsutake* (Japanese wild
    mushrooms) or ceps (porcini)
4 tiger prawns (large shrimp) with shells
8 mangetouts
12 gingko nuts, shelled
1 lime, cut into wedges, to serve

FOR THE SOUP:
560ml/1 pint/2½ cups dashi (see page 56)
    or chicken stock (broth)
½ teaspoon sea salt
1 tablespoon light shoyu (Japanese
    soy sauce)

1 Thinly slice the chicken into 4cm/1½in diameter discs and cook in boiling water for 1–2 minutes or until just cooked. Drain and wash with running water.
2 Trim the root of each *matsutake* with a sharp knife as if sharpening a pencil, carefully clean with a wet cloth or kitchen paper (paper towels) and pat dry. Cut each *matsutake* about 5cm/2in from the top of the cap and thinly slice lengthways. If the remaining pieces are longer than 5cm/2in, cut each into 2 and thinly slice lengthways.
3 Remove the head and vein from each prawn (shrimp). Quickly plunge into boiling water and pat dry. Remove the rest of the shell except the tip of the tail.

4 Cook the mangetouts in lightly salted boiling water for 1–2 minutes or until soft but still crunchy. Drain and immediately place under running water. Pat dry and, if large, cut in half crossways diagonally.
5 Warm the dashi or chicken stock (broth) in a saucepan over a moderate heat, then add salt and bring to the boil. Add a little shoyu to taste and remove from the heat.
6 Put a quarter of chicken, *matsutake*, prawns, gingko nuts and mangetouts into each individual *dobin* (tea pot) and pour over the soup. Place the *dobin* on a moderate heat and bring to the boil. Remove from the heat and serve with a lime wedge on each *dobin* lid.

Clear soup with clams

Hamaguri no ushio-jiru

Hamaguri, *a hard clam, is in season from winter to early spring, and is a popular shellfish. It has a full* umami *(rich flavour), and its pretty shape also makes an interesting addition to a* kaiseki *tray. Because of its* umami, *simple cooking is best, as shown here.*

SERVES 4

5cm/2in square piece of dried *konbu* (kelp)
2 tablespoons sake
600ml/22fl oz/2⅔ cups water
4 large clams in shells, cleaned
1 teaspoon sea salt
½ cake (125g/4½oz) tofu, cut into 12 cubes
1 box of cress, trimmed

1 Wipe the *konbu* with damp kitchen paper (paper towels) and soak in the sake and water in a saucepan for 20 minutes.
2 Add the clams to the pan, and bring to the boil. Remove the *konbu*, then lower the heat and cook on a medium heat, occasionally removing the scum, until all the clam shells open. Season with ¾ teaspoon of sea salt first, and add the remaining salt if necessary.

3 Add the tofu cubes and cress, and simmer for 2–3 minutes until the tofu is warmed through to the core. Remove from the heat, and arrange 1 clam, 3 tofu cubes and some cress in each of 4 individual bowls. Pour the soup into the bowls and serve immediately.

Family miso soup with tofu and wakame

Tofu to wakame no miso-shiru

This is a standard sort of daily miso soup that many Japanese households have for breakfast. In the old days vendors on bicycles used to come round early in the morning selling tofu or clams. You can use daikon, spinach, mushrooms, mangetouts or even potato.

SERVES 4

5g/¼oz dried cut *wakame* (young seaweed), soaked in water for 5–10 minutes
3 tablespoons medium miso
450ml/16fl oz/2 cups dashi (see page 56)
½ cake (125g/4½oz) tofu, cut into tiny dice
1–2 spring onions (scallions) or 5–6 chives, finely chopped
ground *sansho* pepper (optional)

1 Drain the *wakame* and cut large leaves into small pieces.
2 Dilute the miso with 3–4 spoonfuls of the dashi. Heat the dashi on a moderate heat (do not boil) and add the diluted miso. Add the *wakame* and tofu to the pan and turn up the heat. Just before it reaches boiling, remove from the heat and add the chopped spring onions (scallions) or chives. At no stage should the soup boil. Serve hot in individual soup bowls, sprinkling with a little *sansho* pepper if you like.

Ishikari hotpot

Ishikari-nabe

Ishikari, the name of a river in Hokkaido, the northern island of Japan, is well known for salmon, hence the name of this soup, whose main ingredient is salmon. Chunky salmon pieces cooked with various vegetables and tofu products in a miso soup make this not just a soup, but a substantial hotpot dish eaten as the main course for dinner. Konnyaku *is a kind of yam potato cake.*

SERVES 4

2–3 salmon steaks (250g/9oz), scaled
1 cake (270g/9½oz) *konnyaku* (optional)
2 potatoes, peeled
1 carrot, peeled
1 onion, peeled and sliced into half-moons
10cm/4in piece dried *konbu* (kelp) (optional)
3–4 tablespoons miso
4 fresh shiitake or oyster mushrooms, trimmed
1 cake (250g/9oz) firm tofu, cut into cubes
8 mangetouts
salt
2 spring onions (scallions), chopped, to garnish

1 Cut the salmon steaks into chunky pieces, sprinkle with salt and leave for 5–10 minutes. Rub salt into the *konnyaku*, if using, then wash under running water, and roughly cut, using a tablespoon as a blade, into chunky bite-sized pieces.
2 Cut the potatoes and carrot into similarly chunky pieces. Plunge the potatoes in water and drain. Put the potatoes and carrots separately in saucepans with cold water, and parboil. Drain and set aside.
3 Half fill a large pot with water, add the *konbu*, if using, and bring to the boil.

Remove the *konbu* and lower the heat. Dilute the miso in a bowl with some of the hot liquid, then stir back into the pan. Add the onion slices, potato, carrot, shiitake, *konnyaku* and salmon, then cover and cook over a moderate heat for 7–8 minutes. Add the tofu and mangetouts, and simmer for 3–4 minutes.
4 Arrange 1–2 pieces of each ingredient into each of 4 individual bowls and pour over the soup. Serve hot, sprinkled with chopped spring onions (scallions). There may be some more left in the pan for a second serving.

Tofu vichyssoise

Tofu no surinagashi [v]

This is a tofu version of the all-time favourite vichyssoise, and is very easy to make. The point is to draw water well from the tofu in order to make it easier to pound into a smooth consistency, before mixing with the soup stock. It is delicious as well as healthy.

SERVES 4

1 cake (250g/9oz) firm tofu
½ teaspoon sea salt
1 tablespoon light shoyu (Japanese soy sauce)
1 tablespoon sake
2 teaspoons mirin
dash of *yonezu* (Japanese rice vinegar)
280ml/½ pint/1¼ cups vegetable stock (broth)
chopped chives, to garnish

1 Wrap the tofu with a clean tea towel, and roll it in a *makisu* (bamboo sushi roller). Place a weight (a stone or unopened can of food) on top and leave for 1 hour to squeeze the water out of the tofu. Finely grind the tofu in a *suribachi* (Japanese mortar) or a food processor until smooth and shiny.

2 Add to the tofu paste the salt, shoyu, sake, mirin and *yonezu*, and mix well. Pour the stock into the tofu mixture, a little at a time, and stir to make a thick soup. Check the seasoning, and add more salt if necessary. Chill in the refrigerator before serving in 4 individual soup bowls, garnished with chopped chives on top.

Okinawan pork liver soup

Okinawa no buta leva sinji

Sinji, an Okinawan word for slow-cooked dishes, derives from the method used for making herbal remedies. In Okinawa, many nutritious foods such as liver, koi carp and funa *(round crucian carp), are cooked for a long time together with herbs and vegetables.*

SERVES 4

250g/9oz pork liver, cut into bite-sized pieces
225ml/8fl oz/1 cup milk
250g/9oz pork red meat, cut into pieces
2–3 tablespoons sake
800ml/1½ pints/3½ cups dashi (see page 56)
1.5cm/¾ in square of root ginger, peeled and thinly sliced
3 cloves garlic, peeled and thinly sliced
1 medium potato, peeled and cut into pieces
2 medium carrots, peeled and cut into pieces
¼ teaspoon sea salt
1 tablespoon mirin
4–5 tablespoons miso
green vegetables, to serve (optional)

1 Soak the pork liver in the milk, and rub with your hands to wash off the blood. Drain, and wash under running water, then pat dry with kitchen paper (paper towels). Put the liver and the pork meat together, sprinkle with sake and rub it into the meats with your hands. Set aside.

2 Put the dashi in a large saucepan, add the pork mixture, ginger and garlic and cook, covered, on a medium heat for 30–35 minutes. Using a tablespoon or ladle, occasionally scoop off the scum from the surface. Add the potato and carrots, and bring to the boil. Lower the heat and simmer for a further 15–20 minutes. Season with salt, mirin and miso, and adjust the strength to your liking by adding more. Add green vegetables, if using, a few minutes before removing from the heat. Serve in individual bowls along with bowls of hot rice.

Red miso soup with nameko, shiitake and daikon

Nameko to shiitake daikon no akadashi [v]

There are numerous varieties of miso available even outside Japan nowadays, but they are roughly divided into three types: aka *(red),* ordinary *(khaki) and* shiro *(white). The darker the colour, the stronger the flavour.* Aka-miso *is normally used for strongly flavoured soups and simmering dishes, and* shiro-miso, *also known as* Saikyo *(the western capital, Kyoto) miso, is often used for marinating and simmering in* kaiseki *meals. Unless specified, if the recipe says miso, use ordinary, khaki-coloured miso.* Akadashi *has a strong bean flavour as it is mainly made of soya beans (soybeans).*

SERVES 4

4–6 fresh shiitake
5cm/2in piece of daikon
2 tablespoons red miso
1 can (85g/3oz) *nameko*
  mushrooms (optional)
mitsuba or cress, to garnish

1 Cut off the stem from the shiitake, and thinly slice across the cap, inserting the blade slightly diagonally. Peel the daikon and thinly slice lengthways first, and then finely shred into 5cm/2in long matchstick pieces.

2 Put the daikon shreds in a saucepan with 560ml/1pint/2½ cups water and cook over a medium heat for about 3 minutes until half cooked. Add the shiitake shreds and continue to cook for 2 minutes. Meanwhile, dilute the miso with some liquid from the saucepan, and gently mix back in to the pan. As soon as the miso is mixed through, lower the heat: miso soup should never be boiled, otherwise much of the aroma and flavour will be lost.

3 Add the *nameko*, if using, and when heated through after about 1 minute, remove from the heat. Pour a quarter of the soup into each of 4 individual soup bowls, garnish with a sprig of *mitsuba* or cress, and serve immediately, with a bowl of hot rice.

Clear soup with egg and prawns (shrimp)

Ebi-iri sukui-tamago no sumashi-jiru

KAZUNARI YANAGIHARA, Japanese cookery expert and broadcaster, is the descendant of a long line of the *cha-kaiseki* (tea ceremony meal) sect, Kinsa-ryu. His Tokyo cookery school is one of the highly regarded training grounds for daughters and wives of fine families, who retain the Japanese culinary heritage. Here he shows how to make dashi (fish stock or broth), the most important ingredient in Japanese cooking, and, a clear soup.

SERVES 4

FOR THE DASHI (FISH STOCK OR BROTH):

10cm/4in square of dried *konbu* (kelp)

900ml/32fl oz/4 cups water

30g/1oz *kezuribushi* (dried bonito or skipjack tuna flakes)

¾ teaspoon salt

1 teaspoon light shoyu (Japanese soy sauce) or 600ml/22fl oz/2½ cups dashi

4 prawns (shrimp) with shells

2 tablespoons sake

½ teaspoon salt

1 *matsutake* or 4 small fresh shiitake

100g/3½oz *shungiku* (chrysanthemum leaves), or spinach

yuzu or lime rind, to garnish

FOR THE STEAMED EGG:

2 large eggs, beaten

140ml/10fl oz/⅔ cup dashi (see page 56)

½ teaspoon salt

½ teaspoon light shoyu (Japanese soy sauce)

1 teaspoon mirin

Sukui-tamago, *meaning 'spooning egg', is so-called since you spoon the hardened egg into the clear soup. This recipe shows how to make dashi from scratch and is taught at my Yanagihara Cookery School in Akasaka, Tokyo. KY*

1 First make the dashi: quickly rinse the *konbu* under running water, put in a saucepan together with the water and bring to the boil on a medium heat. Just before it reaches the boil, take out the *konbu* and add the *kezuribushi* to the pan and remove from the heat. Briefly let it sit until the *kezuribushi* begins to settle to the bottom. Strain through a sieve lined with kitchen paper (paper towels).

2 Take the head off each prawn (shrimp) and de-vein with the shells on using a cocktail stick (toothpick) inserted between the shells. Mix the sake and salt in a saucepan, and stir-cook the prawns (shrimp) until bright red. Shell them and cut into dice.

3 Mix all the steamed egg ingredients in a mixing bowl, and sieve into another bowl through a fine mesh. Take out about a ladle of the egg mixture into a cup and keep aside.

4 Place the bowl of the sieved egg mixture into a boiling steamer, and steam on a low heat for 30–35 minutes or until just hardened. Remove from the steamer, add the chopped prawns (shrimp), and then pour the uncooked egg mixture on top. Return the bowl to the steamer and continue to steam for another 15–20 minutes until the surface is hardened.

5 Heat the dashi and season with salt and light shoyu, to taste. Remove from the heat and keep warm with a lid on.

6 Clean the *matsutake* under running water. Pat dry with kitchen paper (paper towels). Trim the bottom, and slice thinly lengthways. If using shiitake, cut off the stems and make a cross slit across the caps. Blanch the *shungiku* or spinach in lightly salted boiling water, drain, and cut into 4cm/2in long pieces.

7 Put 110ml/4fl oz/½ cup of the dashi soup in a saucepan, bring to a boil, and then blanch the *matsutake* slices or shiitake in it. As soon as it boils, remove from the heat and add the *shungiku*.

8 Ladle a quarter of the steamed egg into each soup bowl and arrange some *matsutake* and *shungiku* on top. Pour 2 ladles of the dashi soup into each and garnish with *yuzu* or lime rind.

3

Vegetables
and Salads

Vegetable tempura

Yasai no tempura [V]

TETSUYA SAOTOME, the multi-talented tempura chef and artist, says tempura frying is a science. Each material has its own unique property, and the frying should comply with it. The batter should be the right thickness, the oil the correct temperature and the frying time the right length. Tempura should be eaten straight away, so at Mr Saotome's restaurant, Mikawa, in Tokyo, diners sit at the counter. This is a simple tempura recipe, but it takes a little practice.

SERVES 4

FOR THE BATTER:

140g/5oz/1 cup light plain (all-purpose) flour
1 egg, beaten
225ml/8fl oz/1 cup water, chilled

FOR THE VEGETARIAN *TEN-TSUYU* SAUCE:

340ml/12fl oz/1½ cups water
2–3 dried shiitake, soaked in the above
    water overnight
5 tablespoons light shoyu (Japanese soy sauce)
5 tablespoons mirin

½ large aubergine (eggplant)
½ sweet potato, or 1 medium potato
vegetable oil and unrefined sesame oil
    (optional), for deep-frying
8 asparagus tips
½ small carrot, peeled and finely shredded
1 small parsnip, peeled and finely shredded
75g/2½oz mangetouts or fine beans,
    finely shredded
plain (all-purpose) flour, sifted, for sprinkling
10cm/4in piece of daikon, peeled and finely
    grated, to garnish
2.5cm/1in piece of root ginger, peeled and
    grated, to garnish (optional)

Frying reduces the water content of ingredients, so only those whose taste is thereby improved should be fried, and then to the right degree. Tempura chefs are said to fry by sound rather than sight, meaning they listen carefully to the sound of the water evaporating. Tempura needs very light frying, and the batter should not totally enclose the ingredient to enable some water to escape. Thin batter with lots of holes is ideal. TS

1 Sift the flour for the batter twice and leave in the refrigerator to chill overnight.
2 Prepare the *ten-tsuyu* sauce: remove the shiitake from the water, squeezing out as much liquid as possible, and discard the shiitake or use for other cooking. Mix the shiitake water with the shoyu and mirin in a saucepan, bring to the boil and remove from the heat.
3 Quarter the aubergine (eggplant) lengthways, and cut off most of the white flesh leaving thin skin squares with a little flesh left. You should have 4 pieces about 5cm/2in square, with the skin on one side and white flesh on the other. Make 4–5 deep, hidden slits horizontally to both sides of the skin to allow it to easily cook. Cut the sweet potato or ordinary potato into 4 rounds, about 8mm/⅓in thick, and slit a cross on each side.
4 Heat the oil in a deep-fryer to about 170°C/340°F. If using sesame oil, mix with equal parts of vegetable oil.
5 Meanwhile, prepare the batter: sieve the beaten egg through a fine mesh, and gradually mix with the chilled water, a little at a time. Sift the chilled flour again into the egg and water mixture, and very lightly fold in with just 5–6 strokes using a few *hashi* sticks or a fork. Do not stir; the batter should be loosely mixed but lumpy.
6 Dip the aubergine (eggplant) pieces, one by one, into the batter and fry in the hot

oil for 2–3 minutes or until the bubbles ease off and the batter is light golden and crisp. Drain on a wire rack. Fry the potato rounds in the same way but at a slightly lower oil temperature, 165°C/330°F, and for 5–6 minutes until golden brown. Dip each asparagus tip, using *hashi*, in the batter tip-side down, shaking off any excess batter, and fry in the same way as the aubergine (eggplant). From time to time scoop out bits of loose batter from the oil, and adjust the heat to keep the oil temperature at 170°C/340°F.
7 Finally, fry the mixed tempura: put the carrot, parsnip and mangetout or fine beans shreds together into a mixing bowl, sprinkle with a little flour, and mix together. Pour over the remaining batter, and mix well. Take a ladleful of the vegetable and batter mixture, and gently slide into the oil. Fry for 2–3 minutes, turning once or twice, until crisp and golden brown, then drain on a wire rack. Repeat this process for the rest.
8 Arrange a quarter of each tempura on absorbent decorative paper on individual plates, and serve hot together with an individual bowl of reheated *ten-tsuyu* sauce, garnished with a small mound of grated daikon and a little grated ginger, if desired. Diners mix their own *ten-tsuyu* sauce with the daikon and ginger, and dip in the tempura to eat.

Hawaiian ahi poki salad

Hawai no ahi poki salada

KEN TOMINAGA, chef/patron of the Hana restaurant in the Bay area of north San Francisco presents this recipe inspired by Hawaii. Located midway between Japan and America, Hawaiian food and cooking inspired him to create this dish.

SERVES 4

100g/3½ oz tuna, cut into 5mm/¼ in
   thick cubes
1 teaspoon *tobiko* (flying-fish eggs) or red
   lumpfish caviar
½ spring onion (scallion), finely chopped
1 teaspoon white sesame seeds
mixed green salad

FOR THE *POKI* SAUCE:

1 tablespoon shoyu (Japanese soy sauce)
½ tablespoon Thai chilli sauce
1 teaspoon sesame oil
½ clove garlic, finely grated
1 teaspoon olive oil

FOR THE SALAD DRESSING:

3 tablespoons *yonezu* (Japanese rice vinegar)
   or white wine vinegar
1 tablespoon extra-virgin olive oil
2 tablespoons shoyu (Japanese soy sauce)
½ onion, finely grated
½ clove garlic, finely grated
1 tablespoon lemon juice
salt and pepper

FOR THE GARNISH:

1–2 tablespoons vinegared ginger slices (see
   page 70), finely chopped
handful of chives
12 wonton skins, deep-fried

My whole family, including aunts and uncles, love playing golf and have been to Hawaii together many times for this reason. I saw a poki *(poke in Hawaii) – a marinated seafood dish – at a market on my honeymoon there. Their* poki *is rather salty and used as a preserve, but here I have arranged it as a fresh salad dish without using salt. KT*

1 Mix the tuna cubes, *tobiko* or red lumpfish caviar, chopped spring onion (scallion) and sesame seeds in a mixing bowl. Combine the *poki* ingredients and add to the tuna mixture. Allow to marinate while you mix all the salad dressing ingredients together in a bowl.
2 Arrange a quarter of the mixed green salad, tossed in the dressing, on one side of each individual plate, and a quarter of the marinated tuna mixture heaped on the other side. They form 2 mounds side-by-side on the plate with a little space between them.
3 Garnish the tuna mixture with the vinegared ginger slices (see page 70) and a few lengths of chive, and serve with 3 deep-fried wonton skins on each plate.

Grilled aubergine (eggplant) with miso

Shigi-yaki nasu [v]

KAZUNARI YANAGIHARA, *cha-kaiseki* expert and broadcaster from Tokyo, shows here the best way to appreciate this dish. Japanese aubergine (eggplant), *nasu*, is a lot smaller, thinner and more intense in flavour than its Western counterpart. Although it is available all year round nowadays, it is at its best in autumn. There are numerous ways to cook this very beautiful vegetable, but simple grilling (broiling) is best suited to bring out its delicate flavour, and not spoil its soft flesh and crunchy skin.

SERVES 4

4 aubergines (eggplants)
2 tablespoons white sesame seeds

FOR THE MISO SAUCE:
2 tablespoons Sendai or
   any standard (khaki) miso
2 tablespoons granulated sugar
2 teaspoons sake

Japanese aubergine (eggplant) is a slim vegetable with a long stem. The shape resembles that of shigi *(snipe), hence the name of this dish. It's very easy to make and very delicious to eat. What more could you hope for when cooking? KY*

1 Trim the stem from the aubergines (eggplants), but do not cut the calyx. Halve them lengthways, and thread 2 halves crossways on 2 metal skewers. Brush both sides of the aubergine (eggplant) halves with vegetable oil, and braise on a metal mesh over a moderate heat for about 3 minutes each side until soft but not burnt.

2 Toss the sesame seeds in a small dry saucepan over a moderate heat until the first seed pops up.
3 Mix all the miso sauce ingredients in a small saucepan over a low heat, stirring continuously, for about 5 minutes until it becomes shiny.
4 Arrange 2 aubergine (eggplant) pieces on each of 4 individual plates, and spoon some miso sauce on top. Garnish with the toasted sesame seeds and serve.

Simmered aubergine (eggplant)

Nasu no nimono

The pulp-like flesh of aubergine (eggplant) absorbs flavours so well that it's often cooked with meat, chicken and fish, and in soup. One problem is that the flesh tends to disintegrate as it becomes soft in a very short time. To avoid this, aubergine (eggplant) is cooked whole in this recipe to enclose the flesh, while the numerous slits on the hard skin allow it to absorb the dashi well.

SERVES 4–6

4 medium aubergines (eggplants)
1 tablespoon vegetable oil
450ml/16fl oz/2 cups dashi (see page 56)
   (or use vegetarian stock or broth or shiitake
   soaking water if you prefer)
4 tablespoons shoyu (Japanese soy sauce)
4 tablespoons mirin
root ginger, peeled and finely
   shredded, to garnish

1 Trim off the stems of the aubergines (eggplants) and make many fine slits, about 5mm/¼in apart, lengthways on the skin of each aubergine (eggplant).
2 Heat a shallow saucepan, large enough to lay 4 aubergines (eggplants) flat, and add the vegetable oil. Spread the oil over the base by tilting the saucepan and fry the aubergines (eggplants) on a moderate heat until all their skins wilt.
3 Add the dashi and 2 tablespoons each of shoyu and mirin to the aubergines

(eggplants). Bring to the boil over a high heat, then lower the heat and cook, covered, for about 10 minutes or until just cooked. Add the remaining shoyu and mirin and simmer for a further 5 minutes or until well cooked and soft. Remove from the heat, leave to cool and leave in a refrigerator in the liquid overnight.
4 Cut the aubergines (eggplants) into 3–4 rings and arrange on a serving plate or individual plates garnished with finely shredded fresh ginger.

Vinegared salad with cucumber and octopus

Kyuri to tako no sunomono

Sunomono, 'vinegary dishes', are an important part of Japanese cooking, and also a fixture in the kaiseki *(multi-course meal). The vegetables are salted first to draw water to take off the chill, then mixed with a vinegary dressing.*

SERVES 4

FOR THE *SANBAI-ZU* DRESSING:
5 tablespoons light shoyu (Japanese soy sauce)
5 tablespoons *yonezu* (Japanese rice vinegar)
3 tablespoons granulated sugar

1 small octopus tentacle
1 lemon, halved
½ cucumber
1cm/½in piece of root ginger
salt

1 Mix all the ingredients for the dressing, and stir well until the sugar dissolves.
2 Rub the octopus with salt, massage well to clean and wash under running water. Boil water in a saucepan, add the octopus and lemon and cook over a moderate heat for 10 minutes until soft. Drain, discard the lemon, and when cool cut the tentacle into 5mm/¼in thick slices slightly diagonally. Sprinkle with 1–2 tablespoons of the *sanbai-zu*, mix well and set aside.
3 Cut the cucumber in half lengthways, then into almost transparent half-moon

slices. Soak in salted water (1 teaspoonful of salt to about 110ml/4fl oz/½ cup) for 5–10 minutes, drain and pat dry with kitchen paper (paper towels). Sprinkle with 1–2 tablespoons of the *sanbai-zu*, mix and set aside.
4 Peel and shred the root ginger. Plunge into cold water to reduce the bitterness. Drain on kitchen paper (paper towels).
5 Arrange a quarter of the octopus and cucumber on each of 4 small individual dishes, pour over the remaining *sanbai-zu* and serve garnished with shredded ginger.

Wakame and mushroom salad with miso dressing

Wakame to kinoko su-miso aé [v]

This is a version of sunomono, *'vinegary dishes', using miso in the dressing.* Su-miso *is also used with sashimi, octopus or shellfish in particular. Spring onion (scallion) with clams or other shellfish mixed with this* su-miso *is called* nuta.

SERVES 4

5g/¼oz dried cut *wakame* (young seaweed)
1 bunch of *shimeji* or 8–12 fresh mushrooms

FOR THE *SU-MISO* DRESSING:

2 tablespoons white miso
2 tablespoons *yonezu* (Japanese rice vinegar)
1½ tablespoons granulated sugar
1 teaspoon light shoyu (Japanese soy sauce)
½ teaspoon mustard
white sesame seeds, lightly roasted, to garnish

1 Soak the *wakame* for 5 minutes in water. Drain, plunge into boiling water and drain again. Pat dry with kitchen paper (paper towels).
2 Trim the soiled part of the mushroom stems, and for *shimeji* and *enoki-dake*, separate the stems. Plunge in boiling water for 30 seconds (*enoki-dake*) to 1 minute (*shimeji*), depending on the thickness of the mushroom. Do not cook. Drain and immediately put under running water. Pat dry with kitchen paper (paper towels).

3 Mix all the ingredients for the *su-miso* dressing in a bowl, and using a small whisk stir well until smooth.
4 Mix the *wakame* and mushrooms in a mixing bowl and dress with the *su-miso*. Arrange a quarter on each of 4 individual salad bowls or plates and serve garnished with lightly roasted sesame seeds.

Hijiki seaweed with fried tofu and shiitake

Hijiki no nimono [v]

Hijiki *is regarded as one of the best health foods as it is rich in calcium, iron and vitamins, and is usually available in dried form from Japanese supermarkets. Remember, when handling* hijiki, *to plunge it, once softened, into boiling water before cooking.*

SERVES 4

60g/2oz *hijiki* seaweed
½ medium carrot, peeled and shredded
2 *abura-agé* (fried tofu), 15 x 7cm/6 x 3in)
3–4 dried shiitake, soaked in 450ml/16fl oz/
  2 cups water overnight

FOR THE SOUP:

6 tablespoons granulated sugar
5 tablespoons shoyu (Japanese soy sauce)
2 tablespoons sake
1 tablespoon mirin

1 Soak the *hijiki* in warm water for about 20–30 mintues. Drain and wash in a few changes of cold water. Plunge into boiling water, and bring back to the boil. Remove from the heat, drain and set aside.
2 Parboil the carrot shreds on a high heat for 1–2 minutes and drain.
3 Pour boiling water over the *abura-agé* to draw out the oil. Cut in half lengthways, and then crossways into thin shreds.
4 Drain the shiitake, retaining the water, and squeeze out excess water from the shiitake with your hands. Cut across into thin shreds.

5 Mix the ingredients for the soup in a saucepan with the shiitake soaking water, add the *hijiki* and cook over a moderate heat for 7–8 minutes, stirring occasionally. Add the *abura-agé* and shiitake, and continue to cook for 7–8 minutes. Add the carrot and simmer for about 5 minutes until the soup has reduced to almost nothing. Do not stir too often after adding the *abura-agé*, and shiitake. Remove from the heat.
6 Put all in a serving bowl and place in the centre of the table for diners to help themselves. This dish is nice with hot rice.

Wax gourd and eel hotpot

Togan to unagi no tamago-jimé nabe

NAOYUKI SATO, executive chef of Nadaman, Changrilla Hotel, Hong Kong, shows here one of his many *nabe* (earthenware pot) dishes using *togan*, a very popular ingredient in Hong Kong. As soon as the leaves on the trees start to change to bright red and yellow autumn colours, the *nabe* season arrives in Japan. *Nabe* cooking is the very essence of Japanese cooking: fresh ingredients cooked very lightly in front of you and eaten immediately.

SERVES 4

¼ small *togan* (wax gourd) or ½ marrow or
   2 courgettes (zucchini)
560ml/1 pint/2½ cups chicken stock (broth)
1 ready-prepared *kabayaki* eel
   (150–200g/5–7oz), cut crossways into
   about 20 pieces
3 eggs, beaten
mitsuba or cress, to garnish
sprinkling of *sansho* powder, to serve

FOR THE SOUP:
560ml/1 pint/2½ cups dashi (see page 56)
6 tablespoons sake
2½ tablespoons light shoyu (Japanese
   soy sauce)
2 tablespoons mirin

Yanagawa nabe, using a freshwater fish called dojo, *is one of Japan's very traditional* nabe *dishes, but unfortunately* dojo *is not easily available outside Japan. This is a dilemma faced by all Japanese chefs abroad every day. Instead of* dojo, *I use* kabayaki *eel and cook it with* togan *(wax gourd). The contrasting flavours and textures of the rich* kabayaki *and the light watery* togan *complement each other, and the delicious soup is topped with beaten eggs. NS*

1 Cut the *togan* or marrow into 5cm/2in thick wedges, peel and cook in chicken stock (broth) until cooked but still crunchy. Drain and slice crossways into 1cm/½in thick pieces. If using courgettes (zucchini), cut into 1cm/½in thick rings.

2 Place the vegetable in the bottom of a shallow pan or a frying-pan (skillet), and add the *kabayaki* eel slices on top. Pour in all the soup ingredients just to cover, bring to the boil and lower the heat. Pour over the beaten egg evenly on top, garnish with *mitsuba* or cress, and serve hot together with a jar of *sansho* powder. Alternatively, place the pot on a portable fire on the table, and let diners help themselves.

Steamed kabocha squash on a bed of azuki

Mushi kabocha to azuki [v]

Kabocha is undoubtedly the best in flavour and texture of all squashes and pumpkins. It has a dense texture and nutty sweet flavour, so it's best appreciated very lightly cooked as here.

SERVES 4

½ kabocha squash, de-seeded
100g/3½oz azuki beans, soaked in plenty of
    water for 4 hours
3 tablespoons mirin
1 tablespoon granulated sugar
freshly milled sea salt

1 Place the squash, cut-side down, on a chopping-board, and trim off the calyx and any dirty part of the skin, but keep most of the skin on. Cut into 4–6 wedges, and chop each wedge into bite-sized pieces.
2 Put the azuki beans together with the soaking water in a saucepan, and bring to the boil over a high heat, then lower the heat and gently simmer for 20 minutes. Drain, retaining the liquid, and put the beans back in the saucepan with 110ml/ 4fl oz/½ cup of the cooking liquid. Add the mirin and sugar, and gently simmer for about 10 minutes. Remove from the heat and keep warm.

3 Put the kabocha either in a large bowl or directly in a steaming basket, and steam in a boiling steamer over a moderate heat for 10–15 minutes until soft but still crunchy. Pierce with a cocktail stick (toothpick) to test the softness. Remove from the heat and leave, still covered, for 5 minutes.
4 Lay the azuki beans in the centre of a serving dish, and neatly arrange the kabocha on top. Sprinkle the kabocha with sea salt, and serve hot.

Simmered sato-imo with minced meat sauce

Sato-imo no soboro-ni

Sato-imo, or taro, is a kind of potato with a dense flesh and slippery surface. Simply boil whole with the skin on, peel with your hands (the skin comes off very easily) and eat with a little shoyu; it's a very good snack particularly for children, and a much better and healthier alternative to crisps. Sato-imo is also used in many simmered dishes as it doesn't disintegrate easily, as shown here. This recipe shows how to handle this unique vegetable, and one of the popular meat sauces, soboro.

SERVES 4

8 *sato-imo* (taro) (approximately 450g/1lb)
200g/7oz minced chicken meat
1.5cm/¾ in piece of root ginger, peeled
   and shredded
2 teaspoons *katakuriko* (potato starch)
   or arrowroot
salt
lime rind, finely shredded, to garnish

FOR THE SOUP:
2 tablespoons granulated sugar
1 tablespoon sake
4 tablespoons shoyu (Japanese soy sauce)
1 tablespoon mirin

1 Using a scourer, scrape off dirt and hair from the *sato-imo* under running water, and peel. Sprinkle with salt, and rub into the *sato-imo* until the slimy substance comes away. Wash off under running water, and put in a saucepan with water just to cover. Bring to the boil, lower the heat and simmer on a medium heat for 2–3 minutes. Drain, put under running water again, and set aside to drain.
2 Mix the minced chicken, shredded ginger and all the ingredients for the soup in a saucepan, and stir well to separate the minced chicken. Place on a high heat and cook until the meat becomes granular. Remove from the heat and set aside.

3 Put the *sato-imo* in a separate saucepan and pour over the cooked minced chicken together with the soup. Add 400ml/ 14fl oz/1¾ cups of water, cover and bring to the boil. Lower the heat to medium, and simmer for about 15 minutes or until the *sato-imo* is cooked – if it can be pierced with a cocktail stick (toothpick) it's cooked.
4 Dissolve the *katakuriko* or arrowroot in 1–2 tablespoons water, and gradually pour into the soup, shaking the pan so it mixes evenly. When the soup thickens, remove from the heat and divide into 4 individual bowls. Serve hot, garnished with finely shredded lime rind on top.

Vinegared ginger slices

Gari [v]

Gari, a sushi shop jargon for vinegared ginger slices, is always served with sushi and sashimi. It works as a palate freshener inbetween different tastes. It is widely available in packets at supermarkets but is also very easy to make at home. Make a bulk in a jar and it can be kept in the refrigerator almost indefinitely.

MAKES A 560ML/1 PINT JAR

250–300g/9–10oz root ginger
2 teaspoons salt
225ml/8fl oz/1 cup *yonezu* (rice vinegar)
110ml/4 fl oz/½ cup water
3 tablespoons granulated sugar

1 Separate the ginger into lumps and peel. Rub salt all over the pieces and leave salted overnight.
2 Mix the rice vinegar, water and sugar in a sterilized jar. Stir to dissolve.
3 Slice each piece of ginger lengthways along the vein as thinly as possible (use a

mandolin if you have one). Blanch in boiling water for 30 seconds. Drain and marinate in the vinegar mixture. The ginger pieces will turn slightly pink. It will be ready to eat after 2–3 days. Store in the refrigerator almost indefinitely.

Broccoli with sesame and tofu dressing

Broccoli no shiro-aé [v]

Japanese salads are wet salads, which means that vegetables are either salted or blanched before being mixed with a dressing. Sunomono, 'vinegary dishes', are those with a vinegary or citrus dressing. Popular dressings include ground sesame seeds, miso, tofu, egg yolk mixed with vinegar or even sea urchin. Shiro-aé, white dressing, is very easy to make, very delicious to eat and very pretty to look at. Use at least some green vegetables for a beautiful colour contrast.

SERVES 4

FOR THE *SHIRO-AE* DRESSING:

1 cake (250g/9oz) firm tofu

3 tablespoons white sesame seeds,
   lightly roasted

2 tablespoons granulated sugar

¼ teaspoon sea salt

2 teaspoons light shoyu (Japanese soy sauce)

1 head of broccoli (approximately 300g/
   10oz), separated into small florets

2 medium carrots, peeled and cut into
   bite-sized pieces

lemon rind, to garnish

1 First make the dressing: roughly break the tofu with your hands, put into boiling water, and bring back to the boil. Drain into a colander lined with muslin (cheesecloth) or a clean tea towel. When cool, wrap the tofu with the cloth and squeeze out as much water as possible. Remove from the cloth and set aside.
2 Using a *suribachi* (Japanese mortar) or ordinary mortar and pestle, grind the roasted sesame seeds into a smooth paste. Add the crushed tofu and the seasoning (the sugar, salt and shoyu), and further grind together until it becomes a smooth paste. Add some water, a little at a time, to make a slightly runny dressing. Check the seasoning, and add salt if necessary.
3 Cook the broccoli and carrots separately in lightly salted boiling water until soft but still crunchy. Drain and pat dry with kitchen paper (paper towels). Put the broccoli and carrots together in a large mixing bowl, pour over the dressing and lightly mix together.
4 Arrange a quarter of the salad heaped in the centre on each of 4 individual plates, and serve garnished with lemon rind on top.

Vinegared young ginger shoots

Hajikami shoga [v]

In spring, new ginger shoots with long green stems become available at oriental supermarkets, and will make a delicious and pretty garnish when marinated in a sweet vinegar mixture. This ginger is normally used to garnish grilled (broiled) dishes.

MAKES A 560ML/1PINT JAR

10 fresh young ginger shoots with stems

150ml/5½fl oz/⅔ cup *yonezu* (Japanese
   rice vinegar)

5 tablespoons water

2 tablespoons granulated sugar

1 Separate the shoots to make each shoot into the shape of a long pen and clean. Pour boiling water over the shoots and leave to drain.
2 Mix the rice vinegar, water and sugar in a saucepan and bring just to the boil on a moderate heat, stirring continuously until the sugar dissolves. Pour the mixture into a tall sterilized jar and marinate the ginger shoots standing in the jar. As they will turn pinkish up to the marinade level it is advisable to keep the shoots' green stems above the marinade. It will be ready to eat in 2–3 hours and will be good if kept in the marinade in the refrigerator for several weeks. The marinade keeps almost indefinitely though, so each time you take some out, add some more.

Ebi-imo simmered in white miso

Ebi-imo no shiromiso-ni

AKIHIRO KURITA is chef/patron of a so-called 'counter *kappoh*' restaurant, Kurita, in Kyoto. *Kappoh* is an old word for Japanese 'hands-on' cooking, still used by restaurants in their names to imply they serve freshly cooked food individually to order. They are mostly small restaurants with a counter in the centre, inside which the chef cooks, serves food and talks with diners.

SERVES 4

4–8 medium *sato-imo* (taro)
2–3 tablespoons rice bran (optional)
900ml/32fl oz/4 cups dashi (see page 56)
400g/14oz white miso
10cm/4in piece of large carrot, peeled
100g/3½oz spinach
½ *yurine* (lily bulb) or 1–2 turnips
4 dried decorative *fu* (gluten product), to
    garnish (optional)
few drops of mustard, to garnish

This is a typical Kyoto dish, using ebi-imo *(pictured), white miso and lily bulb, all of which are Kyoto specialities.* Ebi-imo, *meaning 'prawn potato' on account of its shape, is in season in winter, and those from Tanba have the best reputation. Outside Kyoto, I suggest you use* sato-imo *(taro), which is slightly coarser in texture. Use white or ordinary miso with a little sugar added. AK*

1 Peel the *sato-imo* into a neat, hexagonal round shape, slightly larger than a golf ball, and put in a saucepan with the rice bran, if using, and water to just cover. The rice bran brings out the *sato-imo*'s so-called *aku* – a kind of bitterness. Bring to the boil on a high heat, stirring until the rice bran has dissolved, and simmer on a moderate heat for about 20 minutes until the *sato-imo* is soft but still crunchy. Remove from the heat and immediately rinse under running water. Drain and keep warm.
2 Warm 675ml/24fl oz/3 cups of the dashi in a saucepan on a moderate heat (do not boil), add the miso and stir until the miso dissolves. Remove from the heat.
3 Ladle about 200ml/7fl oz/1 cup of the miso soup into another saucepan, and add the remaining dashi. Gently bring almost to the boil, then add the cooked *sato-imo* and simmer, covered, on a low heat for 10 minutes. Gently shake the pan to turn each piece. Remove from the heat and keep warm in the pan.
4 Meanwhile, prepare the accompanying vegetables. Cut the carrot in half, then quarter each piece lengthways to get 8 x 5cm/2in long rectangular pieces. Blanch in lightly salted boiling water until soft and drain. Blanch the spinach, also in lightly salted water, for 1–2 minutes, drain, and immediately place under running water. Squeeze out excess water with your hands, then divide into 4 and set aside. Sprinkle salt over the *yurine*, if using, and steam in a boiling steamer for 10 minutes until cooked. Divide into petals. Cut each turnip, if using, into 4 and boil in lightly salted water for 5 minutes until soft. Soak the *fu* in water for 5 minutes to soften.
5 Return the saucepan of *sato-imo* to a moderate heat, and add all the vegetables, except the spinach, to warm up. Arrange 2 pieces of each and a small bunch of spinach on 4 deep dishes. Garnish with a piece of *fu*, if using, and a little mustard on top, and pour over some miso soup to fill half the bowl. Serve hot.

4

Fish
and Shellfish

Red snapper simmered in sake with tofu

Wakasa guji saka-mushi

MASAHIRO KURUSU, the chef/patron of Tankuma, one of the oldest *kaiseki* restaurants in Kyoto, took over from his father when he was only 31, and is still one of the youngest owners of such established restaurants. Here he provides a typical Kyoto dish.

SERVES 4

1 red snapper (approximately 675g/1½lb), scaled and filleted
4 fresh shiitake
100g/3½oz *mizuna* or young spinach
dried *yuba* (tofu skin), (optional)
20 x 20cm/8 x 8in *konbu* (dried kelp)
1 cake (250g/9oz) silken tofu, cut into 4 cubes
2 limes, halved, to garnish

FOR THE STEAMING SOUP:
450ml/16fl oz/2 cups dashi (see page 56)
7 tablespoons sake
½ teaspoon sea salt
2 tablespoons shoyu (Japanese soy sauce)

Wakasa Bay lies north of Kyoto, and is one of the renowned fisheries of Japan. This recipe is usually made with guji, *but as that is unique to this area, use red snapper instead. As is the case for any good, delicate fish, it is best when lightly simmered and minimally flavoured. MK*

1 Carefully remove all bones from the snapper fillets and halve each fillet. Place the fish pieces in a colander and pour over boiling water. Immediately place under running water and wash away any remaining scales. Drain and pat dry with kitchen paper (paper towels).
2 Cut off the stem from each shiitake and make a cross slit on each cap. Plunge the *mizuna* or young spinach leaves into boiling water, drain and squeeze out excess water with your hands. Cut roughly into 5cm/2in long pieces.
3 Roll the dried *yuba*, if using, into 4 cylinders, about 4cm/1½in long.

4 Mix all the steaming soup ingredients in a saucepan, bring to the boil, stirring to dissolve the salt, and remove from the heat.
5 Place the *konbu* in the base of a large, deep, heat-resistant dish or bowl, put the fish on top and add the shiitake and tofu. Pour the steaming soup over just to cover all the ingredients. Cover the dish with a *makisu* (bamboo sushi roller), and place a tea towel over it, then steam in a boiling steamer for about 15 minutes.
6 Add the *yuba* and *mizuna* or young spinach, and continue to steam for a further 3 minutes.
7 Arrange a piece of fish, shiitake, *yuba*, tofu, and *mizuna* in each of 4 individual bowls, and pour over the steaming soup to half fill each bowl. Garnish with a half lime per person, and serve.

Sake simmered sea bream and turnip

Tai kabura

MASAHIRO KURUSU, the third generation to run one of Kyoto's most successful *kaiseki* restaurants, Tankuma, teaches at a number of cookery schools and also frequently appears on television. Sea bream, the red variety in particular, is often used for *kaiseki* cooking, probably because of its colour, and also for the fact that it's an expensive, upmarket fish.

SERVES 4

1 large sea bream (approximately
   900g/2lb), filleted
2 *kabura* (giant turnips, pictured), or ½ large
   daikon, peeled
8 mangetouts, trimmed
450ml/16fl oz/2 cups dashi (see page 56)
½ tablespoon shoyu (Japanese soy sauce)
225ml/8fl oz/1 cup sake
3 tablespoons mirin
light shoyu (Japanese soy sauce), to taste
salt
rind of ½ *yuzu* or lemon, finely shredded,
   to garnish

The Japanese make use of every part of most fish, and none is more used than sea bream. Grilled (broiled) whole sea bream is called okashira-tsuki, *meaning 'with head', and is a cherished dish for celebratory meals. We normally use sea bream head for this dish but here the body of the fish is simmered in sake and served* kaiseki-*style. MK*

1 Cut each sea bream fillet lengthways into 2 and each piece crossways into 3. Sprinkle with salt all over and set aside.
2 Cut each turnip into 8 wedges and, using a sharp knife, cut off the sharp edges to make each wedge into a smooth, round shape. Cook in boiling water for 5–6 minutes until soft but still crunchy. (Use the milky water from washed rice to reduce the bitterness of the turnips.)
3 Cook the mangetouts in lightly salted boiling water for 1 minute, and drain. In a mixing bowl mix 3 tablespoons of dashi, the shoyu and a pinch of salt to taste, and marinate the cooked mangetouts.

4 Blanch the sea bream pieces in boiling water. Put all in a saucepan together with 200ml/7fl oz/⅞ cup of the sake and the mirin, then bring to the boil over a high heat. Skim off the scum that rises to the surface. Add the remaining dashi and the turnips, season with salt and light shoyu, and cook for about 10 minutes. Towards the end of the cooking, add the mangetouts and cook for a further minute. Remove from the heat.
5 Arrange a quarter of the sea bream, the turnip and the mangetouts in each of 4 individual bowls, garnished with finely shredded *yuzu* or lemon rind on top.

Salmon grilled (broiled) with koji

Sake no koji-yaki

HIDEAKI MORITA is the chef/patron of the Matsumi restaurant in Hamburg, Germany. Today there are more Japanese businesses in Düsseldorf, but Hamburg used to be the first gateway to Europe for Japanese exports, and all major Japanese companies had their European headquarters there. Mr Morita came to the Hamburg branch from the parent restaurant in Tokyo where he worked in the eighties, and has stayed ever since, eventually taking over Matsumi from the previous owner on his retirement in 1987. This simple but delicious grilled (broiled) dish subtly flavoured with *koji* (a type of yeast) is one of his favourites.

SERVES 4

100g/3½oz/½ cup Japanese rice
75g/3oz/just under ½ cup rice *koji*
110ml/4 fl oz/½ cup sake, or 60ml/2fl oz/
    ¼ cup rice *shochu* (distilled rice spirit),
    heated to lukewarm (35°C/95°F)
4 salmon or any fish steaks (each weighing
    approximately 120g/4oz)
mirin, to glaze
salt
4–8 ready-made *hajikami shoga* (vinegared
    young ginger shoots, see page 71), to
    garnish (optional)

Koji, a kind of yeast, is a vital agent for making the fundamentals of Japanese food such as miso and shoyu, and for brewing sake. It takes a couple of days to make rice koji *mash and another couple of days to marinate the fish in it, but it's worth every effort. This is a centuries-old method and, according to my old teacher, they even used to take the rice* koji *to bed with them at night. It was very warm from active fermentation, so it wasn't just for the sake of the* koji! *If you do not find the* koji *agent in your area, you can use sake-kasu (sake pulp) on its own, without rice, but then the dish is called* kasu-zuke, *and is altogether quite different. HM*

1 Cook the rice following the method on page 152 (Three kinds of nori-rolled sushi, step 1).
2 Fan to cool the rice to body temperature, 30–35°C/86–95°F, then add the *koji* and the sake or *shochu*. Swiftly transfer the mixture into an *ohitsu* (Japanese wooden rice container) or a large plastic container, and tightly put a lid on. Wrap the whole container with an old towel or blanket, and keep in a warm place such as an airing cupboard for 2 days without disturbing. (It can be kept in the electric rice cooker, if using, for the whole process, but it means the cooker will be out of use for 4–5 days.) On the third day, remove the lid, and stir well with a wooden spatula so the fermentation spreads evenly; if it is progressing well it should be warm. Place the lid back on and return to the warm place. Repeat this stirring twice a day for 2–3 days. The rice *koji* mash is now ready for marinating.
3 Generously salt the salmon steaks, and leave salted in the refrigerator for 2–3 hours. Pat dry with kitchen paper (paper towels), and bury each fish steak completely in the rice *koji* to marinate for 3–4 days in the refrigerator. (The fish keeps in the rice *koji* for up to 7 days.)
4 Remove the salmon steaks from the rice *koji*, shaking off any excess, and grill (broil) under a medium heat, skin-side up, for 7–8 minutes until golden brown. Remove from the heat, and brush the fish with a little mirin to give a glow.
5 Arrange 1 salmon steak on each of 4 individual plates, garnish with *hajikami shoga* if desired, and serve.

Tuna steak with wasabi Chardonnay sauce

Tuna steki wasabi shadonei sosu

KEN TOMINAGA, chef/patron of the Hana restaurant in the Bay Area, north San Francisco, introduces his version of grilled tuna steak with two kinds of dressing. Tuna is the most popular fish used by Japanese chefs abroad, and apart from sushi and sashimi, they have created other innovative recipes using tuna, such as grilled (broiled) steak, seared in salad and tartar.

SERVES 4

4 tuna steaks (about 125g/4½oz each)
vegetable oil, for frying
4 fresh shiitake, trimmed and shredded
½ each red, green,and yellow (bell) peppers,
    de-seeded and shredded
1 teaspoon sake
1 teaspoon shoyu (Japanese soy sauce)
½ teaspoon root ginger juice
salt and pepper
200g/7oz mashed potatoes, to serve
Italian parsley, to garnish

FOR THE WASABI CHARDONNAY SAUCE:
110ml/4fl oz/½ cup Chardonnay or
    other white wine
1 tablespoon finely chopped shallots
1 teaspoon wasabi paste
2 teaspoons single (light) cream
½ teaspoon unsalted butter (sweet butter)
salt and pepper

FOR THE CABERNET SAUCE:
225ml/8fl oz/1 cup red Cabernet or
    other red wine
1 teaspoon mirin
1 teaspoon unsalted butter (sweet butter)

Such a delicate fish as tuna is best eaten raw or very lightly cooked. This is a simple grilled (broiled) dish, so a little excitement in the dressing and a variety of accompanied salads is needed. That's why I thought of the two kinds of dressing, and various vegetables to serve with it. The result is a beautiful delicious dish, which has become a fixture in my restaurant. KT

1 Sprinkle a pinch of salt and pepper on both sides of each tuna steak, and grill (broil) both sides under a direct heat for about 1–2 minutes until only the surface is seared and the inside is still rare. Slice each steak, inserting the blade diagonally, into 1cm/½in thick sashimi pieces.
2 Heat a frying-pan (skillet), add about 1 tablespoon vegetable oil and sauté the shredded shiitake and all the peppers. Season with the sake, shoyu, ginger juice, and salt and pepper to taste.
3 Make the wasabi Chardonnay sauce: mix the white wine and the shallots in a saucepan, and simmer on a moderate heat for 20–25 minutes until reduced to one fifth of the original volume. Add the wasabi, cream and butter, and season with salt and pepper. Leave to cool.
4 Make the Cabernet sauce: boil the red wine until it becomes ⅓ of its original volume, and add the mirin and butter. Leave to cool.
5 Arrange a quarter of the mashed potatoes in the centre of each individual plate, and one portion of tuna slices around it. Add a quarter of the sautéed shiitake and peppers on top of the mashed potato. Pour the wasabi Chardonnay sauce and the Cabernet sauce around it in an artistic manner, garnish with the parsley, and serve.

Swordfish teriyaki

Kajiki no teriyaki

Due to its sweet flavour, teriyaki, literally meaning 'glow grill', is joining the league of Japanese dishes that are more popular today in the West than in Japan. The teriyaki sauce is a mixture of shoyu, sake, mirin and sugar, the sugar giving a glow to the grilled (broiled) food. Fish, chicken and beef are all good for teriyaki. Here, swordfish is used; the effect of the rich sauce on an otherwise dry fish when cooked is quite remarkable.

SERVES 4

4 swordfish steaks (each weighing
  approximately 150g/5½oz)
1 cucumber
2 tablespoons vegetable oil
sea salt
4 ready-made *hajikami shoga* (vinegared
  young ginger shoots, see page 71), to
  garnish (optional)

FOR THE *TERIYAKI* SAUCE:

3 tablespoons shoyu (Japanese soy sauce)
3 tablespoons sake
3 tablespoons mirin
1 teaspoon granulated sugar

1 Sprinkle sea salt evenly over the swordfish steaks, and set aside.
2 Quarter the cucumber lengthways, and de-seed each quarter by running the blade between the seed part and the flesh. Thinly shred the green and white part of the cucumber, and plunge into cold water. (This freshens the cucumber shreds and makes them crisp.) Drain, and divide among 4 individual plates.
3 Mix all the *teriyaki* sauce ingredients in a small saucepan, bring to the boil and simmer over a medium heat until the sugar dissolves. Remove from the heat and set aside.
4 Heat the vegetable oil in a frying-pan (skillet), lay in the swordfish steaks and fry for 1–2 minutes on each side, shaking the pan constantly to prevent the fish from sticking. The fish should still be rare inside. Remove from the heat, turn into a colander and pour boiling water over the fish to expel excess oil.
5 Return the fish to the pan with the juice still in it, place on a medium heat, and then pour over the *teriyaki* sauce. Cook for 2–3 minutes until the sauce begins to bubble, then turn over the fish. Cook for a further 1–2 minutes, tilting the pan occasionally to coat the fish well. Remove the fish from the pan and place on a bed of shredded cucumber on each of the 4 individual plates. Continue to heat the remaining sauce, stirring continuously, for 1 minute to further thicken it. Remove from the heat and spoon a little sauce onto each fish steak. Serve hot, garnished with *hajikami shoga*, if using.

Steamed salmon with citrus sauce

Sake no ponzu-mushi

Like any other fish, salmon is also best very lightly cooked, and steaming retains the moisture of what tends to get too dry and flaky very easily. This is an extremely easy dish that can be made in no time.

SERVES 4

4 spring onions (scallions)
1cm/½in piece of root ginger, peeled
4 fresh salmon steaks (500g/18oz in total)

FOR THE *PONZU* (CITRUS SHOYU) SAUCE:

2 tablespoons shoyu (Japanese soy sauce)
2 tablespoons lemon or lime juice
½ tablespoon *yonezu* (Japanese rice vinegar)
1 tablespoon sake

1 Cut the spring onions (scallions) crossways diagonally into 2.5cm/1in thick pieces. Finely shred the ginger, and plunge into cold water. Leave to drain.
2 Combine all the *ponzu* sauce ingredients. Place the salmon steaks on a large plate, and sprinkle evenly with the *ponzu* sauce. Add the spring onions (scallions) evenly on top, and steam in a boiling steamer on a high heat for 10–12 minutes or until lightly cooked. Alternatively, cover with cling film (plastic wrap), and put in a microwave oven for 8 minutes (500W). Leave in the steamer or microwave oven for 2–3 minutes to settle. Remove, and serve hot, garnished with fresh ginger on top.

Sardine sauté with salad

Iwashi no soté salada

Sardines are nutritionally sound and rich in protein and oil. There are restaurants in Tokyo specializing only in these. They are eaten in many ways, such as grilled (broiled) over a barbecue, simmered with vegetables, deep-fried and marinated in nanban *sauce or pan-fried, as here.*

SERVES 4

12 large sardines, filleted
2 tablespoons curry powder
6 tablespoons plain (all-purpose) flour
2 tablespoons vegetable oil
4–5 iceberg lettuce leaves, 2–3 spring onions
   (scallions), and ½ cucumber, all shredded
salt and pepper
3–4 *shiso* leaves, shredded, to garnish

FOR THE SAUCE:

4 tablespoons *yonezu* (Japanese rice vinegar)
3 tablespoons lemon juice
⅓ teaspoon salt and sprinkling of pepper

1 Trim the sardine fillets neatly, pat dry with kitchen paper (paper towels), and sprinkle with salt and pepper.
2 Mix the curry powder and the flour in a flat dish. Dredge the sardine fillets in the flour mixture, piece by piece, shaking off any excess. Heat the vegetable oil in a frying-pan (skillet), and fry the sardine fillets, skin-side down first, on a medium heat for 1–2 minutes until the skin is crisp. Turn over and fry the other side for another 1–2 minutes until crisp. Drain on a wire rack or kitchen paper (paper towels).

3 Combine all the sauce ingredients together. Mix all the vegetable shreds and arrange a quarter on each of 4 individual plates. Arrange 6 fried sardine fillets decoratively on each bed of salad, and pour the sauce mixture over the sardines. Serve, garnished with the shredded *shiso* leaves.

Seared tuna tataki with citrus sauce

Maguro no tataki ponzu aé

Tataki is a form of sashimi, and this one is seared before slicing into sashimi. The searing is not to cook, but simply to braise just the outside while the inside remains raw. In effect, the slightly hard texture and smoky flavour of the exterior makes the somewhat plain taste of the tuna more interesting. This is the technique often used for katsuo *(bonito or skipjack tuna) shown on page 42 (Skipjack tuna* tataki *salad), but here more widely available tuna is used and dressed with* ponzu, *a popular Japanese citrus dressing.*

SERVES 4–8

300g/10oz tuna
vegetable oil, for frying
1 tablespoon white sesame seeds
mixed green salad leaves such as red and
　　green oak leaf, red chard, flat leaf parsley,
　　rocket (arugula), baby spinach and
　　lamb's lettuce

FOR THE DRESSING:

juice of 1 lime
1½ tablespoons shoyu (Japanese soy sauce)
1 tablespoon *yonezu* (Japanese rice vinegar)
2 teaspoons granulated sugar
1 tablespoon sesame oil

1 Quickly braise, or pan-fry with a little vegetable oil, the tuna over a high heat until all the surfaces are seared but the inside is still raw. Plunge into ice-cold water. Drain and pat dry with kitchen paper (paper towels). Slice very thinly into small discs, no more than 5cm/2in in diameter.

2 Mix all the dressing ingredients and stir until the sugar dissolves.

3 Heat a small dry saucepan, add the sesame seeds and lightly roast, shaking the pan continuously, until the first seed pops up. Remove from the heat and transfer to a mortar. Lightly pound the sesame seeds with a pestle until a third of the seeds are crushed.

4 Put the mixed green salad leaves in a large mixing bowl, add the seared tuna slices and pour the dressing over the top. Lightly mix and arrange a quarter on each individual plate. Sprinkle sesame seeds over the salad and serve.

Prawn (shrimp) tempura

Ebi tempura

TETSUYA SAOTOME, chef/patron of the tempura restaurant Mikawa in Tokyo, says cooking tempura is a science, but he treats it as art as well. He is an artist in his own right and socializes with artists and architects. He also collects antiques and actually makes use of them in his restaurant. Tempura and prawn (shrimp) are synonymous, and here Mr Saotome shows how best to make it.

SERVES 4

FOR THE DIPPING SAUCE:

450ml/16fl oz/2 cups dashi (see page 56)

2 dried shiitake, soaked in the above
dashi overnight

7 tablespoons light shoyu (Japanese
soy sauce)

7 tablespoons mirin

8 uncooked tiger prawns (shrimp) with shells

vegetable oil, for deep-frying

unrefined sesame oil (optional) (see recipe)

1 large white onion, cut into 4 rings

8 pieces of okra, trimmed

4 large fresh shiitake, the stems cut off

4 *shiso* leaves (optional)

5cm/2in piece of daikon, peeled and grated

2.5cm/1in piece of root ginger, peeled
and grated

FOR THE BATTER:

225ml/8fl oz/1 cup ice-cold water

1 egg, beaten

140g/5oz/1 cup light plain (all-purpose)
flour, sifted twice then left in the
refrigerator overnight

Prawn (shrimp) is full of water containing rich 'umami', the source of its fundamental flavour as well as its strong fishy and iron-like smell. Tempura frying, if done properly, reduces this unwanted smell while bringing out its umami. So the timing is everything in tempura frying. For prawns, the right point is when the inside is still uncooked, so at my restaurant, in order to keep the prawn's inside temperature at 40–50°C/104–122°F and its outside very crisp, we fry them very quickly at a high temperature. We use a mixture of vegetable oil and unrefined sesame oil, normally in equal measure and make the batter just before frying. TS

1 First make the dipping sauce: remove the shiitake from the dashi, squeezing out excess liquid from the shiitake. (Use the shiitake for another dish.) Put the shiitake-flavoured dashi in a saucepan together with the shoyu and mirin on a medium heat, and bring to the boil. Remove from the heat and set aside.

2 Shell the prawns (shrimp), leaving the tail intact, and de-vein. Cut the tip of the tail diagonally from each prawn (shrimp), releasing the water in the fins so that it won't splash oil when deep-fried. Make several slits across the belly of each prawn (shrimp) to avoid it curling when heated.

3 Make the batter: stir the icy water into the beaten and sieved egg, then sift in the chilled flour, and lightly fold several times using a few *hashi* sticks or a fork. Do not stir: the batter should still be lumpy.

4 Heat plenty of vegetable oil, or vegetable oil mixed in equal measure with sesame oil, in a deep frying-pan (skillet) or a wok. Just before frying, raise the temperature to170°C/340°F or until a drop of the batter comes up to the surface without touching the bottom of the pan.

5 Fry the vegetables first: plunge the onion rings into the batter by taking one piece at a time and gently sliding into the hot oil. Fry for 2–3 minutes, turning over once or twice, until golden brown, and drain on a wire rack. All vegetables should be fried in this way for 1–5 minutes, adjusting the length of time depending on the thickness and hardness of the vegetable. For shiitake and *shiso*, only one side is dipped in the batter, so the dark brown colour of the shiitake caps and the bright green of the *shiso* remain intact. Fry the shiitake for 2–3 minutes, turning over a few times, *shiso* for 5–10 seconds on the battered side only, until the batter becomes golden.

6 Holding each prawn (shrimp) by its tail, dip in the batter and then fry in the hot oil for 2–3 minutes or until golden brown. Several prawns (shrimp) can be fried at the same time. Drain on a wire rack. Repeat this until all the prawns (shrimp) are fried.

7 Arrange 2 prawns, 1 onion, 1 shiitake, 2 pieces of okra and 1 *shiso* tempura on each of 4 individual plates garnished with a mound of the grated daikon and ginger. A sheet of Japanese paper is normally placed under the tempura to absorb excess oil. Serve the tempura hot with the dipping sauce.

Monkfish hotpot

Ankou nabé

TAKESHI YASUGE, an expert in *fugu* (puffer fish), serves *fugu-chiri* (*fugu* hotpot) at his *fugu* restaurant, Asakusa Fukuji, in Tokyo, but shows here another popular fish hotpot, using monkfish. *Nabé* (pot) cooking is easy; just prepare the ingredients, bring them to the table, and the diners do the rest. There's little in the way of rules as long as you have a source of protein and vegetables. The famous *sukiyaki* and *shabu-shabu* are also *nabé* dishes, using beef.

This recipe shows you how to make an original ponzu *sauce, which does actually take two weeks to make. However, it may be easier to buy it ready-made in jars from a Japanese supermarket. Fugu is caught in tropical and sub-tropical seas all over the world, but the richest fishery lies between Japan and Korea in the Japan Sea, East China Sea and Yellow Sea. The season is from the autumn to spring equinox, so it's really a winter fish. There isn't a better dish than hot* nabé *to have in winter, so all* fugu *restaurants serve* fugu-chiri *as the main course following* nikogori *(see page 41) and sashimi. Ankou (monkfish) is also a winter fish, and although in my opinion there is no comparison to* fugu, *the most delicious fish in the world, it's probably the nearest alternative. The rice cooked in the rich soup, the product of all the cooked ingredients, is also just incomparably delicious. TY*

SERVES 4

FOR THE *PONZU* (CITRUS SHOYU) SAUCE:

110ml/4fl oz/½ cup *daidai* (Japanese bitter
   citrus fruit) juice, or lemon and lime juice
170ml/6fl oz/¾ cup shoyu (Japanese
   soy sauce)
2 tablespoons mirin
2 tablespoons dashi (see page 56)
1 tablespoon sake
10g/⅓oz *kezuribushi* (bonito or
   skipjack flakes)
5g/¼oz (approximately 5 x 10cm/2 x 4in) dried
   konbu (kelp) (pictured beneath seaweed)

1 monkfish (about 675g/1½lb), boned and
   cut into thin slices, bones reserved
8–12 hakusai leaves, chopped into pieces
250g/9oz *shungiku* (chrysanthemum leaves)
   or spinach, trimmed
1 cake (250g/9oz) firm tofu, cut into 8 cubes
12 fresh shiitake, stems removed
20cm/8in dried *konbu* (kelp)
450g/1lb/3 cups cooked rice
2 eggs, beaten
1 spring onion (scallion), finely chopped
shoyu (Japanese soy sauce), to taste
salt

1 First make the *ponzu*: mix all the ingredients in a mixing bowl and leave in the refrigerator for 2 weeks. Strain through a colander lined with muslin (cheesecloth) or kitchen paper (paper towel), and discard the *kezuribushi* and *konbu*.

2 Arrange the monkfish, hakusai, *shungiku* or spinach, tofu and shiitake on 1–2 large serving plates.

3 Put the *konbu* with plenty of water in a large pot together with the bones from the fish, and bring to the boil. Remove the *konbu*, discarding it, and simmer on a

medium heat for 5 minutes. Remove the bones, and transfer the pot on to a portable fire on the table, then put some of each ingredient into the pot. Skim the scum and froth from the surface with a perforated spoon, and adjust the heat during cooking. When cooked, diners help themselves, dipping the food in the *ponzu* sauce served in small individual bowls. Add more fish and vegetables to the pot as they are eaten.

4 After all the ingredients are cooked and eaten, skim off any remaining bits with a perforated spoon, and season the soup with salt, shoyu and *ponzu* to your liking. Add the cooked rice and simmer on a moderate heat, adding the beaten eggs on top, if desired, and when the egg hardens, remove from the heat. Divide into the 4 individual rice bowls and serve, sprinkled with the chopped spring onion (scallion).

Fried saury marinated in nanban sauce

Sanma no nanban-zuké

Sanma (saury) is a synonym for autumn in Japan, and the smell of smoke in the neighbourhood from grilling (broiling) sanma *is a daily occurrence. It is a relatively cheap fish, but very delicious and nutritious. Deep-fried* sanma *marinated in this* nanban *sauce can be eaten whole with the bones. Nanban, literally meaning 'southern barbarians', is a term used to describe foreign imports or things, such as food, painting or furniture, which have a foreign influence upon Japanese cooking or design. Nanban sauce is a piquant citrus sauce, which is used to marinate fish and vegetables.*

SERVES 4

4 *sanma* (saury, pictured) or 8 sardines,
   cleaned and scaled
1 teaspoon root ginger juice
1 tablespoon shoyu (Japanese soy sauce)
1 tablespoon sake
2 spring onions (scallions), chopped
1 dried red chilli, de-seeded and finely cut
   into rings
katakuriko (potato starch) or cornflour
   (cornstarch), for dipping
2 tablespoons vegetable oil
2.5cm/1in square piece of root ginger, peeled
   and shredded, to garnish

FOR THE MARINADE:
4 tablespoons shoyu (Japanese soy sauce)
3 tablespoons *yonezu* (Japanese rice vinegar)
1 tablespoon granulated sugar
½ tablespoon sesame oil
110ml/4fl oz/½ cup water

1 Cut the head and tail from each *sanma*, and cut the body crossways into 1cm/½in thick slices. Mix the ginger juice, shoyu and sake, and soak the fish in the mixture for 10–15 minutes. If using sardines, use whole, with no further preparation before frying.

2 Mix all the ingredients for the marinade in a large mixing bowl, add the chopped spring onions (scallions) and the chilli rings, and set aside.

3 Drain the *sanma* or sardines, and pat dry with kitchen paper (paper towels). Dredge the *sanma* slices or whole sardines with potato flour or cornflour (cornstarch), shaking off any excess, and pan-fry with the vegetable oil in a heated frying-pan (skillet) on a medium heat for 2–3 minutes until golden brown. Turn over, lower the heat and fry for another 4–5 minutes. Drain on a wire rack or kitchen paper (paper towels).

4 Put all the grilled fish in the marinade, and leave to marinate for 5 minutes. Arrange a quarter of the *sanma* slices or 2 sardines on each of 4 shallow individual bowls, pour a little marinade over and garnish with some shredded ginger on top. Serve with freshly boiled rice and miso soup.

Prawn (shrimp) and crabmeat balls on a skewer

Ebi to kani no shinjo

Shinjo is an old cooking term for fish or shellfish paste mixed with mountain potato as a binding agent, and made into a ball or terrine. Yuan-ji was created by the tea ceremony expert Yuan in the nineteenth century, hence the name, and is a mixture of mirin, shoyu and sake.

SERVES 4

150g/5½oz shelled prawns (shrimp)
150g/5½oz crabmeat
1 egg white
salt
katakuriko (potato starch) or cornflour
   (cornstarch), for dusting
2 tablespoons vegetable oil
2 limes, halved, to garnish

FOR THE *YUAN-JI*:
5 tablespoons mirin
3 tablespoons shoyu (Japanese soy sauce)
2 tablespoons sake

1 Finely grind the prawns (shrimp) in a *suribachi* (Japanese mortar) or ordinary mortar with a pestle, or in a food processor, until very smooth. Separate the crabmeat, and add to the ground prawns (shrimp) together with an egg white and a pinch of salt. Grind further until smooth.
2 Spoon 1 heaped tablespoon (approximately 20g/⅔ oz) of the prawn (shrimp) and crabmeat mixture into a wet hand, and make into a ball, about the size of a golf ball. Repeat this process to make a total of 16 *shinjo* balls.
3 Toss the *shinjo* balls in the *katakuriko* or cornflour (cornstarch), patting off the

excess flour. Heat the vegetable oil in a frying-pan (skillet), and pan-fry the *shinjo* balls, 8 at a time, on a medium heat for 5–6 minutes until light golden all over, continuously tilting the pan so as to cook evenly. Add half the *Yuan-ji* mixture, and continue to cook until the sauce reduces to almost nil. Repeat this process with the remaining *shinjo* balls and *Yuan-ji*. Remove from the heat, and thread 2 balls onto each bamboo skewer. Arrange all on a large serving plate, or 2 skewers on each of 4 individual plates, and serve, garnished with halved limes.

Mackerel marinated in ginger sauce and deep-fried

Saba no Tatsuta-agé

Tatsuta-agé is a deep-fried dish of ginger-marinated fish or meat, often mackerel or chicken. This is very easy home cooking, and even if the mackerel is not ultra-fresh, marinating in ginger will revive it. The deep-frying makes it very crispy.

1 large mackerel (675g/1½lb), filleted
110g/4oz/1 cup *katakuriko* (potato starch) or
   cornflour (cornstarch)
vegetable oil, for deep-frying
lemon wedges, to garnish

FOR THE MARINADE:
4 tablespoons sake
3 tablespoons shoyu (Japanese soy sauce)
2.5cm/1in piece root ginger, peeled
   and finely grated

1 Remove the large bones from the mackerel fillets, and slice crossways into 1cm/½in thick pieces, inserting the blade diagonally. Lay them flat on a plate.
2 Combine the ingredients for the marinade, and sprinkle evenly over the mackerel slices. Leave to marinate for 10–15 minutes.
3 Drain, keeping bits of ginger on the mackerel, and dredge the mackerel slices

in the *katakuriko* or cornflour (cornstarch) to dust thoroughly.
4 Heat the oil in a deep-fryer or wok to 160°C/320°F. Slide the mackerel slices into the hot oil, a few pieces at a time, and fry for 2–3 minutes until golden brown, turning over 2–3 times. Remove from the oil and drain on a wire rack.
5 Arrange a quarter of the fried mackerel on each of 4 individual plates, and serve hot, garnished with lemon wedges.

Steam-baked lobster with vegetable sauce

Ise-ebi no moto-yaki yasai sosu soé

HIROSHI MIURA, when he was only 32 years old, was appointed head chef of the Unkai restaurant when it opened at the ANA (All Nippon Airways) hotel in Sydney in 1992. He has a classical *cha-kaiseki* (tea ceremony meal) and *ryotei* (old-style and upmarket entertainment house) training, having worked at a number of reputable establishments before a spell as head chef for Japanese in-flight catering, where he learned a quite different concept of cooking. Here he introduces one of his more Westernized dishes with a Japanese-style vegetable sauce.

SERVES 4

FOR THE VEGETABLE SAUCE:

2 egg yolks, beaten

6 tablespoons vegetable oil

½ teaspoon sea salt

1½ tablespoons finely chopped carrot

2 tablespoons finely chopped courgettes (zucchini) (green part only)

4 tablespoons finely chopped button mushrooms

4–5 scallops, finely chopped

2 lobsters with shell, halved lengthways

pinch of salt

iceberg lettuce, shredded, to serve

2 *shiso* leaves, shredded, to serve (optional)

lemon wedges, to garnish

FOR THE *AMA-MISO* SAUCE:

2 tablespoons miso

2 tablespoons granulated sugar

dash of *toban jian* (Chinese chilli bean sauce)

½ tablespoon white sesame seeds, lightly roasted

The most popular way to eat lobster in Japan is iki-zukuri, *live sashimi, which is so fresh that even after it is chopped and prepared, diners can often see the tail and tentacles still moving. However, this sort of live presentation does not appeal to everyone, particularly outside Japan, so we do not do this here in Sydney. Members of the prawn (shrimp) family, including lobster, are easily overcooked and become hard. So when cooking lobster it is recommended to cook it very lightly and indirectly by steam-baking it. HM*

1 First make the vegetable sauce: beat the egg yolks well in a mixing bowl and add the oil, a little at a time, continuously beating until smooth. Add all the other ingredients and mix well.

2 Steam the lobster halves in a boiling steamer for just 1 minute, then remove from the heat. Separate the flesh from each shell, sprinkle with a pinch of salt and cut into bite-sized pieces. Make 4 'bowls' using the lobster shells, and arrange a quarter of the flesh in each cup. Pour over the vegetable sauce, place in a deep, about 5cm/2in, baking tin (pan), then place the tin (pan) in another larger and similarly deep baking tin (pan) filled with about 2.5cm/1in water. Put the whole tin (pan) into a pre-heated oven at 180°C/ 350°F/Gas 4, and steam-bake for 11 minutes, or until the surface is golden brown. Remove from the heat.

3 Combine all the ingredients for the *ama-miso* sauce. Arrange a lobster half on a bed of shredded lettuce on each of 4 individual plates, and a small mound of the *ama-miso* sauce on top. Serve hot, sprinkled with shreds of *shiso* leaf, and garnished with lemon wedges.

Skipjack belly tartar

Toro katsuo no yukké

NAOYUKI SATO is executive chef of Nadaman, Hong Kong. *Toro* is the word originally used for the fatty and tender part of tuna, but is now used for other fish as well, such as *toro* salmon. A certain amount of fat makes any meat, fish or animal tender, so the best meat is considered by the Japanese to be fatty, but fat that is evenly spread in tiny dots. This dish ideally uses *toro katsuo* (bonito or skipjack tuna).

SERVES 4

300g/10oz frozen skipjack, salmon or
  swordfish fillet, half-thawed
1 small pear, peeled and cored
½ medium white onion, finely chopped
2 spring onions (scallions) (white part only),
  finely chopped
8 lettuce leaves, to serve
4 quail eggs, uncooked, to serve (optional)
2 tablespoons pine nuts, to garnish

FOR THE *TARÉ* SAUCE:
2 tablespoons sake
4 tablespoons shoyu (Japanese soy sauce)
1 tablespoon granulated sugar
2 teaspoons sesame oil
½ tablespoon grated garlic
1 tablespoon ready-made *Kochujian* (Korean
  chilli miso sauce), or stir-fry a mixture
  of 1 teaspoon shoyu (Japanese soy sauce),
  ½ teaspoon each of mirin, miso, granulated
  sugar and chilli powder, and a pinch of salt
  and grated garlic on a moderate heat for
  5 minutes

This is a fish version of Korean yukké *(a beef tartar dish), and can be eaten like sashimi. The point is to serve the* toro katsuo *while still not completely thawed, although this may not be preferable for some tastes. Instead of* katsuo, *any fatty fish such as salmon, swordfish or yellowtail can be used. Or try* shimofuri *('frosting'– meaning meat, often pink, with fat spread in tiny dots) beef – it's in the original* yukké. NS

1 Cut the half-frozen skipjack, salmon or swordfish into about 5mm/¼in thick slices, and then cut into thin 4–5cm/about 2in long shreds.
2 Cut the peeled and cored pear into matchstick shreds.
3 Make the *taré* sauce: heat the sake in a small saucepan on a high heat, and tilting the pan catch the flame to burn off the alcohol content. Remove from the heat and add all the other *taré* sauce ingredients, and stir well until the sugar and *Kochujian* dissolve. Leave to cool.

4 Put the fish, pear, onion and spring onions (scallions) together in a mixing bowl and lightly toss with the *taré*.
5 Place 2 lettuce leaves on each of 4 individual plates and arrange a quarter of the mixture on the leaves. Make a well in the centre, put into it a cracked quail egg, and serve sprinkled with pine kernels (pine nuts) on top. Diners mix the raw egg into the fish mixture to eat but you can omit this ingredient if you prefer.

Fish marinated in yuzu-miso and grilled (broiled)

Sengyo no miso-yuzu an-zuké

EIICHI TAKAHASHI is from the fourteenth generation of chef/patrons of the legendary Hyotei, one of the oldest *kaiseki* restaurants in Kyoto. He was brought up playing in the kitchen. He uses *yuzu* here (a Japanese citrus fruit more bitter than lemon) in his marinade. With the subtle flavour and aroma of the *yuzu* added to miso the marinade becomes a pleasantly mild one. It is traditional to serve grilled (broiled) fish garnished with *hajikami-shoga* (vinegared young ginger shoots) in Japanese cooking. If it is not available ready-made (which most restaurants now use), you can make it yourself when young ginger shoots are on the market from spring to early autumn. Simply marinate the ginger in a mixture of *yonezu* (Japanese rice vinegar) and sugar for several days (see page 71). Along with shoyu, miso, the very basis of Japanese cooking, is frequently used to marinate fish, vegetables and meat.

SERVES 4

4 fresh cod steaks (approximately 120g/
 4oz each) or any fresh fish steaks
4–8 ready-made *hajikami-shoga* (vinegared
 young ginger shoots, see page 71), to
 garnish (optional)

FOR THE *YUZU-MISO* MARINADE:
225ml/8fl oz/1 cup sake
110ml/4fl oz/½ cup mirin
3 tablespoons dark shoyu (Japanese
 soy sauce)
3 tablespoons light shoyu (Japanese soy sauce)
140g/5oz/½ cup white miso
½ *yuzu* (pictured) or ¼ each of lemon
 and lime, cut into rings
½ teaspoon grated root ginger

Yuzu-miso is one of the popular marinades and we have served this dish at my restaurant from time immemorial. The point of this dish is to use unsalted fish only. With meat, add more grated ginger and marinate 2–3 days longer than fish, but do not salt the meat either. Yuzu has a distinctive flavour and aroma, and is the most popular citrus flavour we use in Japanese cooking. It is a pity that it's not available abroad. Instead, use half lemon and half lime. ET

1 Cut each fish steak in half, inserting the blade diagonally.
2 For the marinade, put the sake in a saucepan and bring to the boil. While tilting the pan catch the flame to burn off the alcohol content. This alcohol-free sake is called *nikiri-zake* in Japanese cooking terms.
3 Mix the *nikiri-zake* together with the shoyu, mirin and miso in a large plastic container, and use to thoroughly cover the fish steaks, together with the *yuzu*, or lemon and lime rings, and the grated ginger. Leave to marinate in the refrigerator for 1–2 days. The longer it is left to marinate the stronger the flavour will become.
4 Remove the fish steaks from the marinade and grill (broil) under a medium heat for 5–6 minutes on each side or until well cooked and a golden brown. Remove from the heat and arrange 2 slices on each of 4 individual plates. Serve hot, garnished with *hajimaki-shoga* if desired.

Grilled (broiled) sea bass in sweet miso

Suzuki no ama-miso yaki

LINDA RODRIGUEZ, executive chef at the Bond Street restaurant in New York, who has worked at Nobu, both in New York and London, shows here how to make her version of *miso-yaki*. Miso along with shoyu is one of the most important ingredients in Japanese cooking. It is very versatile and, like shoyu, is used as a condiment, sauce, dressing, in soup, as a pickling agent, marinade and so forth. Marinating fish in miso is a very old technique, and so much part of traditional cooking that every household has its own version. Ever since Nobu Matsuhisa of the Nobu restaurants' fame made miso-grilled black cod his signature dish, it has joined the list of the most popular dishes at Japanese restaurants the world over.

SERVES 4

1 large sea bass, scaled and filleted
10cm/4in piece of daikon, peeled and
    cut into small cubes
450ml/16fl oz/2 cups dashi (see page 56)
2 tablespoons light shoyu (Japanese
    soy sauce)
2 tablespoons mirin
1 bunch of pak choi (Chinese cabbage) or
    250g/9oz spinach
2 tablespoons white sesame seeds

FOR THE SWEET MISO MARINADE:
250g/9oz/scant 1 cup white miso
200g/7oz/1 cup granulated sugar
7 tablespoons sake
7 tablespoons mirin

For miso-yaki *only oily and meaty fish such as black cod, salmon, swordfish and sea bass are suitable. We use Chilean sea bass, and marinate it for 2–3 days. When grilled (broiled) it becomes a very appetizing dark caramel colour. It is one of the most popular dishes at our restaurant. LR*

1 Cut each sea bass fillet crossways into 4 slices (8 in total), inserting the blade diagonally.
2 Make the miso marinade by mixing all the ingredients until very smooth. Completely bury the sea bass slices directly into the mixture, and leave to marinate for 2–3 days.
3 Put the daikon cubes into a mixture of the dashi, shoyu and mirin in a saucepan, bring to the boil and simmer, covered, on a medium heat for about 10 minutes. Remove from the heat and leave to cool in the pan. Boil the pak choi or spinach in lightly salted boiling water for 1–2 minutes, drain and immediately put under running water. Drain again and squeeze out excess water with your hands.
4 Remove the sea bass slices from the miso marinade and discard the marinade. Preheat the oven to 200°C/400°F/Gas 6. Place the fish, skin-side up, on a metal rack and bake in the oven for 20 minutes.
5 Remove the daikon cubes from the dashi sauce. Arrange a quarter of the daikon and green vegetables in each of 4 small individual bowls and sprinkle with sesame seeds.
6 Arrange 2 slices of the sea bass decoratively on each of 4 individual plates, and serve with the bowls of vegetables.

5

Poultry
and Game

Chicken simmered with vegetables

Tori no Chikuzen-ni

SUSUMU HATAKEYAMA, head chef at Ikeda in London, shows here his professional version of *Chikuzen-ni*. This is a regional and national dish from Chikuzen, an old name for the area surrounding Hakata in Kyushu, the southern island, where most trading with foreigners took place before the days of air transport. It has a slight foreign, perhaps Chinese, influence in that it uses oil, and all the ingredients are cooked together.

SERVES 4

450g/1lb chicken thigh meat, fat and loose
    skin trimmed away
4 tablespoons sake
1 tablespoon shoyu (Japanese soy sauce)
4–5 dried shiitake, soaked in warm water for
    at least 1 hour
60g/2oz *gobo* (burdock root), peeled with
    scourers (optional)
120g/4oz *renkon* (lotus root) (pictured), peeled
1 medium carrot, peeled
150g/5½oz cooked bamboo shoots
a little vinegar (see method)
1 cake (approximately 270g/9½oz) *konnyaku*
    (yam cake)
20 mangetouts, trimmed
1 tablespoon vegetable oil
2 tablespoons light shoyu (Japanese
    soy sauce)
2 tablespoons mirin
1 teaspoon sea salt
3 tablespoons granulated sugar
225ml/8fl oz/1 cup dashi (see page 56)

This chicken dish, also known as iri-dori *(stir-fried chicken) or* gomoku-ni *('simmered five items'), unusually for a Japanese dish, simmers several ingredients together in a pan. So the point is how each ingredient should be prepared, and in what order they go into the pan. The ingredients used here are fairly traditional ones, but you can use almost anything as long as you get absolutely right both the combination of flavour, texture and colours, and the order in which each is added to the pan. SH*

1 Cut the chicken into bite-sized pieces, and rub with the 1 tablespoon each of sake and shoyu. Set aside.

2 Drain the shiitake, retaining the liquid for use instead of dashi, or for other cooking, and trim off the stems. If large, cut each cap into 4 or 6 triangles. Cut the *gobo*, if using, into bite-sized pieces, plunge into cold water changing it 2–3 times until the water is clear and drain.

3 Cut the *renkon*, carrot and bamboo shoots also into bite-sized pieces, and plunge the *renkon* into lightly vinegared water to prevent it discolouring. Using a tablespoon as a blade cut the *konnyaku* into bite-sized pieces.

4 Cook the mangetouts in lightly salted boiling water on a high heat for 1–2 minutes, remove from the pan with a perforated spoon and immediately place under running water. Drain. Add the

gobo, carrot and bamboo shoots to the same boiling water, cook, still on a high heat, for 2–3 minutes until half cooked, and again remove from the pan with a perforated spoon. Add the *konnyaku* to the remaining boiling water, cook for 2–3 minutes and drain.

5 Heat a large frying-pan (skillet) or saucepan with the oil, add the chicken pieces and stir-fry on a medium heat for 2–3 minutes until they turn white. Add the remaining sake, the light shoyu, mirin and sea salt, and cook a further 5–6 minutes until cooked. Remove the chicken from the pan, and set aside.

6 Add the sugar to the pan and continue to cook on a moderate heat until the sugar dissolves. Add the *gobo*, carrot, bamboo shoots, *konnyaku* and shiitake. Add the dashi, or the same volume of the shiitake soaking liquid, to the pan to cover 80 per cent of the ingredients, put a lid on, and bring to the boil on a high heat. Lower the heat to medium, and simmer for about 10 minutes, stirring occasionally, before adding the chicken and the *renkon* to the pan. Continue to cook for a 20 minutes or until all the juice disappears. Arrange a quarter of the cooked chicken and vegetables in each of 4 individual bowls, and serve garnished with mangetouts if you like.

Chicken cooked in soup

Tori no mizutaki

NOBUO IWASEYA is responsible for the menus and recipes of all Suntory restaurants abroad. He gained a Michelin star with the London restaurant in St James's in 1987. He places the utmost importance on the use of seasonal, fresh local produce to provide constantly high standard dishes, together with the choice of a good combination of ingredients. Here he introduces another traditional dish, using easily obtained winter vegetables.

SERVES 4

FOR THE *PONZU* (CITRUS SHOYU) SAUCE:

6 tablespoons lime juice (2 limes)

6 tablespoons light shoyu (Japanese soy sauce)

3 tablespoons *yonezu* (Japanese rice vinegar)

2 teaspoons sake

2 teaspoons mirin

2 teaspoons orange juice

10g/⅓oz dried *konbu*, (kelp), lightly roasted

1 teaspoon granulated sugar

½ chicken (approximately 600g/1lb 5oz) with bones and skin

1 whole chicken carcass

7cm/3in piece of daikon, peeled

7cm/3in piece of carrot, peeled

8 shallots, peeled and trimmed

2 bay leaves

10–20g/⅓–⅔oz dried *konbu* (kelp)

200ml/7 fl oz/⅞ cup sake

4 litres/7 pints/4 quarts water

1 tablespoon sea salt

about 1 egg cup-full *momiji-oroshi* (see page 124)

2 spring onions (scallions), finely chopped, to garnish

In Japanese cooking, poultry, chicken in particular, and mallard and duck, has a long history as a very important ingredient. There are many ways of cooking chicken such as tori-nabe *(hotpot),* yakitori *(skewered and grilled or broiled),* iri-dori *(cooked with vegetables),* Tatsuta-age *(deep-fried) and even* tori-wasa *(parboiled sashimi with wasabi). The* mizutaki *introduced here originated in the home cooking of Hakata and Nagasaki in Kyushu (southern island), and uses the cloudy soup stock (broth), so characteristic of chicken soup in Kyushu. There are many upmarket restaurants in Japan specializing only in this hotpot dish. NI*

1 Mix all the *ponzu* ingredients in a mixing bowl and set aside.

2 Chop the chicken, together with the bones and skin, into bite-sized pieces. Plunge into boiling water for 1 minute, and then immediately put into cold water to cool. Trim off all feathers and blood stuck to the bone, and wash in cold water. Leave to drain.

3 Roughly chop the chicken carcass and plunge into boiling water, then wash with cold water. Drain.

4 Cut both the daikon and carrot crossways into 1cm/½in thick rounds.

5 Put both the chicken meat and bones together with the vegetables, bay leaves, *konbu* and sake in a large saucepan. Add the water, then bring to the boil on a high heat. Just before reaching boiling point, take out the *konbu* and discard. Lower the heat when foam starts rising up to the surface, and carefully skim off the foam. Simmer for about 30 minutes and remove from the heat, then leave to cool.

6 When cool, take out all the bones and discard. Then take the meat and vegetables one by one from the soup, and set aside. Sieve the soup through a fine cotton or gauze cloth or kitchen paper (paper towels) laid in a wire mesh basket. Spoon a ladle or two of the soup over the chicken and vegetables so that they won't become too dry while draining.

7 Take the *konbu* out of the *ponzu* sauce and discard.

8 When ready to serve, heat up the soup in an earthenware pot, season with the sea salt, and add all the chicken and vegetables, removing from the heat when hot. Do not boil. Serve as it is in an earthenware pot in the centre of the table, or arrange a quarter of the chicken and vegetables in each of 4 individual bowls and pour over the soup. Serve hot with the *ponzu* sauce in individual small bowls, garnished with the finely chopped spring onions (scallions) and the *momiji-oroshi*.

Cold roast duck

Kamo rosu

YOSHIHIRO MURATA is now at the *ryotei* Kikunoi, Kyoto. Although born to a Japanese restaurant owner/chef family, he was not sure what to do after graduating from university, and so in the early seventies went to Europe in search of inspiration. It was the French chefs' confidence in their own cuisine that convinced him to return to Japan to pursue a career in his own cooking heritage. In his eyes, Japanese cuisine is equal, if not superior, to the French, and he felt it was his duty to let the world know of the cuisine. He partly fulfilled this ambition when he presented a *kaiseki* banquet in association with Dom Pérignon in front of the world media in Epernay, France, in 1999.

SERVES 4

1 tablespoon vegetable oil
4 duck breasts
4 tablespoons sake
4 tablespoons dark shoyu (Japanese
    soy sauce)
1 tablespoon granulated sugar
½ cucumber, shredded
1 stick of celery, shredded
1 small carrot, peeled and shredded
2 tablespoons dried *wakame* (young
    seaweed) (pictured on top of dried *konbu*),
    soaked in water
8 *shiso* leaves
few drops of mustard, to garnish

This dish is a Japanese version of the roast duck I learned in France. We normally cook duck by first grilling (broiling) or pan-frying the skin side to draw off the fat, then putting it in a deep container with lightly seasoned dashi and steaming in the liquid. However, with this method it is not always easy to cook the meat exactly how you want it. Here I use a vacuum pack to cook the meat still with the liquid, using the scientific fact that protein starts hardening at 62°C/143°F and releasing water at 67°C/152°F. In between 62°C/143°F and 67°C/152°F the meat should cook without becoming too dry. The vacuum also prevents most of the meat juice from draining away. YM

1 Start cooking this cold roast duck 2 days before the date you intend to eat. Heat a frying-pan (skillet) with 1 tablespoon of vegetable oil, and pan-fry the duck breasts, two at a time, skin-side down, first on a high heat for 3–4 minutes until golden brown and most of the fat is drawn. Turn over and continue to fry the meat side for 2–3 minutes. Put the breasts in a freezer bag together with the heated mixture of the sake, shoyu and sugar, and tightly tie with a string, squeezing out the air to make a vacuum pack.
2 In a large saucepan, heat plenty of water to about 65°C/149°F, and cook the vacuum-packed duck in the water for

20–45 minutes, depending on how you like the meat cooked. During the cooking, the temperature of the water should never exceed 68°C/154°F, otherwise the meat will be overcooked. At the end of the cooking time, raise the temperature to 85°C/185°F and cook for a further 2 minutes. Immediately place the pack in ice-cold water to cool, and keep in the refrigerator for 2 days.
3 Put the shredded vegetables individually in cold water to freshen up, then drain and pat dry with kitchen paper (paper towels). Cut the softened *wakame*, if large, into bite-sized pieces.
4 Remove the duck breasts from the pack onto a chopping-board, and thinly slice crossways inserting the blade slightly diagonally against the chopping-board. Arrange crushed ice or tiny ice cubes in each of 4 individual dishes, and place 2 *shiso* leaves on each. Place a sliced breast on top of the *shiso* leaves and arrange a quarter of each vegetable and *wakame* by the meat. Serve cold, garnished with a drop of mustard.

Chicken teriyaki

Tori no teriyaki

For teriyaki*, chicken is most popularly used. The sweet shoyu flavour and its glow, when cooked, adds an interesting character to a rather common ingredient. Here's a standard method of making a* teriyaki.

SERVES 4

4 chicken legs (each weighing approximately 200g/7oz), boned
2 tablespoons vegetable oil
spinkling of *sansho* pepper, to serve (optional)

FOR THE *TERIYAKI* SAUCE:
6 tablespoons shoyu (Japanese soy sauce)
6 tablespoons sake
6 tablespoons mirin
1 tablespoon granulated sugar

1 Place the chicken legs, skin-side up, on a chopping-board, and pierce the skin with a fork to avoid shrinkage during cooking and also for the chicken to absorb the sauce well.

2 Mix all the *teriyaki* sauce ingredients in a small saucepan, bring to the boil and simmer over a medium heat until the sugar dissolves. Remove from the heat and set aside.

3 Heat the vegetable oil in a frying-pan (skillet), lay the chicken, skin-side down, and fry over a medium heat for about 2–3 minutes until the skin is well browned. Move the chicken constantly to prevent the meat sticking. Turn the chicken, and fry, covered, for about 10 minutes. Remove the chicken from the pan and keep warm.

4 In the same pan with the leftover juice pour in the *teriyaki* sauce mixture, and bring to the boil. After 1–2 minutes the sauce will thicken slightly. Return the chicken to the pan, and continue to cook over a high heat for another 2–3 minutes, while turning the chicken several times to coat well with the *teriyaki* sauce. Remove from the heat when the sauce has been almost completely absorbed.

5 Place the cooked chicken legs on a chopping-board, skin-side up, and cut crossways into 1.5cm/¾in slices, inserting the blade diagonally. Arrange slices from 1 leg in a fan-like shape on each of 4 individual plates, sprinkle on a little *sansho* pepper, if desired, and serve hot.

Minced chicken balls with taré sauce

Tsukune no taré-yaki

Taré, literally meaning 'dripping', is a general term for thickened sweet shoyu sauces, and yakitori and teriyaki sauces are its best-known representatives. It normally consists of shoyu, sake, sugar and/or mirin, and its sugar content thickens the sauce.

SERVES 4

500g/1lb minced chicken
2½ tablespoons sake
20 *kinome* or 5 mint leaves, finely chopped
salt
taré sauce (see below, step 2)
lemon wedges, to garnish
1–2 tablespoons vinegared ginger slices (see page 70), to garnish

1 Put the minced chicken in a mixing bowl, add ½ teaspoon of salt and the sake, and knead to mix well. Mix in the finely chopped *kinome* or mint leaves, and shape into 24 balls, each the size of a golf ball.
2 Cook the chicken balls in lightly salted boiling water, several at a time, for about 1 minute until the surface is hard. Sprinkle 12 balls with salt, and grill (broil) under a medium heat, turning constantly, for

about 5–6 minutes until cooked and golden brown. Grill (broil) the remaining 12 balls also on a medium heat for 4–5 minutes until very lightly golden brown, dip in the *taré* mixture, and return to the grill to complete the cooking.
3 Thread 2 balls on pre-soaked bamboo skewers, and arrange 3 skewers (6 balls) on each plate. Serve hot or cold, garnished with a lemon wedge and vinegared ginger.

Barbecued skewered chicken

Yakitori

Whether or not you can call it cooking is debatable, but skewered meat grilled over charcoal is a food that almost every corner of the world has in some form. In South-east Asian countries it's satay, and yakitori is the Japanese answer to it.

MAKES 24 CHICKEN AND 12 VEGETABLE SKEWERS

12 chicken thighs with skin, boned
12–18 spring onions (scallions), white parts
24 pre-soaked bamboo skewers (15cm/6in)
24 small okra, trimmed
sea salt
lemon wedges, to garnish
sansho peppers and/or *shichimi* (seven-spice chilli) powder (optional)

FOR THE *TARÉ* SAUCE:
4 tablespoons sake
6 tablespoons shoyu (Japanese soy sauce)
1½ tablespoons mirin
1 tablespoon granulated sugar

1 Trim the fat from the chicken thighs, and cut into 4cm/1½in square pieces. Cut the spring onion (scallion) whites into about 4cm/1½in or similar length to okra.
2 Combine all the *taré* ingredients in a small saucepan, bring to the boil on a medium heat. Simmer for 5–6 minutes, stirring to dissolve the sugar. Remove from the heat and set aside.
3 Keep the bamboo skewers soaked in water until the last minute. Thread 3 chicken pieces tightly together onto each skewer to make 24 skewers. Grill (broil) or barbecue on a high heat for 3–4 minutes, then turn over and grill (broil) for 2–3 minutes until both sides are lightly

browned. Remove from the heat, one at a time, baste with the *taré* and return to the heat to dry the sauce. Repeat this process a few more times until all the chicken pieces are golden brown. Alternatively, half the skewers can be white-grilled and sprinkled with sea salt instead of basting.
4 Thread 3 pieces of spring onion and 2 of okra, alternating, on to each skewer to make 12 skewers. Grill in the same way as the chicken, but for a shorter time, about 1–2 minutes on each side.
5 Arrange all the skewers decoratively on a large serving plate and serve hot, garnished with lemon wedges together with *sansho* peppers.

Simmered chicken with kabocha squash

Tori to kabocha no itame-ni

Kabocha squash has a wonderfully nutty, sweet flavour and dense, crunchy texture if it's cooked properly. If it's cooked a minute too long, it goes soggy and mushy, so the timing is particularly important as shown in this recipe cooked with chicken.

SERVES 4

8 chicken thighs with or without skin, boned
½–⅓ kabocha squash (approximately 450g/
   1lb), de-seeded
1 tablespoon vegetable oil
2 tablespoons granulated sugar
3 tablespoons light shoyu (Japanese
   soy sauce)
3 tablespoons mirin
a little shredded root ginger (optional),
   to garnish

1 Cut the chicken thighs into bite-sized pieces. Cut off the dirty parts from the kabocha skin (most of the skin should be kept on), and cut into bite-sized pieces.
2 Heat a saucepan with the vegetable oil, and stir-fry the chicken pieces on a high heat for 4–5 minutes until golden brown. Add 450ml/16fl oz/2 cups of water, bring to the boil, and then simmer, covered, on a moderate heat for about 10 minutes.
3 Add the kabocha together with the sugar, light shoyu and mirin, and lightly stir to mix the seasoning. Increase the heat to medium and continue to simmer, still covered, for a further 10–12 minutes or until the juice is reduced to a quarter. Remove from the heat, and leave covered for 2–3 minutes for the kabocha to absorb more juice.
4 Arrange a quarter of the simmered chicken and kabocha on to each of 4 individual dishes, and serve hot, garnished with shredded ginger if desired.

Duck pan-fried in Yuan sauce

Kamo no Yuan-yaki

Yuan sauce, the mixture of shoyu, sake and mirin, is so-called as it was first created by the tea ceremony expert, Yuan, in the nineteenth century. The duck is fried, then simply mixed with this sauce.

SERVES 4

4 duck breasts, boned but with skin
1–2 tablespoons vegetable oil
handful of watercress, to garnish
1–2 tablespoons vinegared ginger slices (see
   page 70), to garnish

FOR THE YUAN SAUCE:
8 tablespoons mirin
6 tablespoons shoyu (Japanese soy sauce)
4 tablespoons sake

1 Place the duck breasts on a chopping-board, skin-side up, and prick all over the skin with a metal skewer to prevent shrinkage when cooked and also for the meat to absorb the sauce well.
2 Heat a frying-pan (skillet) with the vegetable oil on a medium heat, and lay the duck breasts skin-side down. Fry, occasionally pressing the meat with a fork to draw out the fat, for 4–5 minutes until the skin is golden brown. Turn and continue to fry for another 1–2 minutes.
3 Mix all the Yuan sauce ingredients and pour over the duck. Bring to the boil, and cook on a medium heat for a further 2–3 minutes until all the duck breasts are well coated with the sauce. Remove from the heat, and slice each duck crossways into thin pieces, about 5mm/¼in thick. Arrange slices from 1 breast on a bed of watercress on each of 4 individual plates, and serve hot, garnished with a small mound of vinegared ginger slices.

Duck hotpot

Kamo-nabé

HIDEAKI MORITA, chef/patron of the Matsumi restaurant in Hamburg, uses a whole duck for this Japanese winter favourite. Duck is popular in Japanese cooking. *Ma-gamo*, wild duck or mallard, is used as well as *ai-gamo*, a cross-breed of duck and mallard.

SERVES 4–6

1 duck (approximately 1.5–2kg/3–4lb)
½ hakusai (Chinese leaf)
4–6 shiitake
1 small bamboo shoot
1 thin leek
½ bunch *shungiku* (chrysanthemum leaves)
   or 150g/5oz spinach
1 packet *shirataki* (*konnyaku* noodles)
   (approximately 150g/5½oz) (optional)
1 bunch of *enoki-dake* mushrooms (optional)
1 cake grilled (broiled) tofu (250g/9oz), cut
   into 8 cubes

FOR THE DUCK STOCK (BROTH):
1 duck carcass
3 cloves garlic, peeled and roughly crushed
1 small carrot, peeled and chopped
2 thin leeks, roughly chopped
5cm/2in dried *konbu* (kelp)
1 stick of celery, roughly chopped

The duck soup, in which the diners cook all the ingredients at the table, is seasoned only with shoyu and salt; it shouldn't be too strong to start with. Too strong a taste not only spoils the delicate flavour of the duck but also the hotpot soon thickens since it is on the heat all the time. After all the ingredients are eaten, add noodles or cooked rice, or grilled mochi (rice cake), to cook with the remaining soup. HM

1 Ask your butcher to bone a duck, leaving you with the meat of 2 breasts and 2 legs both with skin, a body carcass and 2 leg bones. Also ask him to mince all the loose meat including the thin fillet loosely attached to the breast meat and the wing meat; you can make duck balls with it later. Roll each breast lengthways, skin-side out, into a thin cylinder, and wrap with a sheet of cling film (plastic wrap). Put in the freezer for a minimum of 2–3 hours or overnight.

2 To make the duck stock (broth), place all the ingredients in a large saucepan and cover with about 2 litres/3½ pints/9 cups water. Just before it reaches boiling, lower the heat and simmer for 2–3 hours, regularly spooning out the scum that rises to the surface. Never let the stock boil. Drain into another saucepan through a fine cloth or kitchen paper (paper towels) laid in a colander. Discard the bones.

3 A couple of hours before serving, take the rolled duck breasts from the freezer to half-thaw and slice crossways into thin rounds. Arrange in circles on a serving plate.

4 Cut the hakusai, shiitake, bamboo shoot and leek into approximately 5cm/2in long shreds, and roughly chop the *shungiku* or spinach and *shirataki*, if using. If using *enoki-dake*, trim the stem and roughly separate the stalks. Arrange all the vegetables, mushrooms, *shirataki* and tofu on a large serving plate.

5 Heat the duck stock (broth) in a *donabe* (earthenware pot) on a high heat, and lightly season with salt and shoyu to taste. Do not season strongly at first as it is heating and thickening all the time. When it starts boiling add some of the duck, vegetables and tofu, and bring back to the boil. Transfer the *donabe* to a portable fire on the table and serve together with the remaining ingredients. Diners help themselves adding the remaining ingredients to the pot as they like.

Fried chicken

Tori no kara-agé

As the name kara-agé, *meaning 'Chinese fry', suggests, this dish comes from China, but is now deeply established as one of the most popular dishes in home cooking. This hot fried chicken goes very well with ice-cold beer in summer, and with warm sake or* shochu *in winter. It is in fact a very versatile dish equally good as a main dish on a dinner table, finger food for a party or as a snack at any time. Once you've cooked this, it will no doubt be added to your regular menu.*

SERVES 4

750g/1lb 10oz chicken thigh meat with skin, fat and loose skin trimmed
2 teaspoons root ginger juice
3 tablespoons shoyu (Japanese soy sauce)
3 tablespoons sake
vegetable oil, for shallow-frying
8–12 pieces okra or asparagus, hard stems trimmed
katakuriko (potato starch) or cornflour (cornstarch), for dipping
sea salt
lemon wedges, to garnish

1 Cut the chicken thighs into about 5cm/2in square pieces. Mix the ginger juice, shoyu and sake in a large mixing bowl and add the chicken pieces. Rub the seasoning into the chicken with your hands, and leave to marinate for at least 10 minutes. Remove the chicken from the marinade on to kitchen paper (paper towels), and pat dry any excess juice with more paper.

2 If using asparagus, cut each into 3–4 pieces.

3 Heat the vegetable oil in a large frying-pan (skillet) to 160°C/320°F, and fry the okra or asparagus for 1–2 minutes or until bright green. Drain on a wire rack, and sprinkle with a pinch of sea salt.

4 Toss the flavoured chicken in *katakuriko* or cornflour (cornstarch), shaking off any excess, and fry in the hot oil, at about 180°C/350°F, for 5–6 minutes, turning a few times, until bright golden. Lower the heat, and continue to fry for a further 3–4 minutes until well cooked. Towards the end of the cooking, turn up the heat for 1 minute to make the exterior really crisp. Remove from the oil and drain on a wire rack. If the frying-pan (skillet) is not large enough to fry all at one go, divide into 2–3 batches.

5 Arrange a quarter of the fried chicken and okra or asparagus on each of 4 individual plates, and serve hot, garnished with lemon wedges.

Simmered chicken with mustard sauce

Tori no rosu-ni mustard sauce

TAKAYUKI HISHINUMA is one of a number of younger chefs with an innovative mind and skills to match, acquired through working at various top Japanese restaurants in Tokyo. He is a serious, respected chef, and his restaurant, Hishinuma, in Tokyo, is very popular with Japanese and non-Japanese alike. He is also one of the few chefs who understand wines, and his daily changing set menus come with his recommendation of wines.

SERVES 4

2–4 chicken breasts with skin
1–2 tablespoons vegetable oil
½ tablespoon powdered mustard
½ tablespoon arrowroot, diluted with
    1 tablespoon water
salad leaves such as chicory, rocket (arugula),
    watercress, to serve

FOR THE COOKING SAUCE:
140ml/5fl oz/⅔ cup dashi (see page 56)
140ml/5fl oz/⅔ cup sake
140ml/5fl oz/⅔ cup mirin
140ml/5fl oz/⅔ cup light shoyu (Japanese
    soy sauce)

Chicken breast tends to be dry when cooked as it hasn't got much fat, so I thought of a way to make it deliciously moist. The result is to cook it minimally and continue to cook without heating by marinating in a hot sauce. The juice will spread within the meat making it moist. It can be kept for a few days, so I suggest you make more than you need for a meal at a time. You can use beef instead of chicken if you like. Use a roast joint of about 600g/1lb 5oz and cook for only 2–3 minutes, then cool down in the cooking liquid. It will make a delicious beef tataki *(seared sashimi). TH*

1 Trim off the fat from the chicken breasts and pan-fry, skin-side down first, with a little vegetable oil on a high heat for 4–5 minutes on each side until golden brown.
2 Mix all the ingredients for the cooking sauce in a saucepan, bring to the boil and cook on a high heat for 2–3 minutes until the alcohol content has evaporated. Add the cooked chicken breasts, cook for 1 minute and immediately remove from the heat. Transfer the chicken to a mixing bowl and pour over the hot sauce. Cover with a lid and leave to absorb the flavour for at least 15 minutes. You can keep it marinated for a few days.
3 Thinly slice the chicken breasts into bite-sized pieces and arrange on 4 individual plates. Put about 110ml/ 4fl oz/½ cup of the sauce in a saucepan and bring to the boil on a moderate heat. Lower the heat, then mix in the mustard and diluted arrowroot to lightly thicken the sauce and pour over the chicken slices. Arrange some of the salad leaves of your choice with the chicken and serve.

Steamed duck with miso sauce

Kamo miso dengaku

HIROSHI MIURA, head chef at the Unkai restaurant at the ANA hotel, Sydney, shows the method in this traditional, yet still very modern duck dish. Japanese cooking is water-based as opposed to oil-based as in other countries, and nowhere is this more evident than in the searing and then soup-steaming method frequently used to cook duck and chicken in Japan. Searing encloses the juice in the meat without making it dry and oily, while steaming in soup adds a subtle flavour and moisture.

SERVES 4

3 large or 4 medium duck breasts
450ml/16fl oz/2 cups dashi (see page 56)
2 tablespoons mirin
2 tablespoons light shoyu (Japanese
    soy sauce)
½ cucumber, de-seeded and shredded
2 spring onions (scallions), finely shredded
green salad leaves, to garnish

FOR THE *DENGAKU* MISO:

1 tablespoon sake
2 tablespoons mirin
4½ tablespoons granulated sugar
140g/5oz/½ cup white miso
1 egg yolk
½ teaspoon sesame oil

Duck is a marvellous food for Japanese cooking; it's meaty, yet not too strong in flavour and smell. It is fatty, so quick searing on a high heat reduces the oiliness and seals the juice at the same time. Steaming in lightly flavoured soup indirectly cooks the meat doubly resulting in very tender, delicately flavoured meat. Dengaku miso is a sweet miso paste. HM

1 Cut off the excess fat from the duck breasts before making a few slits with a sharp knife on the skin lengthways. Heat a non-stick frying-pan (skillet) and pan-fry the breasts, 1 or 2 at a time, skin-side down, on a high heat for 3–4 minutes until golden brown and some fat has melted. Immediately plunge into plenty of water with ice cubes to quickly cool, drain and pat dry with kitchen paper (paper towels). Put into a stainless steel container, skin-side down.

2 Warm the dashi in a saucepan on a moderate heat, and season with the mirin and light shoyu. Do not boil. Remove from the heat, and pour over the duck. Place the vat in a boiling steamer and steam on a high heat for 5 minutes, turn over the meat, then steam for a further 2 minutes. Adjust the steaming time according to the size of the meat. Remove from the heat.

3 Place a duck breast on a chopping-board, poke a skewer from the side of the breast deep into the meat, then gently press to draw off blood. Pat dry with kitchen paper (paper towels), and slice crossways into 1cm/½in thick pieces. Repeat for the others.

4 Mix all the ingredients, except the egg yolk and sesame oil, for the *dengaku* miso sauce in a small saucepan, and place on a moderate heat. Gently stir until the sugar dissolves and it becomes a smooth mayonnaise-like consistency. This will take 15–20 minutes. Do not overheat. If it becomes too hard, add a little water. Gradually add the egg yolk, a little at a time, and continue to stir until all is mixed in well. Add the sesame oil and remove from the heat.

5 Arrange a quarter of the meat slices on each of the 4 plates on a bed of the *dengaku* miso and shredded cucumber, with the shredded spring onions (scallions) on top. Garnish with green salad leaves such as rocket (arugula), lambs lettuce or mizuna, and serve. To eat, wrap a little cucumber and spring onion (scallion) with a slice of the meat.

6

Meat

Family treasure simmered potato with beef

Kaho no niku-jaga

KENTARO is the son of well-known cookery writer and broadcaster Mrs Katsuyo Kobayashi, who specializes in home cooking, so devotion to cooking runs in the family. He started helping his mother in the kitchen at the tender age of two, weighing rice to cook for the family breakfast. *Niku-jaga* (*niku* meaning 'meat' and *jaga* the shortened word for *jaga-imo*, 'potato') is one of the most popular family dishes anywhere in Japan, and here Kentaro introduces his own family recipe.

SERVES 4

200g/7oz beef (roast joint)
5 medium potatoes, peeled
1 medium onion, peeled
1 tablespoon sesame oil
2 tablespoons shoyu (Japanese soy sauce)
1 tablespoon granulated sugar
1 tablespoon mirin

Niku-jaga is normally simmered on a low heat for a long time, but our family niku-jaga, created by my mother Katsuyo, is cooked on a high heat throughout, making it richer in flavour. This is the pride and joy of our family, so I call it our 'family treasure'. It is a simple, unsophisticated peasant dish, but served in a big bowl and placed in the centre of the table this hot gutsy dish makes an otherwise boring family supper a warm, family-bonding occasion. KK

1 Thinly slice the beef and cut into bite-sized pieces. In order for you to thinly slice the beef, completely freeze the joint beforehand and thaw for 30 minutes to 1 hour until it is soft enough to slice, but still firm. Cut the potatoes into chunky pieces and soak in enough water to cover for 5 minutes. Cut the onion in half and thinly slice into half-moons.
2 Heat a frying-pan (skillet) and fry the onion slices with the sesame oil on a high heat for about 3 minutes until soft. Push them to one side of the pan, then add the beef in the empty space, and fry until the meat changes colour to white.

3 Add the shoyu, sugar and mirin and lightly stir-fry the meat and onion for 1 minute.
4 Place the potato chunks on top of the mixture of meat and onion and add water to the level of ⅔ of the potato. Cook, covered, still on a high heat for about 10 minutes until the potato is just cooked. Stir occasionally to cook through.
5 Take the lid off and lightly stir until most of the liquid evaporates. If the liquid disappears before the potato is cooked, add some water during cooking. Serve very hot immediately in a large bowl.

Rolled baby pork tempura with spring onions (scallions)

Kobuta no negi-maki tempura

SUSUMU HATAKEYAMA, the man behind the sushi counter at Ikeda, reputedly one of the best and most well-established Japanese restaurants in London, trained not just in sushi but as an all-round chef in Osaka before coming to London in the late seventies. Tempura is normally used with fish and vegetables, but this pork tempura is a surprising success for Mr Hatakeyama's endeavours to create dishes also for non-Japanese customers.

SERVES 4

450g/1lb loin of pork, trimmed of fat,
    frozen overnight
1 clove garlic, finely grated
6–8 spring onions (scallions),
    diagonally shredded
vegetable oil, for deep-frying plus unrefined
    sesame oil (optional)
5cm/2in piece of daikon, peeled and grated
2.5cm/1in piece of root ginger, peeled
    and grated
sea salt
lemon wedges, to garnish

FOR THE DIPPING SAUCE:

450ml/16fl oz/2 cups dashi (see page 56)
7 tablespoons light shoyu (Japanese
    soy sauce)
7 tablespoons mirin

FOR THE BATTER:

225ml/8fl oz/1 cup ice-cold water
1 egg, beaten and sieved
140g/5oz/1 cup light plain (all-purpose)
    flour, sifted twice then left in the
    refrigerator overnight

Unlike in other countries, including China and other neighbours of Japan, meat is not a strong feature of Japanese cooking. In the current unprecedented popularity of Japanese food and cuisine in the West, we chefs abroad are constantly thinking of new dishes to appeal to non-Japanese customers as well. This often includes the use of meat, and although meat tempura may seem a weird idea, believe me it works brilliantly. It's very good as an appetizer as well as a main course, going well with hot boiled rice. SH

1 Remove the pork from the freezer 2–3 hours before cooking to half-thaw, and slice very thinly, about 5mm/ ¼ in thick, into approximately 10 x 7cm/4 x 3in oval pieces. Place a slice on a chopping-board, put ½ stalk of spring onion (scallion) shreds in a row across the shortest side of the pork, and tightly roll in. Secure the pork roll with a cocktail stick (toothpick). Repeat this process to make 11 more rolls.

2 Make the dipping sauce: combine the dashi, shoyu and mirin in a saucepan, place on a medium heat, and bring to the boil. Remove from the heat and set aside.

3 Heat plenty of vegetable oil, or vegetable oil mixed in equal measure with sesame oil, in a deep frying-pan (skillet) or a wok.

4 Meanwhile, make the batter: stir in the icy water to the beaten and sieved egg, then sift in the chilled flour, and lightly fold several times using a few *hashi* sticks or a fork. Do not stir; the batter should still be lumpy.

5 Just before frying, raise the temperature to170°C/340°F or until a drop of the batter rises to the surface without first touching the bottom of the pan. Dip the pork rolls, one at a time, into the batter, and gently slide into the hot oil. Fry for about 1 minute, turning a few times, until golden brown. About 3–4 pieces can be fried at a time, but do not overcook. Drain on a wire rack.

6 Cut each roll in half diagonally crossways, and arrange 6 halves decoratively on each of 4 individual plates, garnished with a mound of grated daikon and root ginger together with a lemon wedge. A sheet of Japanese paper is normally placed under the tempura to absorb excess oil. Serve hot with the dipping sauce. The pork rolls can be dipped in the sauce and eaten mixed with grated daikon and ginger, or sprinkled with lemon juice or just salt.

Pork simmered in black miso

Buta kakuni

YOSHIHIRO MURATA, celebrity chef and the owner of the *ryotei* Kikunoi in Kyoto, trained for three years at a restaurant in Nagoya before joining his father at Kikunoi. This dish, though originating in Nagasaki, Kyushu, the southern island, is also well established in Kyoto, and was a favourite of his father's. He saw its popularity at the restaurant in Nagoya, and developed it, taking advantage of the slightly different cuisine in Nagoya and Kyoto.

SERVES 4

1 tablespoon vegetable oil
450g/1lb loin of pork with skin
2 tablespoons rice bran (optional)
4 tablespoons water
1 teaspoon black miso
1 teaspoon muscovado sugar
1 tablespoon sake
1 medium potato (approximately 150g/5½oz),
   peeled, boiled and mashed
200ml/7fl oz/⅞ cup dashi (see page 56)
1 teaspoon light shoyu (Japanese soy sauce)
pinch of salt
1 tablespoon arrowroot, diluted with
   2 tablespoons water
7.5cm/3in piece of *togan* (wax gourd)
   or 1 courgette (zucchini)
8 fine beans
few drops of mustard, to serve

FOR THE *HAPPO-JI* SOUP:
5 tablespoons dashi
1 teaspoon sake
1 teaspoon mirin
1 tablespoon *kezuribushi* (bonito flakes)

My father's way of drawing fat from the pork was to boil it wrapped in bamboo bark in the rice-washed milky water. I use rice bran mixed with water instead, which I believe is more effective. In Nagoya, they used their own Haccho *miso, black miso, to cook the meat but I thought it might be too strong, so added black sugar as they do in Kyushu. The red meat is even more delicious if eaten with the fatty skin, so in order to make it easier for the diners to eat the fat, I disguise it by covering with mashed potato sauce. It works brilliantly. YM*

1 Heat a frying-pan (skillet) with the vegetable oil and sear the pork on a high heat for 2–3 minutes on each side until golden brown all over.
2 Wrap the rice bran in a fine cotton cloth, and sealing the cloth with one hand, squash it with the other hand in just enough water to cover the meat in a saucepan to exude the essence to the water. Discard the cloth and rice bran. Place the saucepan with the milky water on a high heat and bring to the boil. Add the seared pork, bring back to the boil, and then slowly simmer on the lowest heat for 3–4 hours. Towards the end of the cooking time, boil water in a separate saucepan, and transfer the meat to it. Continue to simmer the meat for 10 minutes, and remove from the heat. Up to this stage, this can all be done 1–2 days beforehand.
3 Mix the water, black miso, muscovado sugar and sake in a saucepan and bring to the boil. Add the cooked pork and gently simmer on a low heat for another 3–4 hours until the pork has absorbed the flavour.
4 Sieve the mashed potato through a fine mesh. Heat the dashi, light shoyu and salt in a saucepan and thicken with the diluted arrowroot. Add the mashed potato and stir until well mixed and smooth.
5 Cut the *togan* or courgette (zucchini) into 5 x 2.5cm/2 x 1in pieces and cook in lightly salted boiling water for 2–3 minutes until soft but crunchy. Drain. Cook the beans the same way and drain.
6 Mix the dashi, sake and mirin for the *Happo-ji* soup in a saucepan, bring to the boil and then add the dried fish flakes. Simmer for 1–2 minutes and remove from the heat. When the fish flakes settle to the bottom of the saucepan, drain into another saucepan through a colander lined with kitchen paper (paper towels). Discard the fish flakes. This seasoned and strengthened dashi is called *Happo-ji*. Bring the *Happo-ji* back to the boil, add to the *togan* or courgette (zucchini) and gently simmer for 10 minutes. Remove from the heat, then add the fine beans and leave to marinate for 5–10 minutes.
7 Cut the cooked meat into 4 neat, rectangular pieces and arrange a piece on each of 4 individual plates, pour a little mashed potato on top and add a quarter of each vegetable by the side. Serve with a little mustard.

Ginger pork

Butaniku no shoga-yaki

Pork and ginger go very well together as this simple pan-fried pork with ginger testifies. This is another national favourite in home cooking as well as in restaurants. It is so popular that in Japan just referring to shoga-yaki *means this pork dish.*

SERVES 4

2 tablespoons granulated sugar
4 pork steaks (each weighing 150g/5½oz)
150g/5½oz fine beans, trimmed
5 white cabbage leaves, finely shredded
1–2 tablespoons vegetable oil
salt and pepper

FOR THE GINGER MARINADE:

4 tablespoons shoyu (Japanese soy sauce)
2 tablespoons sake
2 tablespoons mirin
2 tablespoons root ginger juice

1 Rub the sugar into the pork steaks with your hands. Combine the ginger marinade ingredients, and pour over the pork steaks arranged flat in a shallow dish. Leave to marinate for 10–15 minutes.
2 Cook the fine beans in lightly salted boiling water for 1–2 minutes until soft but still crunchy. Drain and leave to cool. Plunge the shredded cabbage into cold water and drain.
3 Heat a frying-pan (skillet) with a little of the vegetable oil. Remove the pork steaks from the marinade and pan-fry on a high heat for 2–3 minutes until golden brown

on one side. Turn over, lower the heat and fry, covered, for a further 3–4 minutes until well cooked. Remove from the pan. Add the ginger marinade to the pan and simmer on a medium heat for 5 minutes to thicken the sauce. Return the pork to the pan and continue to cook on a low heat for 2 minutes to coat with the marinade.
4 Heat a clean frying-pan (skillet) with a little of the oil, and quickly stir-fry the cooked fine beans. Sprinkle with a pinch of salt and pepper. Arrange a pork steak on the bed of shredded cabbage on each plate, and serve hot garnished with the beans.

Rolled pork with burdock

Butaniku no gobo-maki

They say in Okinawa, the largest island in the southernmost archipelago halfway between Kyushu and the Philippines, that they eat every part of the pig except their squeaks. Pork ear sashimi may not appeal to everyone, but this rolled red meat with burdock surely will.

SERVES 4

350g/12oz pork thigh meat (red meat only), frozen overnight
1 *gobo* (burdock root) or 2–3 carrots, peeled
white sesame seeds, lightly roasted, to serve

FOR THE COOKING SAUCE:

300ml/11 fl oz/1⅓ cup dashi (see page 56)
3 tablespoons granulated sugar
2 tablespoons mirin
5 tablespoons shoyu (Japanese soy sauce)

1 Remove the pork from the freezer 2–3 hours before cooking to half-thaw. Cut very thinly, about 5mm/¼in thick, into 12–15 x 7cm/5–6 x 3in oval pieces.
2 Cut the *gobo* or carrots into 5cm/2in pieces or a little shorter than the shortest side of the pork. Cut the thick part lengthways in half or quarters. Soak the *gobo* in water for 1–2 minutes so it is less bitter. Cook in lightly salted boiling water for 5–6 minutes until soft. If using carrot, parboil for 1–2 minutes, and drain.

3 Put a piece of *gobo* or carrot across at one end of a piece of pork, and folding both sides of the meat, roll in. Secure with a cocktail stick (toothpick). Repeat.
4 Place the sauce ingredients in a pan, bring to the boil and place the rolled pork on the base. Cover with a lid and simmer, turning a little, on a moderate heat for 12 minutes or until most of the sauce reduces. Remove and cool in the pan.
5 Remove the sticks, cut the pork in half crossways and serve with sesame seeds.

Char-grilled (broiled) beef

Gyuniku no sumi-yaki

The traditional steak is transformed here to a lighter, yet no less sumptuous and juicy incarnation by simply grilling (broiling) on a direct heat. Barbecuing on real charcoal adds an extra smoky aroma, but gas or electricity can be used. The juice is quickly sealed and fat drawn; it has the goodness of both steak and roast beef. Let's call it 'roast beef, Japanese-style'; it is eaten with a sweet vegetable-flavoured sauce.

SERVES 4

4 beef steaks (each weighing approximately 170g/6oz)
¼ cucumber, shredded
2–3 spring onions (scallions), shredded
½ small carrot, peeled and shredded
4 handfuls of green salad leaves, to serve
salt and pepper

FOR THE *TARÉ*:
140ml/5fl oz/⅝ cup shoyu (Japanese soy sauce)
4 tablespoons mirin
300ml/11fl oz/1⅓ cups tomato juice
1 small onion, peeled and finely chopped
1 large clove garlic, peeled and finely chopped
2.5cm/1in piece of root ginger, peeled and finely chopped
1 small carrot, peeled and finely grated
7 tablespoons runny sugar syrup

1 Make a few slits vertically on the fat strip of each steak to prevent shrinkage during cooking. Sprinkle a pinch of sea salt and freshly milled black pepper over the steaks, and set aside. Plunge the shredded cucumber, spring onions (scallions) and carrot in cold water to make them crisp, and leave to drain.
2 Make the vegetable *taré*: combine all the *taré* ingredients, except the sugar syrup, in a saucepan and cook on a medium heat for about 10 minutes, stirring continuously, until the liquid is reduced by about 20 per cent. Add the syrup and continue to heat until the syrup dissolves. Strain through a fine sieve, and leave to cool.

3 Heat a wire grilling (broiling) rack over a high heat, and place the steaks on it, one or two at a time. Immediately lift up and put down again on the same spot to reduce the chances of the steaks sticking to the rack. Grill (broil) each side for 30 seconds to 5 minutes depending on how you like it done. Turn over only once. Remove from the heat and cut each steak crossways into 1cm/½in thick slices, inserting the blade slightly diagonally.
4 Arrange some green salad and a quarter of the shredded salad in the centre of each of 4 individual plates, and put 1 steak on top of each. Pour over the *taré* sauce, and serve hot.

Fried pork fillet with miso sauce

Hirékatsu

Hirékatsu *is a typical Japanese-english name for a foreign-influenced dish,* hiré *being the Japanese 'fillet', and* katsu *that of 'cutlet'. This is a kind of* tonkatsu, *deep-fried pork cutlet, but using pork fillet instead of loin or chops. It is simply deep-fried, breaded pork – cooking cannot be easier than this; Japanese fast food perhaps, but a lot more nutritious than hamburgers.* Tonkatsu *is one of the national favourites in home cooking, and there are numerous restaurants specializing only in* tonkatsu *in Japan. It is normally eaten with* tonkatsu *sauce, a thick brown sauce, but miso sauce is an interesting alternative, as shown here.*

SERVES 4

1 large pork fillet (approximately 600g/1⅓lb)
plain (all-purpose) flour, for dipping
2 eggs, beaten
dried breadcrumbs, for dipping
vegetable oil, for deep-frying
¼ small white cabbage, finely shredded
sea salt and pepper
lemon and tomato wedges, to garnish
mustard, to serve

FOR THE MISO SAUCE:
2 tablespoons miso
1 tablespoon shoyu (Japanese soy sauce)
2 tablespoons mirin
2 tablespoons sake
3 tablespoons water

1 Sprinkle salt and pepper over the pork fillet, and cut crossways into 1.5cm/½in thick rounds. Dredge each round in flour shaking off any excess. Plunge into the beaten eggs and toss in the breadcrumbs to coat the meat well.

2 Heat oil in a deep-fryer or a wok to 180°C/350°F. Gently fry the coated fillet cutlets in the hot oil, 1–2 at a time, for about 7 minutes, turning once, until lightly golden. Remove from the oil, and drain on a wire rack. Turn the heat up for 30 seconds and return the fillets, 2–3 at a time, to the oil for a second frying of 1–2 minutes until golden brown all over.

The second frying ensures the cutlets are very crisp and well cooked. Drain on a wire rack again.

3 Meanwhile, mix all the ingredients for the miso sauce in a small saucepan, and simmer on a moderate heat for 3–4 minutes until the sauce has slightly thickened.

4 Arrange a quarter of the fried cutlets on a bed of very finely shredded raw cabbage on each of 4 individual plates. Garnish with some lemon and tomato wedges, and serve with the miso sauce and a little mustard on the side.

Beef and vegetables simmered in sweet shoyu

Sukiyaki

Sukiyaki *was probably the best-known Japanese dish abroad before the sushi phenomenon started in the nineties. Along with its sister dish* shabu-shabu, sukiyaki *is still perhaps virtually the only meat dish known outside Japan. Both use paper-thin slices of beef and more or less the same kinds of vegetables cooked on the table for the diners to help themselves, but the difference lies in their cooking methods and sauces. Whereas* shabu-shabu *is cooked in broth,* sukiyaki *is coated in sweet shoyu sauce.*

SERVES 4

450g/1lb sirloin or topside of beef

2 thin leeks (white part only)

8–12 fresh shiitake or button mushrooms, stalks removed

150g/5½oz *shungiku* (chrysanthemum leaves) or spinach, trimmed

1 cake (250g/9oz) *yaki-dofu* (seared tofu) or ordinary tofu, cut into 16 cubes

1 packet (200g/7oz) *shirataki*, roughly cut (optional)

1 bunch *enoki-daké* or *shimeji* mushrooms, trimmed (optional)

5cm/2in square of beef fat, or a little vegetable oil

2–3 tablespoons granulated sugar, plus extra to serve

5 tablespoons sake

6 tablespoons shoyu (Japanese soy sauce)

225ml/8fl oz/1 cup dashi or water, plus extra to serve

4 eggs, beaten individually (optional)

1 Trim off any fat from the beef and cut it into about 7cm/3in wide, 4cm/1½in thick chunks (any length). Put in separate freezer bags and freeze for 2–3 hours. Remove from the freezer 1–2 hours before cooking or until half-thawed. Cut the beef into wafer-thin slices and arrange in a circular fan-shape on a large serving platter.

2 Slice the leeks crossways diagonally into 1.5cm/½in thick pieces. Make a decorative cross cut on each shiitake cap. Arrange all the vegetables, mushrooms, tofu and *shirataki*, if using, decoratively on a large serving platter.

3 Place a *sukiyaki*-pan or a cast-iron frying-pan (skillet) on a portable gas ring or electric hotplate on the table together with the platters of raw ingredients, jugs of dashi or water, the shoyu and sake and sugar pot. Melt the beef fat or add a little vegetable oil to the pan and move around to oil the entire base. Cook a few slices of beef first, then add some of the other ingredients and sprinkle with about 2 tablespoons sugar. Pour in the sake and shoyu, and add dashi or water to taste. (You can make a sauce by combining sake, shoyu and dashi or water in a jug.) Diners serve themselves dipping in a beaten egg, if desired, into their individual small bowls, and add some more ingredients to the pan as they eat.

Meat patties stuffed with aubergine (eggplant)

Nasu no hikiniku hasami-yaki

Aubergine (eggplant) is a versatile vegetable and makes a pretty addition to a dish if properly prepared and cooked. It absorbs juice from other ingredients, so the rich flavour of meat is an obvious choice as companion. With this recipe, meat is stuffed not inside the aubergine (eggplant), but from the skin-side. It looks interesting and tastes remarkably delicious.

SERVES 4

2–3 tablespoons vegetable oil
½ onion, finely chopped
2–3 aubergines (eggplants), calyces removed
plain (all-purpose) flour, for dusting
watercress, to garnish

FOR THE STUFFING:
300g/10oz minced beef and/or pork (use
 either meat alone or mix half and half)
1 large egg, beaten
5 tablespoons fresh breadcrumbs
⅛ teaspoon salt
pepper

FOR THE *PONZU* (CITRUS SHOYU) SAUCE:
1 tablespoon *yonezu* (Japanese rice vinegar)
2 tablespoons lemon juice
2 tablespoons dashi
2 tablespoons shoyu (Japanese soy sauce)

1 Heat a frying-pan (skillet) with 1 tablespoon vegetable oil, and cook the chopped onion on a medium heat for 5 minutes until soft and almost transparent. Remove from the heat and leave to cool.

2 Cut each aubergine (eggplant) lengthways into 4–6 wedges (depending on the size), and make a deep slit vertically in the centre on the skin of each piece. Open the slits slightly with your hands, and pat a little flour on the cut surfaces.

3 Mix the cooked onion with all the stuffing ingredients in a mixing bowl, and using your hands knead well to mix to a smooth consistency. Divide the stuffing into the number of aubergine (eggplant) pieces, and neatly stuff 1 portion into the slit of each aubergine (eggplant).

4 Heat a frying-pan (skillet) with 1–2 tablespoons vegetable oil, tilting the pan to completely oil the base, and lay the stuffed aubergines (eggplants), skin- and stuffed-side down. Fry, a few at a time, for 4–5 minutes until golden brown, turn over and cook, covered, for a further 2–3 minutes. Repeat this process until all the stuffed aubergines (eggplants) have been cooked.

5 Arrange a quarter of the stuffed aubergines (eggplants) on each of 4 individual plates and pour over the *ponzu* sauce mixture. Serve hot, garnished with some watercress.

Fried aubergine (eggplant) dumpling with minced meat

Nasu no agé-gyoza

NAOYUKI SATO is head chef at the renowned Nadaman in Hong Kong. This dumpling is his Japanese version of the Chinese *guo-tie*.

SERVES 4

2 large aubergines (eggplants)
80 per cent vegetable oil, 20 per cent sesame oil, for deep-frying
1 spring onion (scallion), finely chopped

FOR THE STUFFING:
125g/4½oz minced pork
100g/3½oz white cabbage, boiled, chopped
20g/⅔oz chives, finely chopped
1 small egg yolk
½ tablespoon sake
½ tablespoon shoyu (Japanese soy sauce)
½ tablespoon mayonnaise
1 clove garlic, finely chopped
2.5cm/1in square piece of root ginger, finely chopped
granulated sugar and salt, to season

FOR THE BATTER:
110ml/4fl oz/½ cup water
1 small egg yolk
60g/2oz/½ cup plain (all-purpose) flour

FOR THE *MOMIJI-OROSHI*:
5cm/2in piece of daikon, peeled
2–3 red chillies, halved and de-seeded

FOR THE SAUCE:
140ml/5fl oz/⅔ cup dashi (see page 56)
1 tablespoon shoyu (Japanese soy sauce)
1 tablespoon mirin

Dumplings are one of the most popular daily meals even in Japan, and I have come up with the idea of using aubergine (eggplant) instead of flour pancakes to make the dumpling lighter and fresher. Use American fat eggplant if available; if not, slice the European aubergine slightly diagonally to get bigger rounds. The condiment momiji-oroshi *is grated daikon with chilli. It literally means 'grated maple leaf', connecting the red colour with the autumn maple leaves. NS*

1 Slice the aubergines (eggplants) crossways into 16–20 thin rounds, about 2mm/⅛in thick. Mix all the stuffing ingredients, using your hands, to a smooth consistency. Spoon a teaspoonful of the mixture on to the centre of each aubergine (eggplant) round. Fold the aubergine (eggplant) in half, stuffing the meat inside, to make half-moon parcels. Seal the edge tightly; use a cocktail stick (toothpick) to secure the seal if necessary.
2 Make a batter by lightly mixing the water, egg yolk and the flour. Dip the parcels in the batter, and deep-fry in the vegetable oil mixed with the sesame oil at 170°C/340°F for 6–7 minutes, turning once, until light golden brown. Do not try to fry too many in one go; fry 3–4 parcels at a time.
3 Make the *momiji-oroshi*: poke a stick such as *hashi* lengthways into the cut face of the daikon to make 4–5 deep holes. Cut each chilli half into quarters lengthways if necessary. Poke the chilli pieces into the daikon holes. Gently grate the daikon so as to grate the chilli at the same time, making sure the pieces of chilli do not come out.
4 Put the dashi, shoyu and mirin of the sauce ingredients into a saucepan and bring to the boil. Divide the sauce among 4 small individual bowls.
5 Arrange 4–5 aubergine (eggplant) dumplings on each of 4 plates together with a small mound of the *momiji-oroshi* on a bed of finely chopped spring onions (scallions), and serve with the sauce. Diners mix the *momiji-oroshi* and the spring onions (scallions) into the sauce and dip in the dumpling before eating.

7

Eggs
and Tofu

Fried tofu and prawn (shrimp) balls with dashi sauce

Hiryozu no agedashi

TAKAYUKI HISHINUMA shows here how to make mouth-watering, hot, *hiryozu*, with which ordinary *ganmodoki* cannot compare. While *ganmodoki* is usually sold ready-made, *hiryozu* (or *hirousu*) is a home-made *ganmodoki,* literally meaning 'duck look-alike', consisting of tofu and some vegetables.

SERVES 4

1 cake (250g/9oz) firm tofu
few bunches of *kikurage* (wood ear
    mushrooms), softened in water
1 carrot
16–20 gingko nuts, peeled
10 prawns (shrimp), shelled and de-veined
5cm/2in piece of *yamato-ito* (yam potato)
    (approximately 60g/2oz), peeled (optional)
oil, for deep-frying
150g/5½oz oyster mushrooms
5cm/2in piece of daikon, peeled and grated
2.5–4cm/1–1½in piece of root ginger, peeled
    and grated
salt

FOR THE TEMPURA SAUCE:
200ml/7fl oz/⅞ cup dashi (see page 56)
3½ tablespoons shoyu (Japanese soy sauce)
3½ tablespoons mirin

In order to make crispy hiryozu *with a soft and fluffy inside, the excess water should be squeezed out of the tofu before cooking. If this isn't done properly, it won't fry well and the result will be a wet* hiryozu. *On the other hand if too much water is removed from the tofu, it becomes hard and dry. The best method is to weigh it down with something about three times the weight of the tofu, and drain the water slowly over about 12 hours. TH*

1 Wrap the tofu with a clean tea towel, and roll into a *makisu* (sushi rolling bamboo mat) – the traditional way to drain tofu. Put a weight (a stone or unopened can of food) on top and leave overnight to squeeze the water out. It will shrink to two thirds of the original size.
2 Trim the *kikurage*, and cut into fine shreds, and finely shred the carrot into about 5cm/2in long pieces.
3 Cook the gingko nuts in salted water until soft, and drain.
4 Pat dry the prawns (shrimp), and finely chop and crush with a knife on a chopping-board. Transfer to a *suribachi* (Japanese mortar), add a pinch of salt, and finely grind with a *surikogi* (Japanese pestle) or use a food processor. Add the drained tofu, breaking it into pieces with your hands, and grind together with the prawn (shrimp) mixture into a consistent and smooth paste.

5 Grate the *yamato-ito*, if using, to make about 1 tablespoonful, and add to the prawn and tofu mixture. Add the *kikurage*, carrot and gingko nuts, and mix well. Take a handful of the mixture, and make a ball the size of a golf ball. Repeat until you use up all the mixture.
6 Heat plenty of oil in a wok to a moderate temperature (about 120°C/240°F), and deep-fry the tofu balls, a few at a time, until golden brown. Deep-fry the oyster mushrooms until golden brown. Drain both well.
7 Mix the tempura sauce ingredients in a saucepan, and bring to the boil. Arrange 2–3 tofu balls and 2–3 pieces of oyster mushroom in each of 4 small individual bowls. Serve hot, garnished with grated daikon and ginger, and pour over the sauce.

Steamed yuba dumpling with sesame tofu sauce

Yuba no gyoza goma-tofu aé

LINDA RODRIGUEZ first trained in classical French cooking under her mentor Jacqueline Greaud at her restaurant Maison Lacour. Jacqueline also taught her Chinese, Thai, Vietnamese and Indian cuisines along with Cajun-style cooking. For three years prior to the opening of New York's Bond Street restaurant in 1998, where she is executive chef, she worked at the Nobu, both in New York and London.

SERVES 4

8 sheets (approximately 14 x 15cm/5½ x 6in)
   yuba (tofu skin)
8 strips (approximately 20cm/8in long)
   kanpyo (dried gourd) (optional)

FOR THE STUFFING:
½ medium onion, finely chopped
1 tablespoon vegetable oil
2.5cm/1in piece of root ginger, finely chopped
1 clove garlic, finely chopped
150g/5½oz minced chicken
⅓ small carrot, finely shredded
50g/2oz portabello or any mushrooms
   (*matsutake* are pictured), finely chopped
1 tomato, finely diced
50g/2oz spinach, roughly chopped
2 mint leaves
1 tablespoon pine nuts, toasted
½ teaspoon cayenne pepper
1 tablespoon Thai fish sauce
salt and pepper

FOR THE SESAME TOFU SAUCE:
½ cake silken tofu (125g/4½oz)
2 tablespoons sesame purée
pinch of shoyu (Japanese soy sauce)
1 teaspoon granulated sugar

This is another very popular dish at our restaurant, Bond Street, in New York. I have had this on the menu since the opening, and cannot take it off because it's such a big seller. Though it is a dumpling, it is quite original in its flavour and presentation. Kanpyo, used here to tie the dumpling, is a dried gourd string, and is one of the useful ingredients unique to Japanese cooking. You can eat this dish hot or cold, though we steam it and serve it with sesame tofu sauce at Bond Street. LR

1 Soak the *yuba* in plenty of water for 10 minutes and drain. Wet the *kanpyo*, rub a little salt all over and wash in water. Drain.

2 Sauté the onion in a hot frying-pan (skillet) with 1 tablespoon oil until soft and almost transparent, then add the ginger and garlic and continue to stir. Add the minced chicken and cook for 2–3 minutes. Add the carrots and mushrooms, cook for 2–3 minutes, then add the rest of the stuffing ingredients. Cook for a further 1–2 minutes, check the seasoning and remove from the heat. Turn out onto a plate and leave to cool. When cold, chill in the refrigerator.

3 Make the sesame tofu sauce by mixing all the sauce ingredients in a food processor or blender, and purée for 1 minute. Check the seasoning.

4 When the chicken mixture is cold, put one eighth of it in the centre of a softened *yuba* (tofu skin), then fold in the longer sides to cover the chicken mixture and roll so that the stuffing is completely wrapped. Repeat this process until all the *yuba* and chicken stuffing are used up.

5 Secure each *yuba* dumpling by tying with a string of *kanpyo*, (if not using, don't tie the dumplings) and place on a large plate. Steam in a boiling steamer on a high heat for 5–6 minutes. Remove from the steamer.

6 Arrange 2 *yuba* dumplings on each of 4 individual plates and serve hot with the sesame tofu sauce.

Fried tofu with kabayaki eel

Age-dofu to kabayaki no an-kake

SUSUMU HATAKEYAMA is chef at the Ikeda restaurant in Mayfair in London. This recipe is part of the established menu at many Japanese restaurants abroad. Fresh tofu has a very subtle flavour, but for many Westerners it may be too light and bland in flavour. It is often fried to add crunchiness as well as bite and weight, but this recipe goes further to add richness with the addition of *kabayaki* eel. This is very popular with Japanese and non-Japanese alike.

SERVES 4

2 cakes (each weighing 250g/9oz) firm tofu
2 spring onions (scallions), finely shredded
3–4 tablespoons *katakuriko* (potato starch) or
  arrowroot, for dipping
vegetable oil, for deep-frying
1 small *unagi* (eel) or *anago* (sea
  eel) *kabayaki* (i.e. eel grilled or broiled with
  sweet shoyu, see page 9)
wasabi paste, to garnish

FOR THE *AN* SAUCE:
400ml/14fl oz/1⅔ cups dashi (see page 56)
2 tablespoons shoyu (Japanese soy sauce)
2 tablespoons mirin
1 tablespoon sake
¼ teaspoon salt
2 tablespoons *katakuriko* (potato starch) or
  arrowroot, mixed with 2 tablespoons water

This is one of the dishes that evolved abroad in order to accommodate Westerners' tastes by making the simple, rather plain taste of tofu into a more substantial dish. Tofu and eel kabayaki, *two strikingly different flavours and textures, go hand in hand with their tastes complementing each other. In Japan tofu is not fried for this dish, but is layered with* kabayaki *a few times, then steamed. SH*

1 Drain excess water from the tofu by placing a chopping-board on top of the tofu with a weight (such as an unopened can of food) for 30 minutes to 1 hour. Put the finely shredded spring onion (scallion) in ice-cold water. This freshens it and makes it crisp. When ready to serve, drain and pat dry with kitchen paper (paper towels).

2 When water is drawn from the tofu and it is firmer, cut each tofu cake into 4 pieces. Carefully dredge each piece in *katakuriko* or arrowroot and pat off the excess. Slowly slip into hot oil (about 180°C/350°F) from the side of a deep-fryer, and fry for 4–5 minutes until light golden brown. Do not put too many into the oil at the same time; fry only 2–3 pieces at one go. Drain on a wire rack or on kitchen paper (paper towels) and keep warm.

3 Put all the ingredients for the *an* sauce in a saucepan except the *katakuriko* or arrowroot, bring to the boil over high a heat and then lower it. Gently pour in the diluted *katakuriko* or arrowroot, stirring all the time, to thicken the soup – this thick seasoned soup is called *an*. Remove from the heat and keep warm.

4 Cut the *kabayaki* eel into 8 bite-sized pieces, similar in size to the top surface of the fried tofu blocks, and lightly grill (broil) under a hot grill (broiler) or in a microwave oven just to make the surface crispy.

5 Arrange 2 pieces of fried tofu in each of 4 individual dishes, place a piece of *kabayaki* on each of the tofu blocks, and pour the warm *an* sauce over the *kabayaki*. Garnish with spring onion (scallion) shreds and a little wasabi paste on top and serve immediately.

Home-made tofu

Zaru-dofu [v]

AKIHIRO KURITA, a young chef from Kyoto, reveals the secret of easy tofu making. You need a large *zaru* (bamboo mesh tray) to make this tofu. It is increasingly popular in the West, especially for vegetarians. There are many types sold in supermarkets and oriental shops, but no tofu is as fresh and delicious as home-made.

SERVES 4–8

1kg/2lb 2oz/6½ cups soya beans (soybeans), soaked in plenty of water overnight
4 litres/7 pints/4 quarts mineral water
1 (approximately 30cm/12in square) cotton sheet, or a double-layered gauze sheet
1 (over 50cm/20in square) cotton sheet, or a double-layered gauze sheet
1 tablespoon *nigari* (tofu coagulation agent)
1 tablespoon water

For authentic Japanese chefs tofu is one of the most complex materials to handle, and has more depth than you may think. However, this home-made tofu is very easy to make as long as you successfully manage to exude the soya bean (soybean) milk. If the coagulation does not seem to occur, make fried tofu balls instead. Squeeze out the excess water by placing a weight on top, add some plain (all-purpose) flour and make into small tofu balls. Then deep-fry. You can also eat the pulp after the milk is taken: stir-fry with shredded and pre-cooked vegetables. AK

1 When soaked in water overnight, the volume of the soya beans (soybeans) will expand to about 3 litres/5 pints/3 quarts. Discard the soaking water. Put approximately 500ml/18fl oz/2¼ cups of the softened soya beans (soybeans) together with 300ml/11fl oz/1⅓ cups mineral water in a mixer or food processor, and crush well until smooth and creamy. Transfer the crushed beans into a large mixing bowl. Repeat this process another 5 times until all the beans are crushed.

2 Put the remaining 2 litres/3½ pints/9 cups mineral water in a large bowl. Place the cotton cloth or a double-layered gauze sheet flat on one of your palms above the bowl, spoon a ladle of the crushed soya beans on to the cloth and tightly wrap around. Securing the loose end of the cloth in one hand, squeeze the cloth a number of times with the other to get the soya bean (soybean) milk out into the water until the crushed beans become a dry pulp in the cloth. You may need to dip the cloth in the water and continue to squeeze. Transfer the pulp from the cloth into another mixing bowl, and discard, or eat separately. Repeat this process until all the crushed beans are used. Skim off the fine foam that comes up to the surface.

3 Place a large cotton cloth (or a double-layered gauze sheet) into a colander and sieve the soya bean (soybean) milk through it into a saucepan. Wrap the cloth and squeeze out as much milk as possible, and discard the pulp in the cloth (or eat separately). Put the saucepan in a larger saucepan with boiling water. Cook on a moderate heat for 10–15 minutes until cooked. Skim off the foam from time to time. When it's cooked it gives out a mildly sweet aroma, and can be drunk as soya (soy) milk at this stage. Remove from the heat and leave to cool.

4 Dilute the *nigari* with the same volume of water in a large mixing bowl, and pour the warm (70–73°C/160–165°F) soya (soy) milk from high above so the *nigari* water quickly mixes with the soya (soy) milk. Cover with a lid and leave for about 30 minutes until it loosely sets. The loosely set tofu is called *oboro-dofu* and can be eaten at this stage with shoyu (Japanese soy sauce) and wasabi paste.

5 Turn the *oboro-dofu* on to a *zaru* (bamboo mesh tray) and leave to drain for about 30 minutes. The *zaru-dofu* is ready to eat cold with shoyu mixed with wasabi or grated ginger and finely chopped spring onions (scallions).

Egg tofu with prawns (shrimp)

Ebi-iri tamago-dofu

Egg tofu is not really a tofu but a custard mixture of egg and dashi soup in the shape and texture of a tofu. It is a popular hors d'oeuvre dish, eaten cold in summer and hot in winter. Prawn (shrimp) adds extra flavour and bite as well as colour to this plain egg dish.

SERVES 4

4 giant prawns (shrimp) with shells,
   de-veined using a cocktail stick (toothpick)
   inserted between the shells
dash of sake
5 large eggs, beaten
300ml/11fl oz/1⅓ cups dashi (cold) (see
   page 56)
1 teaspoon light shoyu (Japanese soy sauce)
1 teaspoon sea salt
1 teaspoon mirin
2.5cm/1in piece of root ginger, peeled
   and finely grated
salt

FOR THE SAUCE:
400ml/14fl oz/1⅔ cups dashi (see page 56)
2 tablespoons light shoyu (Japanese
   soy sauce)
1 tablespoon mirin

1 Cook the prawns (shrimp) in just enough boiling water with a pinch of salt and a dash of sake for 1–2 minutes until the shells become bright red. The prawns (shrimp) curl to a round shape. Drain and immediately place under running water to cool down quickly. Shell and slice each prawn horizontally into 2 thin discs.

2 Mix the beaten eggs gently with the dashi, shoyu, sea salt and mirin, and sieve through a fine mesh strainer. Put all but 2–3 tablespoons into an oblong, approximately 18 x 15 x 6cm/7 x 6 x 2½in, metal mould, covered with a lid wrapped in a tea towel, and steam in a boiling steamer on a high heat for about 10 minutes until just hardened. If you place a pair of *hashi* (Japanese chopsticks) in between the mould and the base of the steamer, the high heat will not come into contact with the bottom of the mould and it will heat more evenly.

3 When the surface of the egg 'tofu' is lightly hardened, place the 8 prawn (shrimp) slices evenly on top. Pour the remaining 2–3 tablespoons of seasoned dashi onto the prawns and put back into the boiling steamer, covered with a lid, and steam on a moderate heat for 12–15 minutes. Cover the lid with a cotton cloth and steam with the lid slightly off. When the egg 'tofu' is just hardened, remove from the heat and leave to cool.

4 Mix all the ingredients for the sauce in a saucepan and bring to the boil.

5 Remove the egg 'tofu' from the mould, and cut into 8 even-sized cubes. Place 2 pieces in each of 4 small individual bowls and pour over the sauce. Serve hot, or cold, garnished with a little grated ginger on top.

Fried tofu with vegetable dashi sauce

Agedashi-dofu [v]

Agedashi-dofu *is normally made with fish dashi sauce, but as this is a vegetarian recipe you could use vegetable soup instead or the shiitake water formed after soaking dried shiitake mushrooms. You can of course use ordinary fish dashi if you are not vegetarian.*

SERVES 4

2 cakes (each weighing 250g/9oz) firm tofu
4 tablespoons rice flour or wheat flour
4 tablespoons potato starch or
  cornflour (cornstarch)
vegetable oil, for deep-frying
7cm/3in piece of daikon, peeled and
  finely grated
2.5cm/1in piece of root ginger, peeled
  and finely grated
1–2 spring onions (scallions),
  finely chopped, to garnish
shiso flower, to garnish (optional)

FOR THE SAUCE:

6 tablespoons dashi (see page 56)
3 tablespoons shoyu (Japanese soy sauce)
2 teaspoons granulated sugar

1 First squeeze as much water as possible from the tofu: wrap the tofu in a *makisu* (sushi rolling bamboo mat) or a cotton cloth, and leave on a slightly tilted chopping-board (so the water runs down) with another chopping-board and a weight on top for 1 hour. Remove from the wrap, and cut each tofu cake into 4 pieces. Dredge in a mixture of rice or wheat flour and potato starch or cornflour (cornstarch) and shake off any excess.
2 Heat the oil for deep-frying to 180°C/350°F. Gently slide the tofu pieces into the hot oil, 2 or 3 at a time, and deep-fry for 3–4 minutes, turning a few times, until light golden all over.
3 While the tofu is being fried, mix all the ingredients for the sauce in a saucepan on a moderate heat until just warm and the sugar has dissolved. Pour a quarter of the sauce in each of 4 individual bowls, and add 2 pieces of fried tofu to each bowl. Arrange some grated daikon and ginger on top, and serve garnished with finely chopped spring onions (scallions) on top and *shiso* flowers by the side.

Fried Koya-dofu with fish shinjo

Koya-dofu to shinjo no hasami-age

Shinjo is a general term for finely ground white fish or prawns (shrimp), steamed or fried – a sort of Japanese terrine. Ground chicken is also used to make shinjo *and it is called* tori-shinjo (*chicken* shinjo). *Here* shinjo *is sandwiched between pieces of* Koya-dofu (*freeze-dried tofu*), *then fried.*

SERVES 4

FOR THE *SHINJO*:
150g/5½oz cod or any white fish, boned
   and skinned
½ egg yolk, beaten
3 tablespoons vegetable oil
2 dried shiitake, soaked in water overnight
16–24 tinned gingko nuts (optional)
60–75g/2–2½oz crabmeat
salt and pepper

4 cakes (standard size approximately 7 x 5 x
   2.5cm/3 x 2 x 1in) *Koya-dofu*
katakuriko (potato starch) or
   cornflour (cornstarch), for coating
vegetable oil, for deep-frying
2 tablespoons sake
2 tablespoons mirin
2 tablespoons light shoyu (Japanese
   soy sauce)
salt
green salad leaves, to garnish

1 Mash the fish meat to a very fine paste using a *suribachi* and *surikogi* (Japanese mortar and pestle) or a large ordinary mortar and pestle. Put the beaten egg yolk in a small mixing bowl and gradually add the vegetable oil, a little at a time, stirring all the time, to make a smooth egg cream. Add to the fish paste and mix well.
2 Drain the shiitake, keeping the liquid to use later, and cut the softened shiitake into fine shreds. Add to the fish paste together with the gingko nuts, if using, and the crabmeat, and mix well. Lightly season with salt and pepper.
3 Soak the *Koya-dofu* in water for 15 seconds, drain and squeeze out as much water as possible. Cut each piece horizontally into 2 thin slices, and dredge in *katakuriko* or cornflour (cornstarch) to coat all sides. Put a quarter of the *shinjo* on each of 4 *Koya-dofu* slices and cover each one with another slice to make 4 *shinjo* sandwiched with *Koya-dofu*. Lightly pat *katakuriko* or cornflour (cornstarch) onto the exposed *shinjo* sides.

4 Heat some vegetable oil in a deep-fryer to a moderate temperature, about 160°C/320°F, and carefully sliding them in from the side, deep-fry the *Koya-dofu shinjo* for 7–8 minutes until cooked and both sides are a golden colour. Fry 2 or at most 3 at a time. Drain on a wire rack or on kitchen paper (paper towels). Place them all in a strainer and pour boiling water all over to wash out excess oil.
5 Put the shiitake soaking water in a saucepan and add some more water, if necessary, to make it up to about 400ml/14fl oz/1⅔ cups. Bring to the boil and season with the sake, mirin, shoyu and salt. Lower the heat, add the *Koya-dofu shinjo*, then simmer for about 15–20 minutes, turning frequently, until the liquid has almost disappeared. Remove from the heat and leave to cool.
6 Cut each *Koya-dofu shinjo* into 4 and arrange the 4 blocks on a bed of green salad in each of 4 individual plates. Serve hot or cold.

Pan-fried Koya-dofu in egg batter

Koya-dofu no tamago tsuke yaki [v]

Koya-dofu, freeze-dried tofu, *is said to have been developed by the Koya mountain monks, hence its name. Its flavour is very different from that of fresh tofu, and as the texture is firm and spongy, it can be cooked with other ingredients. The egg batter adds an attractive colour and flavour to the* Koya-dofu's *slightly dull appearance.*

SERVES 4

2 cakes (standard size approximately
   7 x 5 x 2.5cm/3 x 2 x 1in) *Koya-dofu*
500ml/18fl oz/2¼ cups vegetable
   stock (broth)
2 tablespoons shoyu (Japanese soy sauce)
1 tablespoon granulated sugar
1 tablespoon mirin
2 teaspoons cornflour (cornstarch)
2 eggs, beaten
1 tablespoon finely chopped parsley
2 tablespoons oil
salt
rocket (arugula) salad, to garnish

1 Most *Koya-dofu* comes in packets with powdered soup in sachets, in which the *Koya-dofu* can be cooked following the packet instructions before cooking with other ingredients. However, the soup sachet normally contains fish dashi stock, so if you are a vegetarian, cook the *Koya-dofu* in a mixture of the vegetable stock, the shoyu, sugar and mirin instead.

2 Lightly squeeze the liquid out of the cooked *Koya-dofu*, then slice horizontally into 2 thin pieces and cut each piece into 8 small triangles.

3 Add the cornflour (cornstarch) and a pinch of salt to the beaten eggs, stir well until the cornflour (cornstarch) has dissolved and then add the chopped parsley. Coat each *Koya-dofu* triangle with the egg batter.

4 Pan-fry the coated *Koya-dofu* triangles in a lightly oiled frying-pan (skillet) for 1–2 minutes on each side. Drain on kitchen paper (paper towels), and arrange 8 *Koya-dofu* triangles on each of 4 individual plates on a bed of rocket (arugula) salad.

Tofu hotpot with oyster and chrysanthemum leaves

Kaki to shungiku no yu-dofu

Yu-dofu, *boiled tofu, an old favourite family winter hotpot, is normally just tofu cooked in* konbu *water, and eaten dipped in shoyu with grated ginger and finely chopped spring onions (scallions). With added oysters and* shungiku, *this simple dish becomes more substantial and is good for growing youngsters too.*

SERVES 4

1 cake (250g/9oz) tofu, cut into
   bite-sized cubes
12 oysters or scallops
katakuriko (potato starch) or
   cornflour (cornstarch), for coating
250g/9oz *shungiku* (chrysanthemum leaves)
   or spinach
10cm/4in dried *konbu* (kelp)

TO SERVE:
8 tablespoons shoyu
4 tablespoons *ponzu* (ready-made citrus
   shoyu) or lemon or lime juice
5cm/2in piece of daikon, peeled and grated
2 spring onions (scallions), finely grated
2.5cm/1in piece of root ginger, peeled and
   finely grated

1 Blanch the tofu in boiling water for 30 seconds and drain. Carefully wash the oysters or scallops, dredge in *katakuriko* or cornflour (cornstarch) and pat off the excess. Roughly cut the *shungiku* or spinach into bite-sized chunks.
2 Place the *konbu* with plenty of water in a *donabe* (earthenware pot) or a wide, shallow saucepan and bring to the boil. Lower the heat and put the tofu, oysters or scallops and *shungiku* or spinach on top of the konbu. Cook gently on a moderate heat for 2–3 minutes until the oysters or scallops are just cooked, and bring to the centre of the table.
3 Each diner mixes about 2 tablespoons of shoyu, 1 tablespoon *ponzu* or lemon or lime juice, or a mixture of lemon and lime juice, some grated daikon and chopped spring onions (scallions) in their individual bowl and serves themselves, dipping the tofu, oysters or scallops and *shungiku* or spinach in the sauce.

Japanese omelette

Tamago-yaki [v]

They say judge a sushi restaurant by its tamago-yaki. *It's probably because* tamago-yaki *is the only topping that is made at the restaurant; all others, such as fish and shellfish, come from the same source: the fish market. Also since* tamago-yaki *is one of the simplest of dishes, the result shows your skill and experience more clearly than others. Here's the basic method for making* tamago-yaki.

SERVES 4

5 medium or 4 large eggs and 1 yolk, beaten

1 tablespoon granulated sugar

1 tablespoon shoyu (Japanese soy sauce), plus extra to serve

1 tablespoon mirin

vegetable oil, for oiling

3–5cm/1¼–2in piece of daikon, peeled and finely grated, to garnish

cooked broccoli, to garnish

1 Use a fork to break the whites of the beaten eggs as small as possible, and strain through a sieve. Add the sugar, shoyu and mirin, and stir well until the sugar has dissolved. Do not whisk or make bubbles.

2 Heat a clean, square pan (12 x 20cm/ 5 x 8in) or an ordinary 18–25cm /7–10in frying-pan (skillet) evenly by moving it over a moderate heat and put in a little vegetable oil. Spread evenly over the base by tilting the pan and wiping off excess oil with kitchen paper (paper towels), while making sure the surface is absolutely smooth. Keep the oiled paper on a plate by the side.

3 Lower the heat and pour a quarter of the egg mixture evenly over the base by tilting the pan. If large air bubbles pop up immediately the pan may be too hot; then remove the pan from the heat and put it back on again when the egg starts to set.

Break air bubbles with a fork and when the egg is about to set, using *hashi* or a fork roll the egg layer 2–3 times from the far side towards you, then oil the empty base with the oiled kitchen paper and push the rolled egg back to the other side. Again using the oiled paper, oil the area where the rolled egg was, then pour a third of the remaining egg mixture evenly over the base by tilting the pan as well as lifting the egg roll so the egg mixture flows under it too. When the egg starts to set, roll again, using the first roll as the core. Repeat this oiling and rolling twice more, using up the remaining egg mixture. Remove from the pan and leave to cool.

4 When the *tamago-yaki* is cool enough to handle, cut crossways into 8. Arrange 2 pieces on each of 4 individual plates, garnished with a mound of the grated daikon with a drop of shoyu on top and the cooked broccoli. Serve warm or cold.

Baked egg in Horaku dish

Tamago Horaku-yaki

YOSHIHIRO MURATA, celebrity chef and owner of the *ryotei* Kikunoi in Kyoto, includes his modern version of the old *Horaku-yaki* which uses a type of earthenware pot. You can use any heat-resistant dish instead. This dish looks fairly modern or even foreign influenced, but the method of baking eggs in a *Horaku* has been around in Kyoto for a long time.

SERVES 4

1 eel, boned and filleted
2 tablespoons sake
2 tablespoons mirin
½ tablespoon each light and dark shoyu
  (Japanese soy sauce)
OR ½ (approximately 60g/2oz) ready-cooked
  kabayaki eel (see page 19)

½ small carrot, peeled
10g/⅓oz *kikurage* (wood ear mushrooms),
  softened in water and finely chopped
110ml/4fl oz/½ cup dashi (see page 56)
1 *yurine* (edible lily bulb) (pictured) (optional)
20–24 gingko nuts, shelled (optional)
½ small *matsutake* or 4 fresh shiitake,
  thinly sliced
4 sprigs of *mitsuba* or spinach leaves
few drops of *yuzu* or lemon juice, to serve
salt

FOR THE EGG SAUCE:
4 eggs, beaten
600ml/22fl oz/2⅔ cups dashi (see page 56)
1 tablespoon light shoyu (Japanese
  soy sauce)
2 tablespoons mirin
1 teaspoon sea salt
2 tablespoons melted butter

When I tasted soufflé in France for the first time in my life, I thought it was a Western version of Horaku-yaki, *but the lightness that melts immediately is not something familiar in Japanese cooking. The more dashi in the egg mixture the softer it certainly becomes, but I still felt there was something missing. Then I thought of adding butter, since what makes soufflé so rich in flavour yet so fragile is the cream and butter. For this dish I use only a little melted butter. YM*

1 If using a fresh eel, gently cook the boned and filleted eel in a saucepan in a mixture of 1 tablespoon each of sake and mirin, and ½ tablespoon each of light and dark shoyu for about 10 minutes until the eel is soft. Remove from the heat and cut into 1.5cm/¾in square pieces. If using a ready-cooked *kabayaki* eel, cut into 1.5cm/¾in square pieces.
2 Dice the carrots and gently cook with the *kikurage* in the dashi, 1 tablespoon each of sake and mirin, and set aside.
3 Sprinkle a little salt over the *yurine*, if using, and steam on a high heat for 10 minutes until soft, then break into sections.
4 If using raw gingko nuts, soak in warm water for 10 minutes, and using the back of a spoon rub the nuts, pressing to the bottom of the pan. This makes it easier to peel away the fine skin.
5 Mix all the egg sauce ingredients together.
6 Place quarter of the eel, carrot, *kikurage*, *yurine*, gingko nuts, *matsutake* or shiitake and *mitsuba* or spinach in each of 4 individual heat-resistant shallow dishes, and gently pour the egg sauce over. Bake in the oven heated to 180°C/360°F/Gas 4 for 35–40 minutes until the surface is golden brown. Sprinkle with a little *yuzu* or lemon juice and serve hot.

8

Rice
and Sushi

Steamed mixed sushi

Mushi-zushi

YUICHI OYAMA presents this wonderful sushi recipe. Though sushi is a national dish, and more or less the same kinds of sushi, traditional and modern, are served nationwide, the traditional Osaka sushi is still the mixed sushi. This sushi is not moulded into any shape, but the vinegared rice is simply mixed with various raw and cooked ingredients. And sushi is not always a cold dish, as this Osaka winter favourite illustrates.

SERVES 4

4 dried shiitake, soaked in
    water overnight

1 tablespoon plus a pinch of granulated sugar

2 tablespoons shoyu (Japanese soy sauce)

1 tablespoon mirin

1–2 pieces of dried *kikurage* (wood ear
    mushrooms), soaked in water for 30 minutes

dashi, seasoned with shoyu and mirin
    (see method)

600g/1lb 5oz/4 cups *sumeshi* (cooked
    vinegared rice, see page 152)

½ grilled *anago* (sea eel), diced, or
    kabayaki eel (see page 19)

2 eggs, beaten

50g/1¾oz white fish meat, ground

1–2 tablespoons vegetable oil

1–2 tablespoons *myoga* (Japanese bulb
    vegetable), or vinegared ginger slices (see
    page 70), shredded, to garnish

Hako-zushi *has now been overtaken by* nigiri-zushi *(finger sushi with a slice of raw fish on top) in terms of popularity and there aren't many sushi restaurants that bother to make it, but another Osaka speciality,* chirashi-zushi *(mixed sushi) is still very popular. This* mushi-zushi *is a type of* chirashi, *but it's steamed and eaten hot. Thus it is also known as* nuku-zushi *(warm sushi). Traditionally in Osaka we mix vinegared rice with cooked* shiitake, kikurage *(wood ear mushrooms) and* anago *(sea eel) or* unagi *(eel)* kabayaki. *Use almost anything as long as the flavour, texture and colour complement each other. YO*

1 Drain the shiitake, retaining the liquid. Put the shiitake and some liquid, about 150ml/5½fl oz/⅔ cup, just to cover the shiitake in a saucepan, and cook over a moderate heat for about 10 minutes, skimming the scum from time to time, until the liquid is reduced by half. Add 1 tablespoon of the sugar, and continue to cook, stirring all the time, for another 10 minutes until the liquid is further reduced by half. Add the shoyu and mirin, and cook until the liquid almost disappears. Set aside, and when cool squeeze out the excess juice and finely chop the shiitake.

2 Chop the *kikurage* into similarly fine pieces, and cook in boiling water for 2–3 minutes. Drain, and cook in the seasoned dashi just to cover on a moderate heat for 5 minutes. Drain and set aside.

3 Put the *sumeshi* in a wooden tub or a large mixing bowl, add the chopped shiitake and *kikurage* and *anago* or *kabayaki*, and gently mix with a wooden spatula. Do not stir. Add a little juice from the sweet shoyu sauce in which the shiitake were cooked, and gently mix again.

4 Mix the beaten eggs, ground fish meat and a pinch of sugar in a small mixing bowl and beat vigorously to make a smooth egg base. Sieve through a fine mesh. Heat a frying-pan (skillet) with a little vegetable oil and add half the egg mixture, tilting the pan so that it spreads out evenly. When the surface is slightly dry, turn the egg sheet over and after a few seconds turn out on to a chopping-board. Repeat this process to make one more egg sheet. Cut finely into about 5cm/2in long shreds.

5 Lay a fine cotton cloth in the bottom of a bamboo steaming dish, add the mixed sushi rice and steam over a high heat for about 5 minutes or until hot. Steam the egg shreds separately. Arrange a quarter of the rice in each of 4 large rice or pasta bowls and sprinkle with the egg shreds on top. Serve hot, garnished with shredded *myoga*, or vinegared ginger.

Swordfish rice bowl with honey shoyu sauce

Kajiki no hachimitsu-joyu dare don

KENTARO's cooking philosophy is easy and quick; so for many single people, as well as mothers with young children, he is not just a television celebrity chef but a friend. One-bowl dishes, such as this one, aim to provide the three main nutrients, vitamins, protein and carbohydrate, at one go. You can use any ingredients as long as the final result is a combination of meat or fish and green vegetables on top of rice. It is an all-round dish to be served at any time of day, and is good to fill hungry youngsters coming home after school.

SERVES 4

3–4 tablespoons vegetable oil

4 cloves garlic, thinly sliced into rings

4 swordfish steaks, patted dry with
    kitchen paper (paper towels)

30g/1oz butter

2 tablespoons shoyu (Japanese soy sauce)

2 teaspoons honey

4 big bowls of hot cooked rice, to serve

4 spring onions (scallions), finely chopped

Swordfish is called kajiki maguro *in Japan. Although* maguro *in fact means tuna, it is not a variety of tuna. When heated, the pinkish, almost transparently white meat turns opaque and firms up just like chicken. The taste and texture are also not very different from those of chicken breast. It has slightly more calories than other white fish such as sea bream, and is rich in vitamin D, which helps digest calcium. Choose fish with a shiny pink to white colour and firm texture. This dish can be cooked within 10 minutes if you have ready-cooked rice. KK*

1 Heat half the vegetable oil in a frying-pan (skillet), and fry the garlic rings on a high heat for about 1 minute or until the garlic turns a crispy golden brown. Remove the garlic to a dish and retain.
2 Roughly wipe the frying-pan (skillet) with kitchen paper (paper towels), then fry the swordfish steaks in the rest of the oil on a high heat for about 2 minutes on each side or until both sides become golden brown. Lower the heat to medium, and cook, covered, for another 2–3 minutes until the fish is well cooked. Remove from the pan.

3 Again, lightly wipe the pan, add the butter, shoyu and honey and bring to the boil, still on a moderate heat. Return the cooked fish to the pan, and spoon the juice evenly on to all the steaks. Remove from the heat.
4 Place 1 steak on top of each of the 4 bowls of rice and pour over the juice. Sprinkle evenly with the fried garlic and the chopped spring onions (scallions) and serve hot.

Tempura rice bowl

Kaki-agé donburi

TETSUYA SAOTOME, chef/patron of the Mikawa tempura restaurant in Tokyo, shows how to make a traditional *kaki-agé* on top of freshly cooked hot rice. This makes a very substantial lunch. Kaki-agé is a tempura with a few ingredients fried together, as opposed to, say, prawn (shrimp) tempura where each single piece is fried on its own. It normally contains vegetables with small prawns or shrimps.

SERVES 4

200g/7oz small shelled prawns (shrimp)
6–8 stalks *mitsuba* or watercress, plus extra
    to garnish
2 eggs
200g/7oz /1 cup light plain (all-purpose)
    flour, sifted
vegetable oil, for deep-frying
4 big bowls of hot cooked rice, to serve

FOR THE SAUCE:
5 tablespoons dashi (see page 56)
6 tablespoons shoyu (Japanese soy sauce)
5 tablespoons mirin

It looks simple, but tempura is one of the most difficult dishes to make properly. I have said it before, and will say it again: make the batter ultra-light by chilling the flour in the refrigerator overnight before mixing it with ice-cold water. You can use any vegetables for this dish, but finely shred big or thick ones such as carrot and fine beans. TS

1 Pat dry the prawns (shrimp) and *mitsuba* or watercress with kitchen paper (paper towels). Chop the watercress into about 3cm/1¼in pieces, and discard the thick stalks. Put the prawns (shrimp) and vegetable in a mixing bowl.
2 Mix 1 beaten egg with 50ml/2fl oz/¼ cup ice-cold water in a mixing bowl, and sift in half the flour, which has been sifted once before and chilled in the refrigerator overnight. Lightly stir to make light, thin batter. Add this batter to the prawns (shrimp) and vegetable, and pour in the other beaten egg.
3 Sift the remaining flour into the mixture of prawns (shrimp), vegetable and batter, and using a pair of *hashi* (Japanese chopsticks) or a fork, lightly stir the mixture. This mixture of ingredients and batter is called *tendané*, tempura base.
4 In a tempura pan or a deep-fryer heat the vegetable oil to about 160°C/320°F. Take a serving spoonful of the *tendané* and gently slide it into the oil. Fry for

2–3 minutes until slightly hardened, and add another spoonful on top. When the 2 stick together into a shape, turn over. Fry for another 2–3 minutes, turning a few times, until cooked to a light golden colour on both sides. Then turn up the heat to get the oil temperature to about 180°C/350°F. Continue to fry until golden brown, remove from the oil and drain on a wire rack or kitchen paper (paper towels). Repeat this process a further 3 times with the remaining *tendané*.
5 While the tempura is being fried, make the sauce. Put all the ingredients together in a saucepan and simmer on a moderate heat until it gets reduced to two thirds of the original volume. Remove from the heat and keep warm.
6 Pour a little sauce on each bowl of rice. Plunge each *kaki-age* in the sauce then place on top of the rice. Serve hot, garnished with a few sprigs of *mitsuba* or cress on top.

Spicy tuna tortilla roll

Maguro no tortilla maki

TOSHI SUGIURA, renowned as the best sushi chef in Los Angeles, takes pleasure in making sushi for schoolchildren in the vicinity. His intention is to introduce the art of sushi making to the next generation.

MAKES 2 ROLLS, 10–12 PIECES

2 tortillas
300g/10oz/2 cups *sumeshi* (cooked vinegared rice) (see page 152)
½ avocado, peeled and thinly sliced
½ box of cress
½ tablespoon finely chopped chives
Mexican salsa, to serve

FOR THE SPICY TUNA:
½ cup minced tuna
4 tablespoons mayonnaise
2 tablespoons *ponzu* (Japanese shoyu) or lemon juice
½ tablespoon chilli oil
pinch of *shichimi* (Japanese seven-spice chilli powder)

Mexican food is very popular in LA, and the idea of rolling sushi with tortilla instead of nori naturally came to my mind. Avocado, a frequently used ingredient in Mexican cooking, happens to go very well with spicy tuna. Children are often fussy eaters, but they or anyone who is not keen on eating raw fish will find it easy to eat this roll and will love it. TS

1 Grill the tortillas lightly on both sides, place a piece on a board, and spread half of the vinegared rice evenly over it.
2 Mix all the spicy tuna ingredients together and place half of the mixture, the avocado, cress and chives in a row across the centre, and roll in. Repeat this process once more.
3 Cut each roll into 5–6 pieces and arrange on a serving plate. Serve with some Mexican salsa in a small bowl.

Super Californian roll

Super California maki

TOSHI SUGIURA, chef/patron of Hama Sushi in LA, runs a sushi school next to his restaurant where apprentices train intensively for three months (this takes years in Japan).

MAKES 2 ROLLS, 10–12 PIECES

1 sheet of nori, cut in half crossways
400g/14oz/2 cups *sumeshi* (cooked vinegared rice) (see page 152)
2 tablespoons white sesame seeds
2 cooked king crab or snow crab claws, or 100g/3½oz canned crabmeat
½ avocado, sliced into 4 wedges
¼ cucumber, shredded
1 large cooked *kabayaki* eel (see page 19) (approximately 200g/7oz)

Californian roll is now so popular that you can eat it anywhere in the world. Sushi restaurants are now looking for something new, and at my restaurant, Hama, in Los Angeles, we tried to put it together with another American favourite, anago kabayaki *(sea eel fillet steamed and then grilled or broiled with sweet shoyu sauce). The result is a very dynamic sushi, which has become one of our most popular dishes. You can use ready-cooked* unagi *(eel)* kabayaki *available frozen in packets from Japanese food shops. TS*

1 Place a half-sheet of nori on a chopping-board, and spread about a cup of vinegared rice evenly over it. Then sprinkle evenly with 1 tablespoon of sesame seeds.
2 Line a side of a *makisu* (sushi rolling bamboo mat) with cling film (plastic wrap) and turn the rice-covered nori on to it rice-side down. Spread half the crab in a row in the centre across the nori, and add 2 avocado slices and half the cucumber along the crab, then roll the ingredients in the nori using the *makisu*. This rice-side-out roll is called *uramaki* (reverse roll). Repeat this process once more using the remaining ingredients.
3 Lightly grill (broil) the eel over a high heat, or in a microwave oven, for 30 seconds and place one half on top of each roll. Cut each roll into 5–6 pieces, and serve.

Rainbow roll sushi

Tazuna-zushi

HIDEAKI MORITA presents this beautiful rainbow sushi, though it's a fairly old-style roll in Japan. There are numerous types of sushi rolls around nowadays, both traditional and modern, and most have been created abroad by chefs using local ingredients. Californian roll, using avocado in place of raw fish, is probably the best-known 'foreign' roll, and the tempura roll, now very popular among Japanese and non-Japanese alike, was most certainly first created outside Japan.

MAKES 4 ROLLS

2 sheets of nori, each cut in half crossways into 10 x 9cm/4 x 3½in sheets
approximately 600g/1lb 5oz/3 cups *sumeshi* (cooked vinegared rice) (see page 152)
1 teaspoon wasabi paste
4 heaped tablespoons mayonnaise
1 avocado, peeled and cut lengthways into 8 slices
4 seafood sticks, each separated lengthways into 2
1 tuna steak, approximately 100g/3½oz (10 x 6cm, 4 x 2½in)
1 salmon steak, approximately 100g/3½oz (10 x 6cm, 4 x 2½in)
10cm/4in piece of cucumber, halved lengthways and de-seeded
1 fillet of ready-made *shime saba* (vinegared mackerel) or 4 slices of smoked trout 10 x 3cm (4 x 1¼in)
1–2 tablespoons vinegared ginger slices (see page 70), to serve
shoyu (Japanese soy sauce), to serve

Tazuna, meaning 'rein' in Japanese, is a twisted rope, and this sushi roll was created using ingredients with various colours to form the shape of a thick rope. It is quite a difficult sushi to roll, but your efforts will be doubly rewarded by the stunningly beautiful result. And the combination of the rich flavours of tuna, salmon and mackerel with fresh cucumber makes this sushi one of the most delicious and sumptuous dishes. HM

1 Make a *uramaki* (reverse roll) first: place a half piece of nori horizontally on a dry chopping-board, and take a quarter of the vinegared rice in your hands, then spread it over the nori evenly. Transfer the nori-rice combination, rice-side down, to a *makisu* (sushi rolling bamboo mat) covered with cling film (plastic wrap) and laid horizontally, and paste a little wasabi and 1 heaped tablespoon of mayonnaise in a line down the centre across the nori. Place 2 slices of avocado and 2 slices of seafood stick in rows on top, and roll away from you, keeping the ingredients inside with your fingers. Repeat this process 3 times more to make a total of 4 *uramaki*.
2 Slice the tuna and salmon thinly into 4 (approximately 10 x 3cm, 4 x 1¼in) pieces. Slice the cucumber lengthways into thin strips. Also thinly slice the vinegared mackerel fillet into 4 similar-sized pieces.
3 Cover the *makisu* with new cling film (plastic wrap), and place horizontally on a chopping-board. Lay the fish pieces sandwiched with cucumber diagonally to make a 20 x 8cm (8 x 3½in) rectangular shape. To do this, start from the left and lay a piece of tuna vertically but tilting

about 45° to the right. Then place 2 cucumber slices tightly next to it, then a piece of salmon, 2 cucumber slices, a piece of mackerel or smoked trout, and another piece of tuna, cucumber, salmon, cucumber and mackerel all next to each other. You should have a beautiful rectangular box (approximately 20 x 8cm, 8 x 3½in) of diagonal stripes of fish and cucumber strips, with empty triangular spaces at the top left and bottom right corners.
4 Place a *uramaki* sushi roll horizontally on the edge of the fish and cucumber rows nearest to you, and using the *makisu*, roll away from you. Press the *makisu* firmly with your hands so that the sushi is rolled tightly. Remove from the *makisu*, and repeat this process of laying the ingredients and rolling another 3 times, using the remaining ingredients.
5 Cut each roll into 5 pieces, inserting the blade in the fish and not in the cucumber, and arrange artistically on a large serving plate with some vinegared ginger slices. Serve with small individual plates and a jug of shoyu for drizzling.

Parisian seafood rice

Pari-fu gyokai maze-gohan

MINORU ODAJIMA loved Paris when he worked there in the late sixties, and every other year he goes back there for a month. This is what he came up with when I asked for a rice dish recipe with Paris in mind. Abalone is a large single-shell shellfish, a delicacy in South-east Asian countries.

SERVES 4

400g/14oz/2 cups long grain rice
300g/10oz fresh abalone (optional)
225ml/8fl oz/1 cup water
225ml/8fl oz/1 cup white wine
12 prawns (shrimp) with shells
100g/3½oz mussels (cleaned and closed
   shells discarded)
8 asparagus tips
200g/7oz *shimeji* (pictured) or
   oyster mushrooms
2 tablespoons virgin olive oil
3 tablespoons shoyu (Japanese soy sauce)
90g/3oz/½ cup white or black olives
100g/3½oz *ikura* (salted salmon caviar)
salt and pepper

For Japanese cooking we always use short grain rice, even when cooking rice with other ingredients. However, when mixed with so many ingredients as in this dish, long grain rice is more suitable as it is drier and stands up better against such varied flavours and textures. Japanese rice is best appreciated for its subtle flavour and soothing softness when freshly cooked on its own. MO

1 Wash the rice and put in a saucepan with 500ml/18fl oz/2¼ cups water, cover and bring to the boil over a high heat. Lower the heat and, still covered, simmer for 10–12 minutes or until all the water has evaporated. Leave covered to keep warm.

2 Gently cook the abalone, if using, in a mixture of the water and white wine for about 2 hours until soft. Drain and thinly slice crossways, inserting the blade slightly diagonally, into bite-sized pieces.

3 Parboil the prawns (shrimp), mussels, asparagus tips and mushrooms, each in a separate saucepan, in slightly salted boiling water. Drain and set aside.

4 Rub the inside of a wooden rice tub or a large mixing bowl with a little virgin olive oil, put in the cooked rice, then while hot, sprinkle with the remaining olive oil and 1 tablespoon of the shoyu. Lightly fold and fan the rice (do not mash) until cool and the grains are separate.

5 Season the cooked mushrooms with the remaining 2 tablespoons of shoyu, and add to the rice, together with the abalone,

if using, prawns (shrimp), mussels and asparagus tips. Season with salt and pepper to taste. Arrange a quarter of the mixed rice heaped in the centre on each of 4 individual plates and serve garnished with olives and *ikura*.

Three kinds of nori-rolled sushi

Ume-jiso, natto and oshinko-maki [v]

Maki-zushi (rolled sushi) is a sushi you make at home, rather than eat at a sushi restaurant. The traditional three colours of maki-zushi are the green of cucumber, the yellow of takuan (pickled daikon) and the red of tuna, but here are another popular three.

MAKES 6 ROLLS (2 ROLLS EACH): 36 PIECES

FOR THE SUMESHI (VINEGARED RICE):
400g/14oz/2 cups Japanese short grain rice
5cm/2in square dried *konbu* (kelp), wiped clean with damp kitchen paper (paper towels) (optional)
5 tablespoons *yonezu* (Japanese rice vinegar)
2 tablespoons granulated sugar
2 teaspoons sea salt

3 sheets of nori, each cut in half crossways into 20 x 10cm/8 x 4in sheets
2–4 *umeboshi* (salted and dried Japanese apricots), stoned
2–4 *shiso* leaves, shredded
½ packet (approximately 25g/1oz) *natto* (fermented soya beans or soybeans), finely chopped
1 spring onion (scallion), finely chopped
shoyu (Japanese soy sauce), to taste and to serve
5cm/2in piece of cucumber, quartered lengthways
10cm/4in piece of *takuan* (pickled daikon), quartered lengthways
2.5–5cm/1–2in piece of carrot, peeled and finely shredded
salt
1–2 tablespoons vinegared ginger slices (see page 70), to garnish

1 First cook the rice: wash it thoroughly in cold water, changing the water several times, until the water runs almost clear, then drain in a fine mesh strainer and leave for 1 hour. (This makes the rice absorb the right amount of water to the core.) Put the rice in a deep saucepan, and add 500ml/18fl oz/2¼ cups cold water and the *konbu*, if using, on top. Cover the pan, then bring to the boil over a high heat and let cook for 1 minute. Remove the *konbu* and discard. Reduce the heat to the lowest setting and simmer, still covered, for 13–15 minutes, or until all the water has been absorbed. Remove from the heat and leave, covered, for 5 minutes. Using a wooden spatula, turn the rice over to separate the grains so that the rice doesn't harden. Cover with a clean tea towel (to absorb the moisture), put the lid back on and set aside for 10–15 minutes.

2 Now make the *sumeshi* (vinegared rice): transfer the cooked rice into a wet wooden sushi tub or a large mixing bowl. Mix the *yonezu*, sugar and salt together and sprinkle evenly over the rice, a little at a time and using a wooden spatula, fold the vinegar mixture into the rice; do not mash. Fan the rice while folding. Leave to cool to body temperature.

3 First make the *ume-jiso* maki: place a *makisu* (sushi rolling bamboo mat) on a chopping-board horizontally, and place a half-sheet of nori on top. Scoop a handful of the *sumeshi* into your hands and shape into a thick log. Place it across the nori, and using your fingers spread the rice evenly over the nori, leaving 1cm/½in margin at the end farthest from you. Close the gaps with some more rice. Put 1–2 pieces of *umeboshi* flesh in a row along the centre of the nori and place half the shredded *shiso* leaves on top. Roll away from you, keeping the ingredients firmly inside with your fingers. Remove from the *makisu* and set aside. Repeat this process to make another roll.

4 For the *natto maki*: mix the finely chopped *natto* and the spring onions (scallions), and lightly season with salt and a little shoyu. Thickly slice off the white part from the cucumber and discard. Finely shred the green side of the cucumber. Spread rice on a half-sheet of nori as for step 3 above. Put half the *natto* mixture in a narrow line along the centre of the rice and add half the cucumber shreds along the *natto* mixture. Roll as before, and repeat this process for another roll.

5 For the *oshinko maki*: trim the *takuan* quarters into about 1cm/½in square cylinders. Make a rice bed on a nori, as before, and place 2 *takuan* cylinders in a row in the centre of the rice. Put half the carrot shreds along the *takuan*, and roll, as before. Repeat this process.

6 Cut across each nori roll into 6 pieces and serve garnished with vinegared ginger and shoyu in a small plate.

Sea bream boxed sushi

Kodai no oshi-zushi

YUICHI OYAMA, executive chef at Yoshino Sushi in Osaka, shows here how to make one example of this popular dish in Japan. In many ways Tokyo and Osaka are two contrasting cities, but nowhere is it more evident than in their culinary difference. Osaka's down-to-earth approach to food is visible in the number of restaurants, particularly in the so-called 'Eat-till-bankrupt' area. While finger sushi with a slice of raw fish on top is a relatively recent Tokyo creation, many other sushi come from Osaka. *Hako-zushi* (boxed sushi) is typical.

MAKES 1 BOX

1 small red sea bream (pictured) fillet
    (approximately 150g/5½oz)
yonezu (Japanese rice vinegar), to marinate
300g/10oz/2 cups *sumeshi* (cooked
    vinegared rice) (see page 152)
1 sheet of nori, cut to the size of the sushi box
salt
watercress, lime wedges and shoyu, to serve

Hako-zushi is called 'kaiseki within two and a half inches' because it contains, within an 8cm (3½in) square box, three types of the finest pressed sushi: sea bream, kokera-zushi (egg omelette, shiitake and prawns/shrimp) and anago (sea eel). This sushi was created by the third generation of the owners of Yoshino Sushi in 1890, and used to be so popular that it was the main sushi at all sushi restaurants in Osaka until the 1950s. Here I am delighted to introduce one of our legendary hako-zushi. YO

1 Start making this sushi the day before serving. Lightly salt the sea bream fillet and leave for 1 hour. Wash off the salt under running water, pat dry with kitchen paper (paper towels) and then marinate in rice vinegar to cover for 10–15 minutes until the surface of the fish turns milky white. Remove from the vinegar and pat dry with kitchen paper (paper towels). Wrap in cling film (plastic wrap) and leave chilled in the refrigerator overnight.
2 Cut the firmed sea bream horizontally into 4 thin slices, and then slice the skin-side piece lengthways into 3 pieces. In a wooden sushi mould (approximately 8cm/3½in square), or a similar-sized

plastic container lined with a large piece of cling film (plastic wrap) (5–6cm/2–2½in should overlap the edges), lay the two most red-coloured skin pieces, skin-side down, along two opposite sides. Fill the gap with the other white pieces. (Discard the remaining skin-side piece, or simply eat it with some vinegared rice.)
3 Put some vinegared rice on top of the fish to fill half of the box from the bottom, and lay the cut nori on top. Add the remaining rice to fill the box, put on the wooden lid and press hard. If using a plastic container, cover the rice with cling film (plastic wrap) and place a hard board on top, cut to fit inside the container. Put a weight (use a book of similar size) on the hard board, and press with your hands, or it can be left pressed for up to 24 hours until serving.
4 When serving, remove the sushi from the wooden box or the cling film (plastic wrap), place fish-side up, and then carefully cut into bite-sized square blocks. Arrange artistically on a large serving platter, garnished with watercress and lime wedges, and serve with a little shoyu in a small dish.

Rice cooked in soup with quail

Uzura zousui

EIICHI TAKAHASHI, the fourteenth generation of the original owner/chef, shows how to make Hyotei's quail *zousui*. Hyotei, an old house built in the property of the Nanzenji temple in Kyoto, started as a teahouse in 1837 to attract worshippers on their way home, and prospered to become one of the most established *ryotei* (old-style *kaiseki* restaurant) patronized by wealthy merchants from Osaka. They used to call very early in the morning on their way home after a night partying and debauchery at nearby geisha houses. Although not open that early, the *ryotei* was obliged to feed them something as they were good, regular customers. This is how the tradition of Hyotei's *asa-gayu* (morning rice gruel) started, and it is still served, now to the general public, for brunch in summer. In winter the more sumptuous *zousui*, rice cooked in soup, is served.

SERVES 4

2 quails, filleted and skinned

2 tablespoons dark shoyu (Japanese
    soy sauce)

400g/14oz/2 cups cold cooked rice

500ml/18fl oz/2¼ cups chicken stock (broth)

500ml/18fl oz/2¼ cups dashi (see page 56)

1 tablespoon light shoyu (Japanese
    soy sauce)

1 bunch of *mitsuba* (pictured) or chives,
    chopped into 1.5cm/¾in long pieces

salt

We started serving asa-gayu in the 1870s, so it has over 100 years' history. The secret of this speciality lies in its Yoshino kuzu-an (thickened dashi soup) poured over the rice gruel, which adds flavour to a simple gruel, as well as making it gentler to the stomach after a night of heavy drinking. Uzura-gayu (though it's zousui, we still call it uzura-gayu as opposed to asa-gayu) has more bite as it contains quail meat, and it uses leftover cold rice. ET

1 Dice the quail meat into 5mm/ ¼in square pieces and sprinkle with the dark shoyu. Leave to marinate for at least 10 minutes: this is to reduce the strong smell of the bird.

2 Put the rice in a fine sieve and wash under running water to separate each grain.

3 Put the chicken stock (broth) and dashi together in a saucepan and bring to the boil on a high heat. Add the washed rice, bring back to the boil, and simmer on a low heat for about 5 minutes. Add the quail meat and season with the light shoyu and a pinch of salt. When the rice becomes puffed up and the soup starts thickening, add the *mitsuba* or chives and immediately remove from the heat. Mix well and divide among 4 individual rice bowls.

Makunouchi bento with Koya-dofu, egg and vegetables

Makunouchi bento [v]

Makunouchi literally means 'within the curtain' at theatres and makunouchi bento, or lunch box, is normally eaten at the interval, hence the name. This is the most elaborate of many types of bento and is traditionally served in a segmented lacquer box. It normally consists of rice, fried food, grilled (broiled) food, simmered food, salad, pickles and sometimes fruits, and is accompanied by sake, beer and/or miso soup.

MAKES 2 BOXES

200g/7oz/1 cup Japanese short grain rice
sesame seeds, lightly roasted, for sprinkling
2 large dried shiitake, soaked in
    water overnight
2 cakes *Koya-dofu* (freeze-dried tofu)
1 tablespoon shoyu (Japanese soy sauce)
1 tablespoon mirin
2 teaspoons granulated sugar

TO SERVE:
pickles
vegetable tempura (see page 60),
    2–3 per box
10–12 cooked gingko nuts (pictured)
tamago-yaki (egg omelette) (see page 139),
    2 per box
carrot, cut into flower shapes and cooked
sake or miso soup

1 Cook the rice following the method on page 152 (Three kinds of nori-rolled sushi), and press into flower or small barrel shapes. Sprinkle a few sesame seeds on top.
2 Drain the shiitake, retaining the liquid, cut off the stems and discard. Soak the *Koya-dofu* in water for 5 minutes until softened, drain and squeeze out excess water. Put about 100ml/3½fl oz/scant ½ cup liquid from the shiitake soaking water in a flat saucepan, bring to the boil and season with the shoyu, mirin and sugar. Add the shiitake and *Koya-dofu* cakes and simmer for 7–8 minutes until cooked and the flavour is absorbed. Drain and set aside.
3 In a *makunouchi bento*, arrange the rice with pickles, *Koya-dofu* with shiitake, vegetable tempura with gingko nuts, egg omelette with carrot flowers on top, and serve with sake or a bowl of miso soup.

Bento with minced meat and scrambled eggs

Soboro bento

Soboro is a term to describe food that is fluffy in texture, such as ground cooked white fish. However, minced meat cooked in the same way is also called soboro, *although the effect with meat is not exactly the same. This lunch box, with rice and chicken* soboro, *and scrambled eggs on top is very easy to make, with contrasting colours that make it attractive. The rice is cooked with a little shoyu, which makes the colour slightly dark – this coloured rice is called* cha-meshi, *tea rice, as the colour resembles that of tea. Eat hot or cold.*

SERVES 4

FOR THE RICE:

400g/14oz/2 cups Japanese short grain rice

1 teaspoon granulated sugar

1 tablespoon shoyu (Japanese soy sauce)

½ teaspoon salt

1 tablespoon sake

oil, for frying

200g/7oz minced chicken

3 tablespoons sake

2 tablespoons shoyu (Japanese soy sauce)

4 tablespoons granulated sugar

3 large eggs, beaten

⅔ teaspoon salt

1–2 tablespoons vinegared ginger slices (see page 70), shredded

12 mangetouts, cooked and shredded

1 Wash the rice thoroughly in cold water, changing the water several times, until the water runs clear, then drain and leave for 30 minutes. Put in a deep saucepan and add 500ml/18fl oz/2¼ cups water together with the sugar, shoyu, salt and sake. Cover the pan and bring to the boil over a high heat. Lower the heat to the lowest setting, simmer for 13–15 minutes or until all the water has been absorbed, and then leave, still covered, for 5 minutes. Using a wooden spatula, turn the rice over to separate the grains so that the rice doesn't harden into the shape of the pan. Cover with a clean tea towel, put the lid back on and set aside for 10–15 minutes.

2 Heat a frying-pan (skillet), add a little oil, and spread evenly over the base. Add the minced chicken together with the sake, shoyu and 1 tablespoon each of sugar and water, and cook for 4–5 minutes, stirring all the time with a fork until the meat is separated into granules. Remove from the heat and set aside.

3 Make sweet scrambled eggs with the beaten eggs, remaining sugar and ⅔ teaspoon salt, stirring all the time with a fork into very fine granules.

4 Arrange a quarter of the cooked rice in each of 4 individual lunch boxes or noodle bowls, and cover half the rice surface in each with a quarter of the meat *soboro* and the other half with a quarter of the scrambled eggs. Arrange some shredded vinegared ginger in the centre and a quarter of the shredded mangetouts in between the soboro and scrambled eggs. Serve hot or cold.

Vegetarian mixed sushi

Chirashi-zushi [v]

There are two types of chirashi-zushi, *meaning 'scattered sushi': vinegared rice mixed with several raw and/or cooked ingredients; and a rice bowl with several kinds of sashimi on top. The former is a very popular family or party dish, suitable for feeding a large number of people. The beauty of this dish is that you can use almost anything to mix with the rice, as long as you choose a good combination of colours. For non-vegetarians use smoked fish such as salmon, trout or eel, or even ham, sausages or minced meat* soboro *(see page 158).*

SERVES 4–8

FOR THE *SUMESHI* (VINEGARED RICE):
400g/14oz/2 cups Japanese short grain rice
5cm/2in square dried *konbu* (kelp), wiped clean with damp kitchen paper (paper towels) (optional)
5 tablespoons *yonezu* (Japanese rice vinegar)
2 tablespoons granulated sugar
2 teaspoons sea salt

4–5 dried shiitake, soaked in plenty of water overnight
4½ tablespoons shoyu (Japanese soy sauce)
3 tablespoons mirin
2 tablespoons granulated sugar
1 small carrot, peeled and shredded into matchstick pieces
7g/¼oz *kanpyo* (dried gourd ribbon) (optional)
50g/1¾oz mangetouts, trimmed
2 tablespoons white sesame seeds
vegetable oil, for oiling
2 eggs, beaten
½ nori sheet, shredded
5cm/2in piece of *takuan* (pickled daikon), shredded into matchstick pieces, or any vegetable pickles sold in packets at Japanese supermarkets
salt

1 Cook the rice and make into *sumeshi* (vinegared rice) by following the method on page 152 (Three kinds of nori-rolled sushi) and set aside.

2 Drain the soaked shiitake, retaining the liquid, remove the stems and discard. Thinly slice the shiitake caps, inserting the blade diagonally, into fine shreds. Put about 100ml/3½fl oz/scant ½ cup of the shiitake soaking liquid in a small saucepan, bring to the boil over a high heat and stir in 1½ tablespoons shoyu, 1 tablespoon mirin and 2 teaspoons sugar. Add the shredded shiitake and simmer on a moderate heat for 10 minutes or until the liquid is reduced to half. Leave to cool.

3 Cook the carrot shreds in lightly salted water for 2 minutes, drain and then cook in the same way as shiitake (using 100ml/ 3½fl oz/scant ½ cup of the shiitake soaking liquid seasoned with 1½ tablespoons shoyu, 1 tablespoon mirin and 2 teaspoons sugar). Set aside to cool.

4 Rub salt on the wet *kanpyo*, if using, and wash in water squeezing in your hands, and cook in boiling water to cover the *kanpyo* for about 10 minutes or until the *kanpyo* becomes almost transparent. Drain, and cut into 2.5cm/1in long strips. Cook in the same way as the shiitake and carrot and set aside.

5 Cook the mangetouts in lightly salted boiling water for 1–2 minutes until cooked but still crunchy, drain and put under cold running water (this maintains their bright green colour). Pat dry with kitchen paper (paper towels) and cut each piece crossways diagonally into 2 diamond-shaped pieces. Toss the sesame seeds in a heated dry saucepan over a high heat until the seeds start popping up.

6 Heat a frying-pan (skillet) on a high heat and spread a little vegetable oil evenly over the base. Rub the base with kitchen paper (paper towels) to make sure the surface is smooth and that the paper absorbs excess oil. Lower the heat, add half the beaten egg mixed with a pinch of salt, and by tilting the pan quickly spread the egg evenly over the base. When the egg is hardened, turn out on to a chopping-board. Repeat this process to make another egg sheet, and cut both sheets into about 5cm/2in long thin shreds.

7 Add the cooked shiitake, carrot, *kanpyo*, mangetouts and the *takuan* into the rice and using a wooden spatula, mix well (do not mash). Sprinkle with the sesame seeds and place the egg shreds on top. Sprinkle it with the nori shreds and serve either in individual plates or in a wooden sushi tub or a serving plate.

Mackerel sushi

Battera

HISASHI TAOKA is a fish merchant and proprietor of Kiku restaurant, London. *Battera*, also known as *saba-zushi*, is the most popular pressed sushi and very easy to make. You can make pressed sushi with any other cured fish, such as sea bream, trout and salmon. For trout and salmon use smoked instead of curing fresh yourself. Mackerel, salted and vinegared as in this dish, can be eaten on its own with hot rice. Here's the authentic *battera*, a speciality from Kyoto.

SERVES 4

2 mackerel fillets (approximately
    200g/7oz each)
225ml/8fl oz/1 cup vinegar
1 tablespoon granulated sugar
2 teaspoons wasabi paste
640g/1lb 8oz/3 cups *sumeshi* (cooked
    vinegared rice) (see page 152)
1–2 tablespoons vinegared ginger slices
    (see page 70), to garnish
2 pieces (10 x 20cm/4 x 8in) *battera konbu*
    (kelp filament) (optional)
2 tablespoons rice vinegar
2 tablespoons water
salt

Mackerel is a wonderful fish indeed: it's beautiful to look at, nutritious, cheap and of course delicious. For sushi, obviously you must use very fresh fish, particularly with mackerel as it goes off very quickly, so quickly that in Japan they say it goes off even while still alive. The battera konbu, *transparent kelp filament, is used to enhance the beautiful silver pattern of the mackerel. HT*

1 In a flat, slightly deep dish, scatter plenty of salt to cover the base well, and lay the mackerel fillets, side by side, flesh-side down. Completely cover the fish with more salt, and leave salted in the refrigerator overnight to draw off its water.
2 Wash the fillets under running water, pat dry with kitchen paper (paper towels) and place, skin-side down, on a chopping-board. Using tweezers, carefully remove all bones; do not miss the small bones hidden under the main spine. Trim off all blood clots, and using your fingers, carefully remove the outer filament from the skin, leaving the shiny silver stripes intact.
3 Mix the vinegar and sugar and add the fish for 10–20 minutes. Drain and pat dry with kitchen paper (paper towels).
4 Return the fillets, skin-side down, to a chopping-board, and inserting the blade of a knife parallel with the board, slice off half the thickness of the thick meat from the tail end to the head. Cut the sliced meat crossways into the ratio of 7 (head end) and 3 (tail). Make shallow, criss-cross slits on the skin.
5 Place a damp cloth on a *makisu* (sushi rolling bamboo mat). Lay a fillet, skin-side down, across it and then put the bigger slice of the meat towards the tail end of the fillet and the smallest on the thick cavity part. Make the fish into a rectangle.
6 Smear a tiny amount of the wasabi paste across the centre. Take half the sushi rice in both hands, and make into a rectangular log shape. Put the rice log across the mackerel, and roll the sushi so the fish and rice stick together. Push the sushi rice in at both edges to make a neat log shape. Remove from the cloth and *makisu*, and slice crossways into pieces about 1.5cm/¾in thick. Make another mackerel and rice log shape in the same way. Arrange a quarter of the sushi on each of the 4 individual plates, and serve garnished with vinegared ginger.
7 If using *konbu*, soak in hot water for 10 minutes, simmer in the rice vinegar and water for 5 minutes, wrap the sushi and trim.

9

Noodles

Cold seafood udon

Umi no sachi no udon pasta

MINORU ODAJIMA, at his restaurant in Sangen-jaya, Tokyo, serves all diners with a set menu he humbly calls *kappo*, which changes monthly. *Kappo*, literally meaning 'cutting and cooking', is an old term denoting fresh cooking in front of the diner: a sort of instant *mini-kaiseki* (formal multi-course meal). The menu consists of an hors d'oeuvre, a small dish, starter, soup, sashimi, grilled (broiled) fish, a Western dish (meat), miso soup, noodle and pickled vegetables, and a dessert. This simple udon noodle dish is served at Odajima's restaurant, not as the noodle dish but as a small starter to settle the diner's stomach before the main courses.

SERVES 4

1 squid, skinned and cleaned
8 medium prawns (shrimp)
8 mussels
100g/3½oz clams
4 sea urchins
1 small head of broccoli, separated
   into small florets
4 asparagus stalks
250–300g/9–10oz dried udon noodles
olive oil, for drizzling
salt and pepper

As it is very thick, udon is not normally eaten cold – so it needs simmering in a strong soup to give it flavour. For this dish udon is treated like pasta, and since the dishes to follow are rich in flavour, the plain udon with its subtle flavour of seafood is a light yet gently filling dish in preparation for the wines to come. This recipe however is written for a more substantial dish and not as the starter that I serve at my restaurant. MO

1 Clean all the seafood and parboil each separately in slightly salted boiling water. Cut the squid into thin rings.
2 Cook the vegetables separately in slightly salted boiling water. Drain. Cut each asparagus stalk diagonally into 4–5 pieces.
3 Cook the udon in boiling water for the time specified on the packet – normally 10–13 minutes. Do not overcook. Drain and immediately place under running water to wash off the starch. Drain again.

4 Arrange a quarter of the washed and cold udon in each of 4 pasta dishes, and scatter a quarter of each type of seafood on top. Add a quarter of each of the vegetables, and sprinkle with salt and pepper, and a little olive oil. Serve cold.

Udon noodle hotpot

Udon-suki

HISASHI TAOKA, the patron of Kiku restaurant, Mayfair, London, demonstrates one of his *nabe-mono* (pot dishes) here. The Japanese idea of good food is to eat freshly made dishes straight from the chef, or from the pot. At good restaurants there are always counter seats where you see your sushi, tempura or *tonkatsu* cooked and served directly.

The beauty of nabe-mono *is that you are not restricted to certain ingredients as long as you have a main source of protein such as meat, fish or tofu and various vegetables. The most well-known* nabe-mono *are probably* sukiyaki *and* shabu-shabu, *in both of which the main ingredient is thinly sliced beef. If you change the main ingredient to fish, for example monkfish, cooked with more or less the same kinds of vegetables, then it is known as* anko nabe. *With chicken it becomes* tori-suki. *This* udon-suki *is a gorgeous* udon nabe *with chicken, fish and tofu, and various vegetables. Use good chicken stock (broth) or vegetable stock (broth) for vegetarians, and any vegetables you may have to hand. HT*

SERVES 4

8 hakusai (Chinese leaves)
1 bunch of *mitsuba* or 150g/5oz spinach
1 medium carrot
10cm/4in piece of daikon
200g/7oz salmon (with skin)
200g/7oz any white fish such as cod, haddock or halibut (with skin)
200g/7oz chicken meat, cut into bite-sized pieces
90g/3oz *shimeji* or shiitake mushrooms, trimmed
90g/3oz *enoki* mushrooms (pictured), trimmed
1 bunch of spring onions (scallions), cut into 5cm/2in pieces
1 cake tofu, cut into 8 cubes
8–12 clams in their shells (optional)
400g/14oz cooked udon noodles
momiji-fu (maple-shaped fu) (optional)
yuzu or lemon wedges, to serve

FOR THE SOUP:

700ml/1¼ pints/generous 3 cups dashi (see page 56)
3 tablespoons light shoyu (Japanese soy sauce)
2½ tablespoons mirin
1 tablespoon sake

1 Boil the hakusai in lightly salted boiling water over a high heat for 30 seconds, drain and immediately put under running water. Plunge the *mitsuba* or spinach into boiling water and immediately drain. Cut the carrot and daikon into 8 sticks, 5mm/¼in square, with both the length and width the same as the white part of the hakusai. Boil them separately in lightly salted boiling water over a high heat for 1 minute and drain.

2 Place a hakusai leaf, right-side up, on a chopping-board, place a piece of carrot, a piece of daikon, and one eighth of the *mitsuba* or spinach across the white, thickest end, and roll up the leaf using a *makisu* (sushi rolling bamboo mat). Repeat this process using the remaining ingredients to make 7 more hakusai rolls. Cut each roll into 2 or 3 cylinders about 5cm/2in long and set aside.

3 Blanch the salmon, white fish and chicken separately in boiling water for 1 minute, drain and immediately put into ice-cold water. Pat dry with kitchen paper (paper towels) and cut the salmon and white fish into bite-sized pieces with skin.

4 Mix the soup ingredients in a saucepan and bring to the boil over a high heat. Remove from the heat and keep warm.

5 Arrange about a quarter of the hakusai rolls, salmon, white fish, chicken, *shimeji* or shiitake, *enoki*, spring onions (scallions), tofu, clams, if using, cooked udon and *momiji-fu*, if using, decoratively in a *donabe* (earthenware pot), and pour over the soup. Place on a high heat, bring to the boil and check the seasoning. Transfer the pot on to a portable fire or a hot plate on the table. Diners help themselves from the pot and sprinkle *yuzu* or lemon juice on top and eat from their individual bowl. Add more ingredients to the pot as they eat.

Cold ramen with ham, egg and cucumber

Hiyashi chuka

Although hot soup ramen is available throughout the year, cold ramen becomes a popular choice in the hot, humid Japanese summer. Various ingredients such as chashu *(long simmered pork), ham, cucumber and egg are placed on top of cold ramen, and eaten with a refreshingly sour* taré *(sweet shoyu sauce). Ramen, toppings and sauce can be served separately and the ramen can be dipped in the sauce.*

SERVES 4

FOR THE *TARÉ* SAUCE:
225ml/8 fl oz/1 cup chicken stock (broth)
7 tablespoons shoyu (Japanese soy sauce)
7 tablespoons vinegar
7 tablespoons granulated sugar
1 tablespoon root ginger juice
2 tablespoons sesame oil

400g/14oz dried ramen noodles
4 dried shiitake, soaked in
   water overnight
2 tablespoons shoyu (Japanese soy sauce)
1 tablespoon granulated sugar
1 tablespoon mirin
vegetable oil, for oiling
2 eggs, beaten
½ cucumber, de-seeded and finely shredded
200g/7oz ham, shredded
10g/⅓oz *ito-kanten* (agar-agar
   threads) (optional)
salt

1 Mix all the *taré* sauce ingredients in a mixing bowl, stirring well until the sugar has dissolved, and leave to stand in the refrigerator overnight. This is to reduce the sharpness of the vinegar flavour.

2 Boil plenty of water in a large saucepan, add the noodles and bring back to the boil. Lower the heat slightly, adjusting to avoid the water boiling over while keeping at the highest possible heat, and cook for the time suggested on the packet – usually 4–5 minutes. Drain and immediately place under running water to wash away the starch.

3 Drain the soaked shiitake, retaining the liquid, and chop into fine shreds. Put about 110ml/4fl oz/½ cup of the shiitake soaking liquid in a saucepan and bring to the boil over a high heat. Lower the heat and add the shoyu, sugar and mirin. Add the shiitake and simmer in the sauce for 7–8 minutes until the liquid is reduced by half. Leave to cool in the sauce.

4 Heat a frying-pan (skillet) over a high heat, add a little vegetable oil, tilting the pan so that the oil spreads evenly over the base, then wipe away excess oil with kitchen paper (paper towels). Add a pinch of salt to the beaten eggs and mix well. Pour half of the beaten eggs into the frying-pan (skillet), tilting the pan so that the egg spreads evenly over the base, and cook for 30 seconds until the surface of the egg becomes dry. Turn out onto a chopping-board. Repeat this process to make another sheet of egg. Finely cut the egg sheets into 5–6cm/2–2½in long thin shreds.

5 Plunge the cooked noodles into ice-cold water and drain. Divide among 4 individual plates, and arrange a quarter each of the shiitake, egg, cucumber, ham and *ito-kanten*, if using, on top of the ramen. Pour the *taré* sauce over and serve cold.

Ramen with mushrooms

Kinoko ramen [v]

Ramen is a Chinese-style noodle, and its difference from other Japanese noodles, such as udon and soba, lies in its springiness. It is the result of adding what Japanese call kansui, *alkali water, to wheat flour and sometimes eggs. Ramen is normally eaten with a variety of ingredients including meat, and as ramen is more sumptuous it is now overtaking udon and soba in popularity in Japan. The ramen phenomenon is now spreading fast in the West, too. Here's a delicious vegetarian ramen using shiitake soaking liquid. For non-vegetarians you could use strong chicken stock (broth) instead.*

SERVES 4

1 bunch of *shimeji* mushrooms, trimmed
1 bunch of *enoki* mushrooms, trimmed
4–6 fresh shiitake, trimmed, or dried shiitake
   soaked in water for 1 hour
30g/1oz dried *wakame* (young seaweed) or
   150g/5½oz young spinach leaves
4 portions (approximately 100g/3½oz) dried
   ramen noodles
100–150g/3½–5½oz cooked *zenmai*
   (Japanese mountain vegetables) (optional)
vegetable oil, for stir-frying
100g/3½oz *nameko* mushrooms (optional)
salt and pepper

FOR THE SOUP:

1.1 litres/2 pints/5 cups shiitake
   soaking liquid
1.5cm/ ¾ in root ginger, peeled
   and crushed
2 cloves garlic, peeled and crushed
6 tablespoons shoyu (Japanese soy sauce)
salt and pepper

1 Break the *shimeji* and *enoki* clumps into individual pieces. Cut the *enoki* in half if large and the shiitake into fine shreds. If using dried shiitake, retain the liquid.

2 Soak the dried *wakame* in water for 10 minutes or until fully expanded and, if large, cut into bite-sized pieces. If using spinach, cook in lightly salted boiling water for 1 minute, drain and immediately place under running water to bring out its green colour. Squeeze out excess water with your hands and cut into bite-sized pieces.

3 Boil plenty of water in a large saucepan, add the noodles and bring back to the boil. Lower the heat slightly, adjusting to avoid the water boiling over while keeping at the highest possible heat, and cook for the time suggested on the packet – usually 4–5 minutes. Drain and immediately place under running water to wash away the starch.

4 To make the soup, heat the shiitake soaking liquid together with the ginger and garlic in a saucepan, and simmer over a moderate heat for 5 minutes. Discard the ginger and garlic, and add the shoyu. Add the cooked noodles just to warm up and check the seasoning by adding salt and pepper to taste.

5 Quickly stir-fry the *shimeji*, *enoki*, shiitake and *zenmai*, if using, together in a frying-pan (skillet) with a little oil until all the mushrooms are just soft. Season with salt and pepper.

6 Divide the noodles and soup among 4 individual noodle bowls and arrange a quarter of the stir-fried mushrooms, *nameko* and vegetables on top. Serve hot.

Cold soba with nori and shiitake

Shiitake zaru soba [v]

The traditional zaru soba *is a simple affair: just soba noodles eaten dipped in a dashi-based sauce with the accompanying condiments of shredded nori, chopped spring onions (scallions) and wasabi. For vegetarians use the liquid in which the dried shiitake were soaked.*

SERVES 4

400g/14oz dried soba noodles
6–8 dried shiitake, soaked overnight in
    700ml/1¼ pints/generous 3 cups water
8 tablespoons shoyu (Japanese soy sauce)
4 tablespoons mirin
1 tablespoon granulated sugar
½ sheet of nori, lightly toasted and cut into
    2.5cm/1in shreds
2 spring onions (scallions), finely chopped
2 teaspoons wasabi paste

1 Boil plenty of water in a large saucepan, add the noodles and bring back to the boil. Lower the heat slightly and cook for 5–6 minutes (see packet). Drain and rinse.
2 Squeeze the shiitake, keep the liquid, and chop into fine shreds. Put 110ml/4fl oz/½ cup of the liquid in a saucepan and bring to the boil over a high heat. Lower the heat and add 2 tablespoons of the shoyu, 1 tablespoon of the mirin, the sugar and the shiitake. Simmer for about 8 minutes and cool.

3 For the dipping sauce, add the remaining shoyu, mirin and shiitake liquid to the pan, bring to the boil, and remove from the heat. Place in 4 teacups.
4 Refresh the noodles under cold running water for a second, and arrange a quarter on each of 4 bamboo trays or plates. Sprinkle the nori shreds on top. Serve with small plates of the spring onions (scallions) and wasabi paste and the sauce. Diners dip the noodles into their shiitake sauce.

Pot-cooked udon noodle

Nabeyaki udon

Because udon is a thick noodle, it is best cooked in soup so it absorbs the flavour of the soup well. This pot-cooked noodle dish makes an ideal supper for cold winter months.

MAKES 2 POTS

100g/3½oz spinach
200g/7oz dried udon noodles
2 prawn (shrimp) tempura (see page 86)
2–4 fresh shiitake, stems cut off
2 slices of *kamaboko* (fish paste) (optional)
2 eggs

FOR THE SOUP:
560ml/1 pint/2½ cups dashi (see page 56)
½ teaspoon sea salt
2 tablespoons shoyu (Japanese soy sauce)
2 tablespoons mirin

1 Blanch the spinach in lightly salted boiling water for 30 seconds, drain and immediately put under running water. Drain again and set aside.
2 Boil plenty of water in a large saucepan, add the noodles and bring back to the boil. Lower the heat slightly so it does not boil over, and cook for the time suggested on the packet – usually 10–13 minutes. Drain and immediately place under running water to wash away the starch. Drain and divide into 2 individual *donabe* (earthenware pots) or put them all in a saucepan.

3 Place a prawn (shrimp) tempura, half the spinach, 1–2 shiitake and 1–2 slices of *kamaboko*, if using, on top of the noodles in the 2 individual pots, or place all the ingredients on top of the noodles in the saucepan, and then pour over the soup. Crack an egg into each of the pots, or both eggs into the saucepan, cover with a lid and bring back to the boil over a high heat. Lower the heat and simmer for 5–6 minutes or until the egg is cooked. Serve hot.

Soup soba with mountain vegetables

Sansai soba [v]

Japan is a mountainous country, and numerous varieties of sansai, *wild mountain vegetables, are picked all over Japan and used in daily cooking.* Sansai *such as bracken, fern and horsetail are now mass cultivated and available in packets at Japanese supermarkets.*

SERVES 4

400g/14oz dried soba noodles
12 mangetouts
100g/3½oz *shimeji* mushrooms (optional)
300g/10oz cooked *sansai* (pre-packaged
   mountain vegetables or any vegetables)

FOR THE SOUP:

1.1 litres/2 pints/5 cups vegetable stock (broth)
4 tablespoons shoyu (Japanese soy sauce)
2 tablespoons mirin
⅔ teaspoon sea salt

1 Boil plenty of water in a large saucepan, add the noodles and bring back to the boil. Lower the heat slightly to avoid the water overboiling while keeping at the highest heat, and cook for 5–6 minutes (see packet). Drain and immediately wash away the starch under running water.
2 Boil the mangetouts in lightly salted boiling water for 1 minute. Drain.
3 Mix all the soup ingredients except the salt in a saucepan, bring to the boil and lower the heat to a simmer. Check the seasoning and, if using plain boiled

sansai, add a pinch of salt. If salted *sansai* is used, do not. Add the *shimeji*, if using, and cook for 2–3 minutes. Remove from the soup and keep warm.
4 Put the *sansai* in a saucepan, add a ladle of the hot soup and heat up on a moderate heat. Remove and keep warm.
5 Plunge the cooked noodles into boiling water to refresh and drain. Divide into 4 bowls. Arrange a quarter of the *sansai* with the juice and *shimeji* on top and pour the soup over most of the ingredients. Serve hot, garnished with mangetouts.

Udon in egg soup

Kakitama udon

Udon is a thick wheat noodle and is normally eaten in hot soup. Kakitama *is a scrambled egg in soup, which in this case is thickened dashi soup. It's a rich, nutritious noodle dish, so it makes a very good lunch or snack after school or late night for growing youngsters.*

SERVES 4

400g/14oz dried udon noodles
3 tablespoons *katakuriko* (potato starch) or
   5 tablespoons cornflour (cornstarch)
4 eggs, beaten
chopped spring onions (scallions), to garnish

FOR THE SOUP

1.1 litres/2 pints/5 cups dashi (see page 56)
¾ teaspoon sea salt
4 tablespoons shoyu (Japanese soy sauce)
3 tablespoons mirin

1 Boil plenty of water in a large saucepan, add the noodles and bring back to the boil. Lower the heat slightly to avoid boiling over while keeping at the highest possible heat, and cook for the time suggested on the packet – 10–13 minutes. Drain and immediately place under running water to wash away the starch.
2 Mix all the ingredients for the soup in a large saucepan and bring to the boil. Lower the heat and slowly add the *katakuriko* or cornflour (cornstarch), first dissolved in water of its own quantity,

stirring all the time. The soup should be lightly thickened.
3 Pour the beaten egg slowly into the thickened soup, cooking for 2–3 minutes over a moderate heat until the egg rises to the surface. Lightly stir to break the egg and remove from the heat.
4 To warm up the cooked udon noodles, plunge them into boiling water, drain and then divide among 4 noodle bowls. Pour a quarter of the soup over each. Serve hot, garnished with finely chopped spring onions (scallions).

Sea bream soup somen

Tai nyumen

EIICHI TAKAHASHI of the legendary Hyotei, in Kyoto, here cooks somen, very fine wheat noodles, in a soup with a piece of *tai* (sea bream) on top. In Japan *tai* is often grilled (broiled) whole for celebratory meals such as wedding receptions and childbirth or graduation parties, due to its beautiful shape and the joyous red colour. The combination of the white of the somen and the red of sea bream makes this one of the most beautiful dishes.

SERVES 4

1 sea bream (preferably red) approximately
    500g/1⅛lb, scaled
4 stalks *mitsuba* or watercress
4 portions (approximately 350g/12oz) fine
    somen noodles
salt

FOR THE SOUP:

1 litre/1¾ pints/4½ cups water
5cm/2in square dried *konbu* (kelp)
3 tablespoons sake
3 tablespoons shoyu (Japanese soy sauce)
1 teaspoon sea salt

thread, to tie noodles

Nyumen, *hot soup noodle, is an established dish as it is very versatile in a* kaiseki *course. It can be served as a clear soup at the beginning, a 'mouth-rest' to cleanse the pallet in the middle, a simmered dish or a substitute for rice at the end. Somen is a very delicate noodle, so it must never be overcooked, and it needs a good, strong soup to go with it. ET*

1 Fillet the sea bream, keeping the head and bone to make the stock, and cut each fillet into two neat pieces, the size of a standard playing card, to fit in the soup bowls. Thread 2 skewers through each fish slice, sprinkle with a little salt and then grill (broil) over a direct heat, skin side first, for 3–4 minutes until golden brown. Turn over and grill the other side for 3–4 minutes until golden brown and the inside is well cooked.
2 Make the fish bone stock (broth): sprinkle salt over the fish carcass, and leave to stand for 10–15 minutes, then pour over boiling water. Place the fish carcass with the 1 litre/1¾ pints/4¼ cups water and the *konbu* in a saucepan, bring to just below boiling point and discard the *konbu*. Lower the heat and simmer for 20 minutes. Continuously skim off the scum that rises to the surface, and season with the sake, shoyu and salt. Remove from the heat and keep warm.
3 Plunge the *mitsuba* or watercress in boiling water and immediately place under running water. Drain and pat dry with kitchen paper (paper towels). Cut neatly into about 5cm/2in long pieces.
4 Tightly tie one end of each bunch of somen with a strong thread, and cook in plenty of boiling water on a high heat for 1–3 minutes according to the packet instructions of the somen you are using. Add a little water each time it comes to the boil. Gently stir while cooking to prevent the somen from sticking together. Drain, and rinse off the outer starch in cold water. Drain again then, holding the tied end out of the water (uncooked), plunge each bunch of somen into the heated soup.
5 Cut and remove the thread, and the uncooked ends of the noodles. Loosen the strands and neatly arrange a bunch of noodles in each of 4 individual soup bowls. Arrange the grilled fish and mitsuba or watercress on top and pour over the soup. Serve hot immediately.

10

Desserts
and Cakes

Figs with mountain grape sauce

Ichijiku no budo an-kaké [v]

KAZUNARI YANAGIHARA, expert in *cha-kaiseki* (tea ceremony meal), teacher and broadcaster, turns a simple fruit into a beautiful, rich dessert. Dessert is not a very strong feature in Japanese meals, as fresh fruits are more usually eaten at the end of a meal. Heavy cakes are eaten at teatime or at the tea ceremony with rich green tea.

SERVES 4

4 large, 8 medium or 12 small ripe figs
110ml/4fl oz/½ cup cranberry juice
110ml/4fl oz/½ cup water
5 tablespoons granulated sugar
1 tablespoon *katakuriko* (potato starch) or
    arrowroot, diluted with 1 tablespoon water
sprinkling of demerara sugar, to garnish

Figs are now widely available, and their season is long, from summer to late autumn, so they are a very useful fruit. The fig does not seem visibly to bear flowers, hence the Chinese character for this fruit, indicating fruit without flowers, but the reddish bits at the centre of the fruit are actually its flowers. Choose ripe, red-skinned figs, which are sweeter. KY

1 Trim off some of the flesh from the top and bottom of each fig into a good sitting position, plunge into boiling water and immediately remove from the heat. Drain and carefully peel the outer skin. Leave in the refrigerator to chill while you are making the sauce.

2 Mix the cranberry juice and water, and bring to the boil. Lower the heat, then add the sugar and stir until it dissolves. Slowly stir in the diluted potato starch to thicken the juice. Remove from the heat and put the bottom of the saucepan in cold water to cool the red sauce.

3 Arrange the chilled figs in the centre of each individual plate, pour over the sauce and serve, sprinkled with some demerara sugar on top.

Coconut milk and red bean paste jelly (jello)

Coconut milk to anko no jelly-yose

HIROSHI MIURA, chief chef at the Unkai restaurant in the ANA hotel in Sydney, shows one of his endeavours. The Japanese idea of a meal does not normally include desserts, and people are happy to have just fruits and green tea after a big meal. However, Japanese chefs overseas are required to come up with interesting desserts for non-Japanese customers.

SERVES 4

60–75g/3–3½oz/½ cup azuki beans, soaked
   in plenty of water overnight
o r 200–225g/7–8oz/1 cup ready-made
   sweet azuki bean paste
3–4 tablespoons granulated sugar
pinch of sea salt
15g/½oz gelatine, soaked in water
6 tablespoons coconut milk or cow's milk
4 teaspoons granulated sugar
1 small egg, hard-boiled (hard-cooked)
   (only yolk is needed)
assorted fruits such as melon, orange and
   strawberry, to garnish

An, sweet red bean paste, is the most commonly used ingredient in Japanese cakes and sweets, but it isn't so popular among non-Japanese customers, probably because of its dense texture and unique sweetness. I have altered the texture slightly by making it lighter and adding gelatine to it, and the result is a notably refreshing, but less sweet dessert. Coupled with coconut milk jelly, the striking contrast of the colours also appeals to Japanese and non-Japanese alike. At our restaurant we mix two parts cow's milk with one part coconut milk to reduce the coconut smell, but at home, because so small a quantity is required, you can use either coconut milk or cow's milk. We also serve matcha (powdered tea) ice cream with this dessert plate, along with assorted fruits at our restaurant. To make matcha ice cream, dilute 1 teaspoon of powdered green tea with a little water, and mix into 500ml/18fl oz/2¼ cups plain ice cream. HM

1 To make the sweet azuki bean paste from scratch, first boil the soaked azuki beans in the soaking water on a high heat, then when boiling add about 1 tablespoon water and remove from the heat. Leave in the hot water for 10 minutes and drain. Put the beans back into a saucepan, add water to just cover the beans and bring back to the boil. Lower the heat and gently simmer for about 30 minutes, adding water from time to time. When most of the water has evaporated, add 3–4 tablespoons sugar and a pinch of sea salt, and continue to simmer, stirring all the time. You want a slightly runny, not hard, paste, so if it's hard add some water. If using the ready-made bean paste, add some water and gently simmer on a moderate heat to mix well. Remove from the heat and leave to cool.
2 When the paste is lukewarm, mix half the soaked gelatine in and set aside.

3 Put the coconut milk or cow's milk in a saucepan on a moderate heat and add 3 teaspoons of the sugar. Remove from the heat and add the remaining gelatine. Pour a little over 1 tablespoon of the mixture into each of 4 small pudding moulds (it should come to about 5mm/¼in from the bottom), and chill in the refrigerator to set. When set, fill the moulds with the azuki mixture. Put back in the refrigerator to set.
4 Sieve the hard-boiled (hard-cooked) egg yolk through a fine mesh and add the remaining 1 teaspoon sugar. Take a teaspoonful in your hands and make a tiny ball. Repeat this process to make 4 balls.
5 Turn out the milk and jelly on to 4 individual plates and place an egg yolk ball on the top of each jelly (jello). Serve garnished with tiny melon balls, orange slices and/or some strawberries.

Azuki paste rice cake

Ohagi [v]

Azuki beans are often used in celebration meals and sweets, probably due to the joyous red colour. You can buy powdered azuki beans and mix with sugar, or ready-made paste in cans. It's also very easy to make your own as shown in this recipe.

MAKES 12 CAKES

200g/7oz/1 cup dried azuki beans, soaked overnight
180g/6oz/scant ¾ cup granulated sugar
pinch of sea salt
150g/5½oz/¾ cup glutinous rice
40g/1⅓oz/3 tablespoons Japanese short grain rice
1–2 tablespoons vegetable pickles, to garnish

1 Put the soaked azuki beans with water in a saucepan, bring to the boil and add 2 tablespoons of cold water. Remove from the heat and leave covered for 10 minutes. Then drain, and put the beans back in a saucepan with plenty of water. Bring to the boil, lower the heat and gently simmer for 1 hour, adding more water when necessary to keep the beans just covered.
2 Add the sugar and a pinch of sea salt, stirring all the time, and remove from the heat. Mash the beans in the cooking liquid. If the paste is runny, put the pan back on a very low heat, stirring, to evaporate excess liquid. Leave to cool.

3 Wash both types of rice together. Drain and leave for 1 hour. Put in a saucepan and add 225ml/8fl oz/1 cup water. Cover and bring to the boil over a high beat. Lower the heat, simmer for 13 minutes and leave aside, covered, for 10 minutes.
4 When the rice is cool, take a small handful and shape into a 4–5cm/1½–2in long oval ball. Repeat for 11 more balls. Spread a heaped tablespoonful of the azuki paste to a thin 12–15cm/5–6in diameter round in the centre of a clean damp cloth. Place a rice ball in the centre and fold the cloth so that the paste wraps it. Repeat. Serve with vegetable pickles.

Steamed milk and egg white with ginger syrup

Gyunyu chawan-mushi with ginger syrup [v]

Dairy products do not feature much in traditional Japanese cooking, but milk can be successfully used in desserts, as shown here.

SERVES 4

500ml/18fl oz/2¼ cups milk
2 tablespoons light plain (all-purpose) flour
1 tablespoon honey
2 egg whites, beaten

FOR THE GINGER SYRUP:
5cm/2in root ginger, peeled and thinly sliced
560ml/1 pint/2½ cups water
2 tablespoons light plain (all-purpose) flour
1 teaspoon honey

1 Mix the milk, light plain (all-purpose) flour and honey in a saucepan and heat on a moderate heat to about 82°C/180°F, stirring all the time. Remove from the heat and leave to cool.
2 Add the milk mixture to the beaten egg whites, and sieve through a fine mesh. Divide into 4 individual glass cups, and gently steam in a boiling steamer on a moderate heat for about 15 minutes.

3 Meanwhile, make the ginger syrup. Put the ginger slices in cold water just to cover, cook for 5 minutes over a high heat, and drain. Then add the measured water, flour and honey, and cook on a moderate heat until the syrup reduces to a third.
4 Pour a quarter of the ginger syrup on top of each cup of steamed milk and egg mixture, still in the steamer, and warm through. Serve hot.

Sweet azuki and kanten cake

Mizu yokan [v]

Yokan, hard-set rich azuki paste, is a very popular cake and is sold ready-made at wagashi *(Japanese confectionery) shops and supermarkets. This* mizu *(water) version is a much softer and lighter cake, and eaten chilled, so it's a very good dessert in summer.*

SERVES 6–12

1 *kanten* (agar-agar) stick (7–8g/about ¼oz), soaked in water for 1 hour
450ml/16fl oz/2 cups water
200g/7oz/1 cup granulated sugar
300g/10oz/2 cups ready-made sweet azuki bean paste
shiso leaves, to garnish

1 Drain the *kanten* and squeeze out the water with your hands. Put in a saucepan together with the water, bring to the boil and gently simmer for 15–20 minutes until the *kanten* is completely melted. Add the sugar and stir until dissolved. Remove from the heat and finely sieve into a bowl.
2 Add the azuki paste to the sweetened *kanten* liquid and stir well until the paste is dissolved. Place the mixing bowl over cold water and gently stir, while cooling down, to prevent the bean paste from settling down at the bottom.
3 After about 15 minutes, as the mixture starts to set, transfer to a metal *kanten* mould or plastic container measuring about 20 x 15cm/8 x 6in, covering the inside with cling film (plastic wrap). Leave to set at room temperature.
4 Take out of the mould using the cling film (plastic wrap), and cut into 6–12 pieces. Serve with *shiso* leaves.

Fruit and kanten salad in cranberry syrup

Fruit kanten [v]

Kanten, agar-agar, *is not only used for setting but is also very nice to eat on its own. Indeed in Japan,* kanten *cubes are eaten on their own mixed with syrup and some red beans, and is called* mitsumame, *syrupy beans.*

SERVES 4

½ dried *kanten* (agar-agar) sticks (3–4g/⅛oz)
225ml/8fl oz/1 cup water
1 tablespoon granulated sugar
1 small red apple, cored, cut into 8 wedges
1 persimmon or other fruit (pear, nectarine)
1–2 bananas, peeled, sliced into thin discs
20 green grapes, halved and de-seeded
10 strawberries, hulled and halved
single (light) cream, to serve

FOR THE SYRUP DRESSING:
225ml/8fl oz/1 cup cranberry juice
6 tablespoons runny sugar syrup

1 Soak the *kanten* for 1 hour. Drain the *kanten*, squeeze out the water and tear into small pieces. Put in a saucepan with the measured water and cook over a moderate heat until the *kanten* dissolves. Stir in the sugar and when it has dissolved, strain into a 500ml/18fl oz square mould or a plastic container lined with cling film (plastic wrap). Leave to cool until set. Chill in the refrigerator.
2 Make the syrup dressing: heat the cranberry juice and syrup on a moderate heat until the syrup dissolves, and remove from the heat. Do not boil. Keep in the refrigerator to chill.
3 Slice the apple wedges crossways into thin half-open fan-shaped pieces and plunge into salted water to prevent discolouring. Drain and pat dry with kitchen paper (paper towels). Cut the persimmon into pieces.
4 Remove the hardened *kanten* from the container using the cling film (plastic wrap), and cut into small, about 1.5cm/¾in cubes. Put the *kanten* cubes and all the fruits in a large salad bowl, pour over the cranberry dressing and fold in. Serve with a jug of cream.

Midori liqueur kanten jelly

Midori likyuru no kanten-yose [v]

NOBUO IWASEYA, the chief chef for all Suntory restaurants abroad, shows how to make a green jelly using *kanten* (agar-agar), a healthy, vegetarian alternative to animal gelatine. This vegetarian version sets quickly at a higher room temperature, so start cooking the *kanten* after all the other ingredients have been prepared. Midori, probably Suntory's most renowned product outside Japan, is a liqueur made from melon. The beautiful green colour makes very attractive cocktails.

SERVES 4

2–3 figs, peeled
juice of ½ lemon
2–3 tablespoons of water
110ml/4fl oz/½ cup Midori liqueur
1 *kanten* (agar-agar) stick (10g/⅓oz)
450ml/16fl oz/2 cups mineral water
4 tablespoons granulated sugar
12 seedless green grapes, peeled and
   halved lengthways
12 blueberries
6 small strawberries
3–4 white marshmallows (optional)

You can of course use gelatine for this dessert if you are making it in individual dishes, but if you make one large jelly and cut it into four, kanten *is a much better choice as it is easier to cut in straight lines. Midori is a strong liqueur, so boil to evaporate all alcohol content before use otherwise it won't set properly. You can use any fruit or a combination of two or three kinds in this beautiful green jelly. NI*

1 First prepare the fruits. If using figs, mix the lemon juice and water in a small bowl, dip the peeled figs in it, and drain on kitchen paper (paper towels). Cut crossways into 3–4 rounds depending on the size.
2 Put the Midori liqueur in a small saucepan and heat over a high heat for 2–3 minutes until the alcohol has evaporated. Remove from the heat and set to cool.
3 Soak the *kanten* in plenty of water for 5 minutes, then drain and squeeze out excess water. Break the *kanten* into small pieces, place in a saucepan with the mineral water, and cook on a moderate heat for 7–8 minutes, stirring occasionally, until it has completely melted. Remove from the heat and strain through a flour sieve into another saucepan. Place the saucepan on a moderate heat, add the sugar to the *kanten* liquid and stir until dissolved. Remove from the heat and leave to cool. When it is about body temperature, mix in the Midori liqueur. It will set quickly so do not leave for long.
4 Arrange the fruits and marshmallows, if using, artistically in a 560ml/1 pint jelly (jello) mould, and pour over the *kanten* and Midori mixture. All fruits rise to the surface, so if you want to avoid this, use half the fruits and half the *kanten* mixture whilst warm, leave in the refrigerator for 10 minutes, and then arrange the remaining ingredients on top when the mixture is about body temperature. Leave to set for 20 minutes. *Kanten* liquid sets very quickly so it needn't be chilled. When set, remove from the mould and cut into 4 pieces. Arrange on individual plates and serve.

11

Drinks
and Liqueurs

Sake

Sake

The Japanese traditional alcoholic drink is of course sake, which is made from rice. Although it is still the drink that is most respected and chosen to drink with authentic Japanese meals, its popularity in Japan has now been superseded by more casual drinks, notably lager beer and whisky, and even wine. Sake is brewed all over Japan, and to meet the increasing popularity outside Japan some large breweries have production operations abroad, mainly in the United States.

The majority of the top-range sake is still made at cottage-style small breweries all over Japan, where the traditional process is still intensively followed by hand throughout. There are about 6,000 such breweries producing as many as 55,000 brands each year. The process is fairly simple: first propagate *koji* (a kind of bacteria, to transform starch into sugar) with steamed rice, then add yeast to break the sugar into alcohol and carbon dioxide, and add steamed rice, some more *koji* and water to ferment. Finally the mush is pressed to produce sake, which is then matured in a tun. Sake is made from autumn through to winter, and is ready in about 60 days. It is best drunk within a year of bottling.

The grading system of sake is very complicated, but if you want the top range, look for the three kinds: *ginjo*, *junmai* and *hon-johzo*. To make sake, the outer part of the rice, which includes unwelcome nutrients such as protein and fat, is removed to get the pure starch of the core. How much is removed determines its quality. To make *ginjo*, a minimum of 40 per cent of the grain must be removed. *Dai-ginjo* (big *ginjo*) is the highest quality, with a minimum of 50 per cent removed. *Junmai* is a pure rice sake whilst *non-junmai* contains some brewing alcohol and sugar. *Hon-johzo* is made from rice with 30 per cent of the grain removed, with an added alcohol content. *Ginjo* should be drunk cold. *Junmai* and *hon-johzo* are drunk either cold or luke-warm. However, only 20 per cent of all sake produced in Japan comes into this top-range category. Unlike wine, it keeps well but once a bottle is opened, but it should be drunk as soon as possible. Store in a cool, dark place away from sunlight.

Plum liqueur

Umé-shu [v]

Although it is known as plum liqueur in the West, the fruit, umé, used to make this drink is actually not plum but Japanese apricot. Fresh, unripe green apricots are soaked in white spirit such as shochu *together with sugar for at least three months.* Shochu *is a distilled spirit made from rice and a mixture of various other grains or even sweet potatoes. The Japanese apricots start coming onto the market in early June in Japan, and most households used to start making* umé-shu *for consumption the following year. It is drunk chilled with ice cubes, and is a good summer drink.*

MAKES ABOUT 4 LITRES/7 PINTS/4 QUARTS

1kg/2¼lb unripe greengages or apricots
750g/1lb 10oz/3½ cups crystallized sugar or
    560g/1lb 8 oz/2¾ cups granulated sugar
1.8 litres/3¼ pints/8 cups *shochu* (distilled
    rice spirit)

1 Remove the calyx from the unwashed fruits, and wipe each one with kitchen paper (paper towels) or a dry clean cloth.
2 Put some of the fruits in a 4 litre/ 7 pint/4 quart air-tight jar and cover with some of the sugar. Repeat the process until all the fruits and sugar are in the jar.

3 Pour the *shochu* into the jar, submerging the fruit. Seal the jar tightly and leave in a dark, cool place, ideally for a year but for at least 3 months. Drink straight with ice cubes or mixed with tomato juice or soda water.

Hot shochu with pickled plum

Umé-jochu [v]

Here, the somewhat rough shochu, *a distilled spirit made from grains such as rice, barley and millet, molasses or sweet potato, is infused with* umeboshi, *dried and salt-pickled Japanese apricots, available ready-made in packets at Japanese supermarkets. It is a down-to-earth, daily drink and, although it's been quite fashionable at times, and is a cheap alternative to sake.*

MAKES 4 TALL GLASSES

4–8 *umeboshi* (salted and dried
    Japanese apricots)
225ml/8fl oz/1 cup *shochu* (distilled
    rice spirit)
boiling water, for topping up
lemon slices, to serve

1 Put 1–2 *umeboshi* in each of 4 glasses. Add a quarter of the *shochu* to each glass and pour in boiling water to fill. Adjust the strength of the drink by the volume of the hot water.

2 Serve hot with a lemon slice on the rim of each glass.

Fish fin sake

Hiré-zaké

TAKESHI YASUGE, chef/patron of the *fugu* restaurant Asakusa Fukuji in Tokyo, says wild *tora-fugu* (ocellate puffer) should be used to appreciate the real thing. Unfortunately, *fugu* is not obtainable in the West, so here red sea bream fins are used. *Fugu* (puffer fish) is a precious little fish, so precious that every part of the fish is used. Even its fins are used for a drink. *Hiré-zaké* is hot sake normally served at *fugu* restaurants in Japan, using *fugu* fins.

MAKES 4 TALL CUPS

fins from 1 red sea bream
900ml/32fl oz/4 cups inexpensive sake

You drink hiré-zaké for its aroma and not really for its taste. At my restaurant we use only wild tora-fugu fins, which have by far the best aroma. It makes sake mild and sweet, and inexpensive sake drinkable. A fugu has four fins, one on each side, one on the back and bottom. You can also use the tail fin. The best way to appreciate this exquisite sake is to drink it at fugu restaurants in Japan that serve only wild fugu like mine. If you want to make your own outside Japan, use sea bream fins instead, although this is not as authentic and superior as the real thing. TY

1 Open up the 4 fins – 2 from the sides, 1 long one from the back and 1 from the tail – into fan shapes, and while wet stick to a large flat surface like a plate so that the fins keep their open shape. Air-dry under natural light for 2–3 weeks until very dry and crisp. Gently grill (broil) on a double metal grill (broiler) over a moderate heat until both sides are a charcoal colour, almost burnt.

2 Meanwhile, put the sake either directly into a saucepan, or in a large *tokkuri* (sake jug, as pictured) or 2 in a saucepan with boiling water, place on a high heat and bring the sake almost to the boil. Put a well-grilled fin in each of 4 tall cups, glasses or mugs, and fill with the hot sake. Cover with a lid or a small plate, and leave to infuse for 5–6 minutes. Drink while hot.

Index

The master chefs

FROM JAPAN

Takayuki Hishinuma
A forerunner of a breed of young chefs creating new-wave Japanese cooking in Japan, Takayuki Hishinuma is the chef/patron of the restaurant, Hishinuma, in Tokyo. While his handling of ingredients is based on a traditional training, he shows his modern artistic skills in its assembly. He also has an understanding of international wines.

Nobuo Iwaseya
Nobuo Iwaseya is the chief chef for all overseas Suntory restaurants, renowned throughout the world for the very high standard of their traditional and authentic dishes. Responsible for opening all the restaurants, compiling menus and recipes and using seasonal local fresh produce as much as possible, he gained a Michelin star with the London restaurant in St James's in 1987.

Kentaro Kobayashi
Kentaro is a young celebrity cookery personality on television, following in the footsteps of his mother, the well-known cookery writer and broadcaster Katsuyo Kobayashi. His cooking style is carefree and easy-going, which appeals particularly to the busy people of today. He has written many books.

Akihiro Kurita
The young chef/patron of a small Kyoto cuisine restaurant bearing his name, where he cooks in front of the diners, Akihiro Kurita's cooking is based on the old *kaiseki* style, but is more approachable and affordable. He is an innovative chef and his little dishes show off his vast knowledge of seasonal Kyoto produce and their handling. He has been the subject of many Japanese magazine features and books.

Masahiro Kurusu
The third generation chef/patron of the well-established *kaiseki* restaurant Tankuma in Kyoto, Masahiro Kurusu also teaches and frequently appears on television. His grandfather, the founder of Tankuma, was the pioneer of the now very popular so-called 'counter *kappo* (cooking)' restaurant, where a chef cooks and serves at the counter.

Yoshihiro Murata
Born into a *kaiseki* restaurant chef/patron family, Yoshihiro Murata travelled the world in search of culinary traditions, when he realized how great his own culinary heritage was and how it was his duty to let the world know of it. His ambition was partly fulfilled when he and his wife presented a *kaiseki* banquet in association with Dom Pérignon in front of the world media in France in 1999.

Minoru Odajima
Minoru Odajima worked at a Japanese restaurant in Paris for a few years before returning to Japan and opening his own Odajima in Tokyo in the early seventies. He was one of the first to start serving meat, such as steak, as the main course and matching wines. 'Simple is the best' is his motto in cooking, and he believes, as many do, that Japanese is the ultimate cooking for the world to follow.

Yuichi Oyama
Yuichi Oyama is executive chef and general manager of the 160-year-old sushi restaurant Yoshino in Osaka. His long career has been entirely devoted to sushi making and he is very proud of being the guardian of the now rarely served *hako-zushi* (boxed sushi), a traditional Osaka-style sushi. Watching his expertise in rolling, pressing and assembling various types of sushi is a magical experience.

Tetsuya Saotome
The multi-talented tempura chef Tetsuya Saotome believes tempura frying is a science, and proves it at his tempura restaurant, Mikawa, in Tokyo. He writes articles about tempura for magazines and appears on television. He is also an artist, calligrapher and collector of Japanese antiques.

Eiichi Takahashi
Born to the chef/patron family of the legendary *kaiseki* restaurant Hyotei in Kyoto, established in 1837, the kitchen was Eiichi Takahashi's playground. As the fourteenth generation he is very proud to be the keeper of his heritage, and leads the army of chefs in the kitchen. As a leading figure in the culinary world of Japan he has written many books on *kaiseki* cooking.

Kazunari Yanagihara
Teacher and broadcaster, Kazunari Yanagihara is the descendant in a long line of the *cha-kaiseki* (tea ceremony meal) school, Kinsa-ryu. His Tokyo cookery school, Yanagihara Ryori Kyoshitsu, is one of the most prestigious training grounds for daughters and would-be wives of fine families from all over Japan. He has done a number of television series on Japanese cooking and written many books including *Kinsa-ryu Seasonal Tastes*, published by Shufu-no-tomo.

Takeshi Yasuge
Although trained in general Japanese cooking, Takeshi Yasuge's expertise now lies in his handling of the unique and extremely poisonous *fugu* (puffer fish). He is the chef/patron of the *fugu* restaurant, Asakusa Fukuji, in Ginza, Tokyo, and believes *fugu* is the most delicious, and probably the most expensive, fish in the world.

FROM THE UNITED KINGDOM

Susumu Hatakeyama
Susumu Hatakeyama, the head chef at the well-established Ikeda restaurant in Mayfair in London, came to London in the late seventies after training in authentic Japanese cooking in Osaka. The key to successful cooking abroad, he says, is understanding the taste of the people and to not be afraid to adjust a little.

Hisashi Taoka
Born to a *ryokan* (old-style hotel) family in a famous spa resort in Japan, Hisashi Taoka is a fish trader and owner of Kiku restaurant in Mayfair, London, established in 1978. Once a wholesaler based at Billingsgate, London's fish market, he now goes to the Mediterranean himself in search of good tuna in season. Due to his profound knowledge of fish, his restaurant reputedly has the best sushi bar in London.

FROM GERMANY

Hideaki Morita
Hideaki Morita trained in Tokyo and came to Hamburg to work at the local branch of the Japanese parent restaurant in Tokyo where he worked in the eighties. He moved to work at Matsumi restaurant, and eventually took it over from the previous owner on his retirement in 1987. His traditional and uncompromising approach to cooking earned him many devotees, including his German partner and manager Petra.

FROM THE UNITED STATES

Linda Rodriguez
Born in Manila, Linda Rodriguez, executive chef at New York's celebrated Bond Street restaurant, was raised in the United States, but spent part of her childhood in Japan, where she first tasted the joy of Japanese food. She first trained in classical French, then in various Asian cuisines along with Cajun-style cooking. She worked at Nobu both in New York and London before moving to Bond Street when it opened in 1998.

Toshi Sugiura
Chef/patron of the Hama restaurant, Toshi is reputedly the best sushi chef in Los Angeles. He travelled the world before reaching LA in the late seventies. Having learned the art of sushi making entirely in LA, he now also runs a sushi chef training school adjacent to his restaurant. Visit www.restaurant-hama.com and www.sushi-academy.com

Ken Tominaga
Ken first came to California as a boy in the seventies and returned to Tokyo to train as a chef, having been brought up with good food and surrounded by gourmets. His cooking is instinctive and innovative, yet based on the traditional techniques and culinary senses that have earned his restaurant, Hana, in the Bay Area, north of San Francisco, the reputation as one of the best 50 in the Bay Area. Visit www.hanajapanese.com

FROM AUSTRALIA

Hiroshi Miura
Hiroshi Miura is the head chef of the Unkai restaurant, in the All Nippon Airways hotel, Sydney. He had a classical *cha-kaiseki* (tea ceremony meal) and *ryotei* (old-style and upmarket restaurant) training, working at a number of reputable establishments before joining the ANA restaurants group and spending a spell as the head chef for an in-flight catering company. When he was 32 that he was appointed the head chef for the newly opened Unkai in 1992.

FROM HONG KONG

Naoyuki Sato
Naoyuki Sato is the head chef of the renowned Nadaman at the Kowloon Changrilla hotel in Hong Kong. Nadaman is one of the oldest *kaiseki* restaurants, established in Kyoto in 1829, and now has 20 restaurants in Japan and seven abroad. Sato is a true Nadaman man, having started his career with the company, and climbing the ladder within the organization ever since.